THE
HEART OF A
FATHER

THE
HEART OF A
FATHER

How You Can Become a Dad of Destiny

KEN CANFIELD, PH.D.
FOUNDER OF THE NATIONAL CENTER FOR FATHERING

NORTHFIELD PUBLISHING
CHICAGO

Cover Design: Smartt Guys
Cover Photograph: Frare/Davis Photography, Brand X Pictures
Editor: Ali Diaz

Library of Congress Cataloging-in-Publication Data

Canfield, Ken R.
    The heart of a father : how you can become a dad of destiny / Ken Canfield.
      p. cm.
    Originally published: c1996.
    Includes bibliographical references (p.   ).
    ISBN-13: 978-1-881273-46-2
    ISBN-10: 1-881273-46-6
      1. Fathers—United States. 2. Father and child—United States. 3. Parenting—Religious aspects. I. Title.

    HQ756.C359 2006
    306.874'20973—dc22

                                                                    2006003476

We hope you enjoy this book from Northfield Publishing. Our goal is to provide high-quality, thought-provoking books and products that connect truth to your real needs and challenges. For more information on other books and products, write to:

Northfield Publishing
215 West Locust Street
Chicago, IL 60610

1 3 5 7 9 10 8 6 4 2

Printed in the United States of America

To fellow pilgrims
in the adventure
of fathering . . .
Keep up the good work!

Contents

A c k n o w l e d g m e n t s

Quality books utilize a team of gifted people. This book is the result of such a team.

Its beginnings go back many years, to my early college days when several had a significant influence on my studies. I am particularly indebted to Verlin Hinshaw, who modeled a lifestyle of sincere scholarship. Professors J. I. Packer and Roy Bell helped me establish my cultural framework and worldview, and Profs. Phillip Carter and Walter Schum put fresh polish on my research skills. They also provided the necessary encouragement and clarity to finish my Ph.D. Other professors have also influenced me significantly, notably: Leroy Brightup, Roland Reimer, John McMillan, Bruce Waltke, Klaus Blockmeuhl, Ken Kennedy, Joyce Terrass, Robert Meisner, and Robert Newhouse.

I have been fortunate to have some "iron sharpening" colleagues who have stimulated me profoundly. The ideas that we have discussed in phone conversations, over coffee, or during the workday now yield a good harvest. I owe a great deal to Rodney Duke, Judd and Nancy Swihart, Suzan

Hawkes, James Furrow, Gale Roid, Gary Klozenbucher, Emerson Eggerichs, Randy Sly, Lowell Bliss, Don Burwell, as well as Walt Mueller, Gordon Dalbey, Bernard Franklin, and Brock Griffin.

This book would not have been completed without the help of the staff at the National Center for Fathering. I am particularly indebted to Brock Griffin and Lowell Bliss. Their literary skills (shaping, editing, and creative illustrations) are second to none. David Warnick helped significantly in shaping section three and giving overall editing suggestions. Other staff who assisted in the research over the years are: Randy Mallon, Lisa Bromlow, Randall Nulton, Kelly Hayes, and Allison Lousch.

The staff and associates at Northfield Publishing must also be commended. They have done a superb job in promoting the ideas and substance of this book.

Finally the vehicle doesn't move unless there is gas in the tank. Many people have contributed to this project indirectly over the years by supporting me or the work at the National Center for Fathering. They include Joe Lee, Peter J. Stokes, Blake Ashdown, Joel Jennings, and Rich Hasley. Other supporters include Lee Paris, Ralph Smith, Daryl Heald, and Melvin Canfield.

You will be encouraged to know that much of my theory and research is grounded in everyday living. My five children, Hannah, Sarah, Joel, Micah, and Rachel, will attest to that. They have had a considerable influence in shaping my fathering practices, for which I am grateful and humbled. And finally I would like to thank Dee, my wife. Without her continuing belief in me I wouldn't be where I am today.

FATHER POWER

Pascal, the famous mathematician and inventor, once wrote, "The heart has its reasons which reason does not know." If this is true (and I believe it is), then what counts is not necessarily what a person knows intellectually. What matters is what that person believes about the world deep down inside—the mystical but very real place of the heart.

I have titled this book *The Heart of a Father* because I believe it's critical that we who are fathers deal with our hearts in order to connect with our children. It is on the level of the heart—that messy, sometimes illogical, often spiritual center of each father—where I believe the best fathering occurs.

The hearts of many fathers ache. Just as women learn to mother by imitating their moms, men learn to father by watching their dads. But a crisis of fatherlessness has removed the models for many men and distorted them for others. Now we fathers desire to give something better to our children and thus break the cycle. But our best plans can go awry, because sheer determination isn't enough. The issues closest to rearing children are rooted in the yearnings of our hearts, the seat of our deepest longings and feelings. And, for most of us, our hearts have been damaged by incomplete relationships with our own fathers.

This book views the "job" of fathering from the perspective of the heart, because fathering is essentially a relationship. Such a perspective will allow us the freedom to acknowledge that our children are not machines; we can't run them in the same way we operate a lawn mower. You have a unique fathering situation, unlike mine or that of any other father, and it includes the distinct personalities of your children. Furthermore, you bring your own strengths and weaknesses to the task.

In *The Heart of a Father,* we will look at our own hearts—shaped by the past, affected by the present, and influencing our children's future. In the process we will begin to learn what it takes to be engaged fathers. Our conclusions are based on a review and analysis of other family research as well as the findings from surveys commissioned and in some cases conducted by the National Center for Fathering (NCF). In addition, we have drawn principles from the center's numerous interviews with fathers during the past two decades. We have reviewed the literature (both current and historical) and have catalogued more than five thousand citations related to tasks of fathering. NCF maintains one of the largest ongoing databases on fathers' attitudes, behaviors, and practices. We also have interviewed children, mothers, and adults who are not parents. And if I were to sum up our findings in three short words, they would be: *Fathers are important.* They make a vital contribution to their children's development and, in truth, can shape the destiny of America.

This book is divided into three sections, each of them centered on a metaphor. The three sections correspond with the past, present, and future and deal with what a father *brings* to fathering, what a father *does* in fathering, and what a father *will experience* in fathering. In other words, we will examine "Father Power" in its source, exercise, and context.

Father Power is what each of us has as men with children. Father Power is about a man's ability to shape his children into responsible adults, even leaders of the twenty-first century. Father Power is about loving, knowing, and influencing our children to the good. In a real sense, that is what the heart of every father desires.

The first section, "The Shape of Your Heart," has to deal with *past* circumstances. The primary influence on the heart of a father is a man's relationship with his own father. Your father has contributed to who you are today, including how you respond to your own children. We will examine both the positive and negative effects that our own fathers had on us. We all bring the legacy of how we were fathered into our own fathering, both for good or bad.

I suspect some of you will be tempted to skip this section to get into the "meat" of the book about present-day fathering. This would be a mistake. Unless you understand how your heart has been strengthened and/or damaged by your own father, you will not understand the condition of your heart. When you apply for life insurance, most insurers will require that you see a doctor. The doctor will complete a medical history, asking you questions about your parents' health in order to get clues about your own health. In a similar manner, before you can effectively father, you need to understand from your past the shape of your heart today.

For some, this process will bring back deep feelings of contentment as you survey your father's careful, committed craftsmanship. If you had a close, meaningful relationship with your dad, you've been given a great legacy. Reviewing that relationship will motivate you to provide the same kind of strength for your kids. I suspect most of us, however, will discover some damage, even with fathers who tried to always give us the best. In some way, your father was probably absent, and it's good to recognize that. You will need to allow time and effort for grieving, healing, and restoring your heart. Once your heart has been "reconditioned," you can move forward.

Gordon Dalbey wrote about his book *Father and Son,* "This book is not about becoming a father, but rather, about the prior and primal step of manhood in becoming a son."[1] It is certainly a critical step, and it's a goal of this book as well.

Part 2, "The Four 'I CANs' of Fatherhood," describes the practices, behaviors, and attitudes of an effective father. We'll give respectful consideration to child development and research experts, yet go beyond that to a practical framework for dealing with our children. Most fathers simply want to know: What is it that effective fathers do? What are the essential issues related to fathering?

We will offer several answers based on findings at the National Center for Fathering. Our earliest research at NCF looked into the tasks of fathering, all the things a father is expected to do. We found that they can be categorized in four overarching dimensions. We call these dimensions the "I CANs" of fathering: Involvement, Consistency, Awareness, and Nurturance. They correspond to the four walls of a house—the exterior walls that provide the essential support, upon which the entire structure is built.

Although much of this material is not new, our findings at NCF confirm and extend important truths about being a good father. I hope this book will bring forth in each man what is basic to rearing his children. Once we understand the basic tasks at the heart of fathering, we can discover (or rediscover) the deep joy of knowing and loving our children. We can learn to satisfy the longing we have to be proud of what we pass on to the next generation.

Fathering is not a sprint; it is a marathon. And what is more essential for such a long run than a strong heart? In part 3, "The Disciplined Heart," you'll become familiar with the changing course of rearing children. Fathering isn't finished until a man is lying six feet under. From a newborn baby to a fully grown adult, the needs of our children change during a lifetime. A man who has a teenager in his home knows that the demands on his fathering are substantially different now than when his child was a toddler.

Here, too, there may be the temptation to skip some of this material and only read about the present life stage of your children. For example, if your children are in preschool, you may not desire to read about the enlightenment stage where those preschoolers have become teenagers.

But it's to our advantage to know what is coming up. Many men consistently engage in planning while on their jobs; they set goals and craft great vision statements. We need to do the same thing with respect to our fathering. We can have our best impact if we discipline ourselves for the grueling yet rewarding challenges that lie ahead of us as fathers.

Father Power must be activated. To help you evaluate your Father Power we have included several inventories that assess your strengths and opportunity areas as a dad. Use these "Father Inventories" as tools to improve your fathering, and don't be afraid to share the results with a friend, in a small group, or with your spouse and children. Remember, fathering is a relationship, not a regimen. And there are no perfect fathers. But a father's heart seeks to be the best he can be. I trust this book will aid you in fulfilling that desire.

THE HEART
OF A FATHER

Whenever I look into my daughter Sarah's face, I think about the power of fatherhood. Her face reminds me I have given her more than just my name. Like me, she has a patch of freckles stretching across the bridge of her nose almost like a Band-Aid. She steps out into the sun and squints. The skin around her eyes crinkles, and the lines match mine. "When Sarah smiles," my mother tells me, "she looks just like you."

Other things in her are reflections of me. I see myself most clearly in her eyes, the windows to her soul. Like me, Sarah has a drive to succeed and will try anything. "Who needs to wait for instructions?" she used to tell herself as she attempted to flip off the high bar in gymnastics class; more than once, she tumbled to disaster. Also, more than once, she executed a perfect dismount.

Sarah Canfield, without a doubt, is her own person. Yet, somehow, in the mystery of fatherhood, I get the unmistakable sense that my life is her life and vice versa. We are connected by nothing less than bone and flesh and spirit. Her face reminds me of the power of fatherhood.

A Wound . . . and a Reminder

But for the past fifteen years when I've looked at her face I've also seen a scar. This, too, reminds me of the power of fathering. Or maybe, better said, the power of fatherlessness. Starting just low enough on her forehead that her sandy blonde bangs do not cover it, the scar stretches down between her eyebrows and comes close to her left eye. The twelve stitches have long been removed; the wound has healed. But the scar remains, placed there by my "fatherlessness."

All those summers ago, Sarah's younger brother, Joel, signed up to play tee-ball. At his first practice, I discovered there was no coach and no other fathers present. Several mothers were there as loyal advocates for their sons and daughters, and if no one came to coach the team, they would. As I walked up and listened to their discussion, you can guess what they were thinking. *He could be the coach. He should be the coach.*

For my part, I was quick to protest: "Actually, I've been pretty busy lately. Making it to practice would be quite a commitment." Some of the women were certainly quite capable of coaching those youngsters through a season of tee-ball. But as I looked into the eager eyes of these "Mighty Ducks," I caught my first whiff of a certain fatherlessness that circles among that team. It was like the women, even the children, were saying, *Yes, you are no doubt busy, and yes, mothers could coach this team if they had to, but don't you see that something is missing?* Maybe it was the nostalgia of baseball, the cultural icon of a father and son out in the backyard playing catch. We—the women, the children, and me—all wanted to hear a strong male voice encouraging the child in the batter's box: "You can do it. Just be patient. Keep your eye on the ball." We all wanted strong male arms reaching to welcome a child into the dugout: "Nice going! I'm proud of you."

So I took the job. Coach Canfield.

Craig, one highly energetic boy on the team, soon became a vivid reminder of fatherlessness. Craig's father had left the family when Craig was very young, but his mother faithfully brought Craig to every practice. The other team members considered Craig to be a "hothead." They told tales about how he was constantly in trouble at school, and how he had difficulty keeping up with his schoolwork.

My most immediate concern with Craig was his tendency to throw the bat after swinging. I can still hear the "ching" of the aluminum bat flung into the backstop, causing his teammates to jump back. After practice I helped Craig work on dropping the bat before running to first. Standing behind him, I wrapped my hands around his on the bat, and we hit the ball together. *I'm going to hit the ball, drop the bat, and run,* I taught him to say through endless repetition, with as much passion as I could muster in my best Norman Vincent Peale imitation. It didn't take long for him to learn.

Or to forget.

One Saturday morning, I had gone into the office and was running a little late for practice. I called and asked Sarah, who is a "take-charge" person (like her father), to go over to the park and get the kids started. Sarah had accompanied me to practice before, and she knew Craig's problem with throwing the bat. She knew the exercises I put Craig through to break his habit.

"OK, Craig," Sarah said, standing a few feet behind him over his right shoulder as her father was miles away at an office, "be sure to hit the ball, drop the bat, and run."

I arrived at the doctor's office just in time to see the twelfth stitch close up Sarah's wound. Sarah, so willing to try anything.

Whenever I see Sarah's scar, I am reminded of the wounds of fatherlessness. Certainly, there is my guilt. I was a father too busy at the office to be where I should have been, coaching my team and protecting my daughter.

Yet on a deeper level, Sarah's scar teaches me of a more painful wound. It belongs to Craig, the little boy who threw the bat, who had no father. It's little wonder he continued to throw his bat, even after hours of coaching— there was no one at home to practice with him, to wrap their arms around him for a strong swing, or to give a powerful hug. And it's no wonder that Craig was constantly in trouble at school.

Sarah, wounded by Craig's bat, shed a few tears as the doctor sewed her, leaving a scar of a couple of inches. If only little Craig, with a wound deep inside from the absence of his father, could be put back together by something as simple as a few stitches.

About Father Power

A father has enormous power. About this, he has no choice. For good or for bad, by his presence or absence, action or inaction, whether abusive or nurturing, the fact remains: A father is one of the most powerful beings on earth. Craig's dad, even though absent, continues to exert power over his son, just as I have over my daughter Sarah.

Today, whenever I look into my daughter's face, I am reminded of that power. This same power is actually localized in you as the father of your children. Certain things are being accomplished in your kids, whether you are aware of them or not. Let's call it, as others have, *Father Power*—a man's ability to shape the leaders and parents of the twenty-first century, whether he does so by his devoted commitment or by his absence.[1]

Think about it. Think of the power, say, in a father's words. "I believe in you, Son." "Why can't you ever do anything right?" "I'm so proud of you." "Why couldn't you be more like your sister?" "I love you." "You lazy bum." Those are words that, one way or the other, will stay with a child for the rest of his or her life.

Fathers give children, for good or bad, what no one else can. "Fathers make unique and irreplaceable contributions to the lives of their children,"[2] says Dr. Wade Horn, U.S. Assistant Deputy Secretary of Health and Human Services.

"Unique and irreplaceable." Fathers are handed a mandate to serve their children. Few people would argue. In *Fire in the Belly*, Sam Keen put it this way:

> In the quiet hours of the night, when I add up the accomplishments of my life in which I take justifiable pride—a dozen books, thousands of lectures and seminars, a farm built by hand, a prize here, an honor there—I know that three that rank above all others are named Lael, Gifford, and Jessamyn [his children]. In the degree to which I have loved, nurtured, and enjoyed them, I honor myself. In the degree to which I have injured them by being unavailable to them because of my obsessive preoccupation with myself or my profession, I have failed as a father and as a man.[3]

Disintegration of Fatherhood

For many dads, though, their father power has dwindled. Dr. Wade Horn's compilation of data in the 2004 *Father Facts* study confirms that many men have diminished or even lost their roles as influential fathers, some even by choice. Their findings are sobering:

- Twenty-four million children (34 percent) live in homes without their biological fathers.
- Out-of-wedlock births have overtaken divorce as the primary cause of father absence since many do not feel required to stick around. In 2000, 1.35 million births (33 percent of all births) occurred outside of wedlock.
- About 40 percent of children in father-absent homes have not seen their father within the past year; and 50 percent of father-absent children have never set foot in their father's home.
- While the divorce rates peaked in the 1980s, in this millennium 40 to 50 percent of marriages are ending in divorce, affecting approximately one million children each year.[4]

But there is more than one way for a father to be absent from his family. Being fatherless does not just mean losing a father through death, divorce, or illegitimate birth. In a survey of more than 1,600 adult men, more than 50 percent said their fathers were emotionally absent while they were growing up.[5] That may help explain why in another survey only 34 percent of adult males could say that they considered their own father to be a role model.[6]

Ward and June Cleaver's ideal neighborhood of the fifties seems to be a nostalgic relic. Dramatic changes in lifestyle and culture have revolutionized the structure of the traditional American family. It is harder for families to simply sit down for a meal together. However, according to a Columbia University study, the risk of stress, poor academic performance, and substance abuse is cut in half for kids who have regular dinners with their families, compared with those who eat together less than twice a week.[7]

In a span of a few weeks, as I was speaking in New York City and then in southern California, I again came face-to-face with the life stories behind the statistics. Only a few of the men I met were still married and living with their children's mother. One man told me a typical story: His wife had left him and moved with their three children to Sacramento; he has since remarried a woman who has three children of her own. "I feel like I'm fathering my stepchildren but not my own children," he said.

My friends on both coasts reflect another facet of lifestyle on fathering. Many of them commute an hour or more every day to work. Some leave at

5:00 or 5:30 in the morning, and often don't get home until 7:30, just in time to watch their children go to bed.

Certainly financial pressures have contributed to the decline in fathering. Those financial pressures cause some men to work longer and harder for hopes of advancement and pay raises. A rise in addictions and sexual irresponsibility are also factors. Yet, I believe there to be deeper reasons for disintegrating fatherhood:

A loss of vision for the future. For years, our society was focused on our posterity, but no longer. For many adults, happiness has become the all-consuming goal. That's putting our personal preferences ahead of our children's needs.

A loss of priorities. Men especially are prone to finding their identity through their work rather than their family, and they confuse achievement, salary, and title with being better as a person.

A loss of sense of duty and commitment. Sacrifice is no longer applauded —who does what is right anymore simply because it is right?

A loss of community. Individualism has gone too far. Involved fatherhood has become a private matter, and fathers rarely communicate with other dads about fathering.

When Fathers Disappear

The late Henri Nouwen, a parish priest and author, accurately predicted in the seventies that the coming generation would be known by its sense of inwardness, convulsiveness, and fatherlessness.[8] The legacy of the disappearing father is nothing to be proud of. Fatherless boys are 63 percent more likely to run away and 37 percent more likely to abuse drugs, and fatherless girls are twice as likely to get pregnant and 53 percent more likely to commit suicide. Fatherless children are twice as likely to drop out of high school and twice as likely to end up in jail.[9]

The statistics can try to measure the tragedy, yet they can never capture the personal pain of thousands. Such as Cathy. One of Cathy's earliest memories was climbing up into the window seat of her bedroom and waiting for the lights of her father's car to pull into the family's driveway. She remembers both fear and longing, a sort of sick feeling. Fear, because he was loud and drunk and often abusive with her and her mother. Longing, because . . . well, just because he was her daddy.

"I remember just wanting to crawl up in my daddy's lap and just feel safe," she says. "He never let me do that." Cathy is now thirty-eight and struggles with her own identity and feels worthless.

Reasons for Hope

We certainly don't intend our children to be among those statistics or individual stories of pain. Yet we may wonder about the culture: Is there any hope for a rebirth of fathering? Will my children be surrounded by Cathys?

Despite the overwhelming deterioration around us, I am encouraged about fathering. In a sense, it is both the best of times and the worst of times. Though many children are growing up fatherless, many dads are now making their children a priority in a new way. I've seen them at our seminars and other speaking engagements around the country. More and more, there is a calling on men to accept their duties as fathers and have a higher commitment to fathering. In the past decade, phenomena such as the Promise Keepers men's movement and the Million Man March on Washington, both calling on men to accept their duties as fathers, suggest a new sense of commitment to fathering.[10]

Some years ago, *Parents* magazine asked me to come up with trends for fathering. I tried to tell the reporter that fathering itself would be the trend. When she didn't seem to understand, I said plainly, "There will be an increased awareness of the importance of fatherhood." This awareness, I explained, would grow out of the pain of a million neglected childhoods, and find its voice in counseling sessions and therapy groups, some with titles such as "Adult Children of Alcoholics" and "Adult Children of Dysfunctional Families."

That awareness has come to pass. It's good, but we must be careful not to overreact—to blame our fathers for all things. One *Newsweek* cover carried the headline "Deadbeat Dads" above a photograph of an unshaven, surly looking man with smudged glasses riding low on his nose.[11] He is one of the images of modern American fatherhood.

From experience I've learned that most of these "deadbeat dads" are little boys in men's bodies, often living in denial and pain after the divorce. The best way to reach them is to help them get in touch with their pain and wait patiently until they have a revelation that being a father is one of the greatest joys a man can experience, and their children are actually a gift that gives them purpose, direction, and hope. As Sam Osherson notes, "Fatherhood is not just a role-provider, disciplinarian, friend—it's also a relationship, one that transforms us as much as our kids."[12]

The yearning of many men today to become good fathers is rooted in our past—we are all children who want our fathers. Something in us yearns to honor fatherhood. James Herzog of Harvard University is credited with coining the term "father hunger," which one of his disciples defines as "a subconscious yearning for an ideal father."[13]

I don't think we necessarily want an "ideal" dad; we just want our dad, and just want to be a dad to our kids. That's why this book isn't a call to restore the "traditional" family; it's a call to restore your family. You need not be like a rerun of Tim Taylor (*Home Improvement*) or Heathcliff Huxtable (*The Cosby Show*), full of laughs and occasional wisdom, to correctly raise your children. You, your father, and your father's father are all unique men qualified to be fathers to your children.

The Need for Model Dads

Men *do* want to be effective fathers, and that's the good news. As fathers, we recognize our powerful influence on our children and want to use it for good. But a key roadblock in recovering our positive power as fathers is that we lack complete and effective models. Historically, men learned to father by following models. They kept their eyes open and watched daily how it was done. Hopefully they were able to do their fathering apprenticeship, studying under their own dads, subconsciously taking notes of who a father is and what a father does.

Today, what can a man deduce about fathering if his primary model walked out on him when he was just a kid? He may say to himself, *Hmm, I guess this means dads are free to come and go as they please.* That may seem like a wild deduction, but it's an operative one, in the suburbs as well as the inner cities.

More often, though, men who had an incomplete model have a sense of the vacuum, and they have a desire to give something better to their children. Dads who are overcomers want to break the unhealthy cycles they've inherited from their fathers. Some do so by overcompensating. "I'm going to be the father I never had," they say. Yet many who made that declaration later admit, "You know, when my first child was born, I told myself, 'I am going to be the father I never had,' but now I find myself doing the very things I disliked so much in my dad." Our fathers are default models: If we reject them as models but fail to replace them with new ones, then we end up using them as our models anyway, in spite of ourselves.

Unfortunately, much of what is being written by experts, sociologists, and journalists about fathering doesn't help. In addition to "deadbeat dads," other models rise up, such as those from pathology, via such thinkers as Lewis Yablonsky and Robert Meister: abusive dads, buddy dads, distant dads, critical dads, seductive dads, idealized dads, egocentric dads, psychopathic dads, and more.[14] These types, which are considered vitally important in research, often make you feel like a college freshman in a psychology course: Nothing in the textbook seems to fascinate us as much as the chapters on abnormal behaviors.

But we're not abnormal fathers. We're just typical Joes trying to win with our kids. We need a simplified plan for being an effective father—a simple plan that makes sense and that considers social research.

Discovering the Joy of Fathering

The heart of the father needs to beat for his children. Ultimately, it's not a matter of what a father *does*—although that is important, and we'll look at research that shows what behaviors help our children. But my overriding purpose is for you to discover the immense joy of fathering.

I wish for each of us to be more like Bob, a father and friend of mine. One day at work during an intense meeting, Bob's eyes started wandering. "Bob," someone said, "did you hear me?"

"Oh sure," Bob said, and his focus snapped back to the person's face. He leaned forward to study some papers and the meeting resumed in full force.

But only a few seconds later, in the middle of someone's comment, Bob waved his hand apologetically. "I'm really sorry," he said, "but I just can't concentrate. Hold your thought; I'll be back in a minute." Out the door he went.

In his wake, he left bewilderment. *Where did he go?* the staff wondered. *What was so important that it couldn't wait twenty minutes?* And, without a clue, they waited. Betty twiddled her thumbs; Helen crossed and re-crossed her legs; Jerry offered to get coffee.

About eight minutes later, Bob shuffled back into the room. "Where were we?" he asked. Everyone looked at him, still perplexed. "OK," he said, "I'm sorry I left, but I couldn't wait. My kids are down at the day care today, and I just had to have a 'kid fix.'"

Dad, I'm warning you: *Fatherhood can be addicting.* Its simple joys can become compelling. Maybe for you it will start with bouts of wrestling when you come home from work, then maybe you'll find yourself sneaking hugs before dinner, or lingering longer than necessary by their beds at night, or uttering words of encouragement when they leave for school. Finally, you'll be looking to score a fix at any moment of the day.

Then, if worse comes to worse, you'll become a pusher. Like me.

Part One

THE SHAPE OF YOUR HEART

EXAMINING YOUR HEART

You may remember Hank Gathers, a big-time basketball star at Loyola University in the 90s. As a college forward, he was one of the nation's leading scorers and rebounders, and he had pro scouts watching him closely. Then, one March evening in the midst of a crucial game, he slam-dunked the ball, smiled, began to run up court, then collapsed on his back.

A little over an hour later, Gathers lay dead in the emergency room of a Los Angeles hospital. To all outward appearances, he was a man at the height of his athletic prowess. To those who had gathered at the hospital, a doctor gave a flat statement: "Much to everyone's chagrin, there was never any evidence of spontaneous heart activity that we could measure on a heart monitor."[1]

Hank Gathers suffered from a congenital heart problem. A doctor had warned him of it earlier that year, but nearly everyone found it difficult to believe that such a gifted and physically fit athlete could be brought down so young. He continued to play, until, at the seeming height of his career, he collapsed and died.

A father, too, can suffer from a bad heart without ever knowing it. I'm not talking about the physical heart, but the emotional and spiritual heart that sustains a family. He may even move gracefully through several stages of fatherhood, a veritable model of parenting. "Did you see the way Phil disciplined his daughter?" Phil's neighbor asks a friend. "Firm, yet compassionate. And how about the tree house he built for his two little boys? It's a great design, and that guy sure is a craftsman with wood. And he makes the time and really enjoys coaching his Little League team, leading Cub Scouts, and teaching a children's Sunday school class. Where does he get his energy? He has such a heart for his kids. I wish I could be half the father that Phil is."

But then, suddenly, something happens. Maybe one of his sons turns into a teenager and rebels; Phil cannot handle the loss of control. Or his daughter is hurt in an accident, and he stubbornly clings to guilt. Maybe it is for no foreseeable reason at all. But, without warning, Phil stops playing as much with his children and disappears into a career. Over time, hugs and outings and spontaneous play are replaced by excuses, fatigue, and defeated resignation. Somewhere along the road, the heart of a father stopped beating.

If an emotional autopsy of Phil's heart could be performed, one might be able to discover the hidden cause. Chances are, Phil's fathering heart was damaged early on in his life, as a child or teen.

The primary influence on the condition of a father's heart is a man's father. In other words, the first step to becoming an effective father is to come to terms with your past by resolving your feelings, attributes, and actions as a son. As the disintegration of fathering continues, dangerous trends worsen. Fathers, damaged by their fathers, pass on the broken baton to their sons. And so on. Unless the cycle is broken, the damage to the emotional and spiritual hearts of future fathers is almost as certain as a defect passed along to the physical heart through a chromosome.

"Boys grow into men with a wounded father within, a conflicted inner sense of masculinity," wrote Samuel Osherson, a Harvard research psychologist. After scores of interviews with men in their thirties and forties, Osherson concluded that "the psychological or physical absence of fathers from their families is one of the great underestimated tragedies of our times."[2]

Despite the overwhelming amount of research confirming the impact of a father on a son's ability to father, many men I have met are reluctant to think about their fathers and deal with underlying feelings. Some of that reluctance is certainly a fear of pain. You can dredge up some hurts that seem to accrue compound interest over the years, and these seem overwhelming.

Other men aren't convinced that an inventory of the past will be productive: "That was then; this is now. I'm too busy raising my own kids to worry about how I was fathered. Besides, the way I was fathered has little effect on my fathering. Right?" Or, "My dad was just like everyone—each one of us has our good points and bad points—and we have to make do with what we are given."

And so these men, unaware of the condition of their hearts, jump blindly into fathering. Some of them fail immediately; others, fueled on the adrenaline of commitment and strong will, run a little longer, maybe even as gracefully as Phil. But eventually, often at what marathon runners call "the wall of pain," their damaged hearts simply fail them.

What Do We Do Now?

Psychologist Donald Joy points out, "Men with a damaged father connection will be healed only to the extent that they can describe the loss and the pain."[3]

A heart damaged by a father is often deeply bruised. Over the years, many movements have sprung up to help men deal with the pain from the damage left behind by poor fathering. Robert Bly, the poet and de facto guru of the "Men's Movement," conducted "Wild Man Weekends" in the 1980s and 90s to help men deal with their pain. Dancing to drum beating and giving emotionally charged personal histories were some of the forms of expression he encouraged men to try as a way to release their father pain. In his book *Iron John* he wrote: "[Father-] hungry sons hang around older men like the homeless do around a soup kitchen. Like the homeless, they feel shame over their condition, and it is nameless, bitter, inexpugnable shame."[4]

Before we run the race of fathering, it only makes sense to have our hearts checked, to see how they have been strengthened or damaged. The first section of this book, "The Shape of Your Heart," explores the relationship between a father and his own father. The goal is to restore whatever is faulty in the relationship with healthy attitudes and actions (to whatever extent that is possible). The section investigates three vital steps in the process: recognition, resolution, and relating.

To begin the process, you first must know the shape of your heart; then you can make healing your goal. To bring healing, what you do next—as well as how and why you do it—is critical. For the damaged heart of a father to heal and remain healthy, it is important that a man seek to establish a new relationship with his own father as well as another Father.

Honoring Our Fathers

I believe there is something in us—a law written on our hearts—that says, "Honor your father and mother." That's how it's stated in the Bible, but you'll find it in all of the world's religions. The ancient Chinese Analects advise, "Surely proper behavior to parents and elder brothers is the [tree] trunk of goodness."

We must consciously attempt, first of all, to find the good in our fathers, no matter how badly they seemed to have fathered us. To put a spin on Marc Antony's cry: "We have not come to bury our fathers under the dirt of our accusations; we've come to praise them for what we have discovered in them and for what they have given us." What our fathers did right is every bit as important as what they did wrong.

If, as C. S. Lewis wrote, "fatherhood must be at the core of the universe," then disrespect for a father means engaging in some very dangerous vandalism.[5] That is true culturally, but also personally. Gordon Dalbey writes, "We had better teach our sons mercy. A man who curses his father . . . curses his own manhood."[6]

The first safeguard against father-bashing is to maintain a high degree of respect for the office, regardless of the man who fills it. Fatherhood is an honorable calling. Certain men may bring dishonor to it, and we wouldn't be so troubled by what these men do unless we had an innate sense that they were severely missing the mark. But being a father is a marvelous thing—to give life and sustain life, to sacrifice your own life for the sake of those who are helpless. We must honor our fathers and embrace our own honorable title as fathers.

If you are a father yourself, you've got a great deal at stake in preserving the integrity of the office, especially in the eyes of your children. That means fulfilling your responsibilities faithfully, but that also means refusing to shame the one who held the office before you—your dad.

And there is hope.

It may surprise you to learn that, in one bit of research at the National

Center for Fathering, we discovered that a man's relationship with his father is not the most significant predictor of his current relationship with his children. In other words, a painful past is certainly an influence, but not the "silver bullet." Your commitment to become a dad of destiny can displace the negative effects resulting from a poor relationship with your dad. You can join the distinguished ranks of the "overcomer dads."

RECOGNIZE YOUR PAST

When he noticed the pain in his chest, recording artist David Meece went promptly to his doctor's office. There the doctor examined him for several hours and concluded the symptoms signaled a heart attack.

David told me the story one day on a Father's Day radio special: "They took me down to the emergency room and then to intensive care and hooked me up. At this point I was hyperventilating because I was flipping out—I didn't know what was going on and I was passing out and then waking up. I thought this was from having a heart attack. They told me later it was from hyperventilating.

"I'm later there, tubes in my arms, tubes up my nose, nurses coming in and sticking things in me, turning me over and rolling me back. Then, after several days in the hospital, my physician came in and told me that I had not had a heart attack—I was physically fit as a horse!"

David was shocked to hear that finding, but the question the doctor asked him was just as unsettling: "David, is there any alcoholism in your family?"

"Yeah, my father," David answered. The response "just popped out of my mouth," David recalls. "It was the first time I'd ever acknowledged that word [alcoholism] at all."

David—who by his own words was an "extreme workaholic"—had never faced his feelings about his father. He knew he hadn't felt anything at his funeral earlier that year, but he still refused to admit how much his father's alcoholism had impacted him.

Many men are like David, unable to recognize the impact of their father's past. To a large degree, your heart as a father is shaped by the heart of *your* father. You and I need to face that, and recognize any damage from our childhood. Without taking this step we run the risk of ending up like David. Even if our symptoms are different, we will assuredly have some type of symptoms—most likely in the way we relate to our families.

Here are the words of some other fathers, each of whom has a family history of what I call "father-heart disease," passed down by their own dads.

Tom, who like David is just beginning to recognize how shortcomings in his father affected him: "You know, my dad gave thousands of dollars to various youth organizations, but he never helped his own kids."

Jim: "I can't tell you whether my father treated me harshly or warmly, because he left almost all interactions with me up to my mother. I guess the truth is, even though we lived in the same house, he was barely involved with me at all."

Tyler: "Dad did little to satisfy my hunger for knowledge. He didn't talk much, either about current events or, especially, about his own past. I knew he had grown up in Ireland, which sounded terribly exotic to me. But it was almost impossible to get him to talk about it."

Dan: "Up until I turned into a teenager, my childhood was wonderful. My father created a magical world for us—one that was filled with imagination, safety, and play. But when I started having ideas of my own, my father and I clashed. I could sense that he didn't like the idea of losing control over me."

Bill: "I wanted my father to be so proud of me. Then all he did was drive me to the graduation ceremony in our pickup, and let me off. He never stayed to see me graduate. He just came and picked me up afterward."

Who You Are

Today, in a culture that has been splintered by marital failure and mobility, our ties to our parents often seem less obvious. Yet, in research literature across the board, from genetics to psychology, it is increasingly clear that we have not escaped our family inheritance. Your father and mother have had a huge influence on who you are. Concerning our fathers, that means for some of us a legacy of pain or loss or feelings of being incomplete. For others, it means a less intense father-hunger, thanks to our dads' involvement. But we cannot deny that our dads have given us much, beginning with our identity.

The first and most important thing we receive from our fathers is our names. I am Ken Canfield, son of Melvin Canfield, who was the son of Merle Canfield. Et cetera.

Up until recent times, a name was more than just what you called yourself. It reflected, in one way or another, a deep connection with preceding generations. If your last name was Baker, for instance, you probably followed the recipe of a long line of men who baked bread for a living. Or Mr. Fuller, Mr. Fisher, Mr. Carpenter—all of these names indicate that early fathers passed on to their sons careers, livelihoods, and lifestyles. Names also could have represented personality traits. Bliss, Hope, Lovejoy. A last name originally was a simple way of saying, "Like father, like son."

There were other obvious connections that tied generation to generation. Inheritances, for example. In the old days, the reading of the last will and testament meant more than receiving a few disconnected items—some china, furniture, and money. It meant, instead, the passing on of a livelihood. Children received the raw material they would need to begin conducting the business, the deed to a farm, or utensils for the kitchen.

In Middle America, some family farms survive. I know some fifth-generation farmers, descendants of original homesteaders. When their parents died, they received the farm, and with it a mission—to grow crops and raise cattle and provide for their families, the next generation. And the inheritance's inventory included more than just acreage and machinery. Sometimes it included poorly managed fields, sucked dry by erosion and overuse. It even included the family operation's reputation. The feed store owner knew how good the family's credit was. The cattle auctioneer knew how pure the family stock was. It was like the father was saying to his son,

"Here you go. This is what I was able to do with what my father entrusted to me. Now it's your turn. When you pass it on to your son, may the assets outweigh the liabilities."

Such concrete ties with preceding generations made it clear to nearly everyone that the passing on of names and livelihoods marked the cycle: What you possess, you have been given, you pass on.

The Power of Our Dads

Cookie-holics and Other Legacies

Some years ago, I was in Wichita visiting my parents. For some reason, I borrowed Dad's car to run some errands, and as I was driving along something caught my eye on the floor of the car, just below my leg. I knew immediately what it was: a sackful of cookies.

I laughed out loud (but stopped long enough to stuff a cookie into my mouth). I remembered that my dad is a cookie-holic. He was in his sixties, but he still drove around munching on cookies as he went about his business. But there was another reason that I laughed: I also used to hide my bag of cookies in the same place. I never knew I was so like my dad.

Certainly this is a silly example, yet I'm sure some fathers and sons stash bottles under the seat instead of cookies. I suspect you'd be surprised to discover the influence your father has had on you, even down to how you imitate some of his gestures, behaviors, and attitudes. How can you help but be influenced by your father? His Y chromosome resides in every single cell of your body. Your very DNA cries out that you owe your person to another. And how can you not be affected by the words and actions of your father that say, *Son, I love you,* or, *Son, I wish you were a little more like so and so?* The impact, biologically and emotionally, is irrefutable and immense.

Wrong Responses to Our Father's Influence

But still there are some who deny their father's influence. In essence, they say, "The past is past; I need to get on with life. I will simply choose to be different from my father." Yet, the underlying issues remain unresolved, and, in time, the son becomes just like the father. Good intentions are simply not enough.

I compare this kind of denial to our country's national debt, which as of 2006, is more than $8 trillion (and though it fluctuates wildly, it can grow by more than $100 million in an hour).[1] "If we wait long enough," we kid ourselves, "one day we'll wake up and it will be gone; the math will rework itself and balance out to a big zero in the end."

The same kind of logic is often also applied to the fathering deficit. The consequences of such denial, on both a personal and community level, are staggering. "The ultimate economic and spiritual unity of any civilization is still the family," writes playwright Clare Boothe Luce.

The other extreme to denial is exacting justice. Some men recognize their fathers' failings, become angry, and want to take revenge. They go to their fathers and demand payment for the way they have treated them.

Like denial, though, taking revenge won't help a man deal with his past. His father, who is probably already feeling guilty, is handed blame that is beyond his capability to resolve. And the son, awash in anger, typically will refuse to move forward until his father does. So, the son is reduced to bashing his father.

Deficits and Assets

Your family, generation after generation, may be passing along a "fathering deficit." Did your father make any deposits in your emotional bank account as you were growing up? If your father hasn't provided affirmation and affection for you, you will most likely run up a big overdraft. The result of continuing overdrafts is emotional bankruptcy. Unless you stop and take a look at the balance of your intergenerational fathering accounts, you will be in danger of passing that "fathering debt" on to your children. One day, someone will have to pay.

And we're not only looking for deficits. We are also looking for the assets—those areas where our fathers excelled and were faithful. We want to be doubly sure that these pools of strength are passed on to our children with no decrease in their value. There are many men who've been given wonderful legacies, but like farmers who let their family farms go to weed, they don't act on what they've been given. In this chapter, we will recognize our past: the influence, good and bad, of our fathers that has made us who we are today. This first step of recognition is not simply for those with traumatic childhoods. It's for every father, and it is the only way we can get a good assessment of our strengths and weaknesses, our assets and liabilities.

Tell Me About Your Dad

For some people, taking an inventory of the past can be a complicated process. If your father abused you as a child—and the statistics suggest that many fathers did—then you may be wise to find a professional counselor who can more thoroughly and personally lead you through this inventory process. For most men, however, the inventory process is a lot less complicated. In fact, once you've dug a core sample, toxic waste really isn't that hard to detect. Memories will come back. And with those memories— emotion. I have a friend named Jeff who felt emotionally overwhelmed after he broke off his marriage engagement. The first person he reached out to was a sympathetic college professor, who listened to Jeff speak for a while and then simply said, "Tell me about your dad." That did it. Jeff broke down weeping.

"Tell me about your dad." That's really all I'm asking in this chapter. Because each of your situations is so varied, this chapter cannot be arranged in a typical, step-by-step, universal problem, universal solution fashion. What follows is a series of interactive questions, which will allow you to get a better grip on your relationship with your father. All of us will find our inheritances lacking to some degree. I trust that whatever lack we identify will motivate us to work on the next step: resolving our feelings, attitudes, and actions as sons.

And remember what author Samuel Osherson writes: "Every man needs to identify the good in his father, to feel how we are like them, as well as the ways we are different from them."[2]

Now for some of you, your father was largely absent. It's hard to even get a handle on the questions in Father Inventory #2. I would suggest trying this exercise twice: once for your natural father, from whatever you know about him, and then once for the man who most treated you like a son.

Before you begin Father Inventory #1, I recommend that you enlist the help of others to complete the inventory. In any relationship as powerful as that with a father, strong emotions are inevitable. And, even if you want to honestly explore the similarities and differences with your father, your perspective may be hopelessly clouded by your feelings. By asking others to help, you are saying, "Do you think I'm assessing myself and my father honestly?"

Your wife is an obvious choice for a sounding board, even though she too may be influenced by your feelings. Close friends and family can be helpful, especially if they are familiar with both you and your father. Some of you, depending on how healthy your relationship with your dad already is, may wish to work through this exercise with him.

Once you finish your lists, you might also want to share them with others (besides those who helped you during the process) before taking any action. Author and psychologist David Stoop writes, "Many people's initial impulse is to go straight to the person who has hurt them—in this case, Dad—and confront him, letting the chips fall where they may. That is seldom a helpful approach to dealing with the kinds of issues we are talking about."[3] Dr. Stoop recommends talking to someone.

A listening ear can help you accomplish what you need to do, namely, verbalize your memories and your feelings, as well as provide a double check on your accuracy.

FATHER INVENTORY #1
Your Father and Your Past

For this inventory, you will evaluate the similarities and differences between your father and yourself to get a picture of his influence on you. Guidelines for completing this inventory can be found on the following pages.

To identify similarities and differences, please write down:

- **Five ways you are like your father**
- **Five ways you are not like your father**

In an effort to give you some clues on what might be included in such lists, here are my responses to Inventory #1, reflections on my own relationship with my dad.

SIMILARITIES WITH AND DIFFERENCES FROM MY FATHER

FIVE WAYS I'M LIKE MY FATHER

1. Frugal Lifestyle

For example, my dad rarely makes car payments. Instead, he buys used cars and saves his money toward the purchase of a replacement. Similarly, I always purchase used cars outright and drive them until they're barely worth fixing anymore.

2. Harder on the Older Children

My father was the oldest child in his family. I was the oldest child in mine. My father raised his oldest son (me) the way he was raised, and I seem to be doing the same. I have higher expectations of my two oldest children, whom I seem more ready to discipline and correct.

3. Ice Cream Late at Night

Vanilla is fine for both of us, just as long as it's three healthy scoops and served after the sun goes down.

4. A Subtle Workaholism

My dad had a tendency to get too many projects going at one time. When the pressure of deadlines built up, he'd end up starting to work at 4 a.m. I am writing this paragraph at 2 a.m.

FIVE WAYS I'M NOT LIKE MY FATHER

1. A Circle of Outside Acquaintances

My father rarely socialized outside the family. Home was a private refuge, not a public watering hole. By contrast, Dee and I entertain friends quite regularly.

2. Spiritual Concerns

My father wasn't very interested in the spiritual side of life, but I've chosen to be active in my church and place high value on a relationship with God.

3. A Real Competitor

My father was president of his senior class and very involved in sports (he was starting quarterback and won a state championship in tennis). I was average athletically and wasn't involved in student government.

4. Leadership Styles

My father likes to be in control, while I am much more laid-back. He will likely take charge in a meeting to assure some productive conclusion. I am more likely to be a consensus leader.

FIVE WAYS I'M LIKE MY FATHER	FIVE WAYS I'M NOT LIKE MY FATHER
5. Emotionally Inexpressive	**5. Variety**
My dad came out of the era when men didn't express feelings. He rarely touched me except for discipline, and only occasionally affirmed me verbally for an accomplishment. I still struggle with this tendency toward emotional distance from my children.	My father demands regularity. I like to travel, while he prefers to stay home. I will take a new route to see the different sights; he beats the same path home every night.

Your list, of course, will be different. That's the idea. Each of us, because we are different and come from varying situations, will develop entirely unique lists. As you work on your list, here are some additional tips:

Start simple. If you have trouble starting your list, begin with physical characteristics. Do you have your father's nose? Is he a stocky man, while you are more trim? These might get you started as you think about comparisons and contrasts, and give you a greater sense of your father's far-reaching influence—even in the way you look. Also, you might want to consider listing what seem like trivial issues, such as eating ice cream at night or hiding cookies under your seat. Listing these incidental observations may be helpful, giving you clues to other deeper issues.

List both positive and negative qualities. The best way to honor a man is to seek to understand him accurately. To err on the side of his negative points is to malign his character; to err on the side of his positive points is to idolize him. If you have experienced a particularly difficult childhood, it may seem unjust to even consider putting your father's positive inheritance in writing. Try anyway. You may have to become creative in your search for positive items. I remember one man who told me about his parents' divorce and how painful it was for him as a young boy. "But you know," this man said, "my dad never once missed a child support payment. He was as regular as clockwork."

Be sure to pay equal attention to your "not like" list. It is possible that your father has influenced your "not like" list as much as he has influenced your "like" list. In other words, while the "like" list may reveal cycles you wish to break, the "not like" list may reveal reactions you wish to avoid. A man may think he's being proactive when in reality he only wishes to avoid being like his father. We need to find the freedom to make our own choices as fathers, choices based on wisdom and effectiveness, not on the pendulum swing of emotion. The "not like" list may reveal some deep psychological insights. Other characteristics will also help you see your genuine independence from your father.

Be specific. Include examples. Fathering knowledge is caught, not taught. As you review your list, probably only a few of your items are things that you and your father ever discussed outright. It's unlikely your dad said, "Son, let me tell you about workaholism, how to fall into it, and why it's good for America." Instead, as sons we've picked up certain traits and behaviors from our dads because they modeled them. By including specific examples to the general traits, the memories will be more vivid and result in greater benefits as you begin to process the items on your list.

Assessing Your Father

Understanding your father as a man is an important step. It is our desire, however, to focus the perspective a little tighter—what kind of a dad was your father? Perhaps the first—and maybe the most critical— aspect that you need to understand about your father was that he, too, was a son. This can be a powerful revelation, allowing you great insight into your father.

My friend Andrew recently showed me a photograph. "That's me," he said. "I'm standing in front of my grandpa's grave." The shot was out of focus and taken from a distance, but Andrew stands before the grave of his father's father with his head bowed. His dark blue jacket is a sharp contrast to the vibrant yellow leaves on the ground and the light marble gray of the tombstones.

"I had never really made the connection before," Andrew told me, "that my father had a father. I mean, I knew Charles Axelrod as Grandpa and I knew my father as Dad, but right then at the grave site, it struck me that these two men were also father and son."

Later Andrew would ask his father, "Tell me about Grandpa," but the information he was really gathering was: "Tell me about your relationship with your dad—how you two interacted, ways you are like and not like him." Andrew came to a better understanding of how and why his father fathered.

By viewing your father as a son, you can make comparisons to your own experience as a son, and you may discover in yourself a well of empathy to help you reconcile with your father. We tend to picture our fathers as all-powerful beings because that's how they appeared in our childhood perspective, but we never stop to realize that they too were once boys, and sons of a father. Many of the wounds we have suffered as sons were handed down from our fathers and their fathers and beyond.

In Father Inventory #2, we will look at some of the fathering fundamentals in order to get a handle on how our fathers fathered us. Some insights may startle you.

The four questions in Inventory #2 are simple questions about the four major functions at the heart of fathering—involvement, consistency, awareness, and nurturance. In the last two sections of this book we will examine these issues in great detail, but for now we simply want to ask, "How'd your dad do?"

FATHER INVENTORY #2
Assessing My Father

The four major questions below will help you evaluate your father's functioning in four major areas of your life: his involvement, consistency, awareness, and nurturance. Take your time in answering these questions; it may even be helpful to write your observations into a journal. It also may be helpful to get another perspective, perhaps of a sibling or someone else who was aware of your relationship with your dad while you were growing up. As you write, try to clear your mind, as much as possible, of emotion.

These questions serve only as a guide to helping you understand your dad as a father. You may, as you write, begin to ask yourself other questions. That's OK. The goal is not to specifically answer *these* questions, but to arrive at a clearer perspective.

1. Was my father *involved* in my life as a child?

Did your father spend time with you? Did he attend those events that were important to you? Did he include you in what he did? Perhaps you can remember a specific time when you were deeply disappointed because your father failed to be involved in something important. Or perhaps you can recall a surge of joy or pride during a specific time when your father participated in a particular moment or event.

2. Was my father *consistent*?

How regular and predictable was your father? Did you know what to expect when you approached him? Could you rely on him to give order to your young world? Reflect on certain moments when he either succeeded or failed in his consistency.

3. Was my father *aware* of my feelings and thoughts?

Did you have a sense that your father was interested in you? Did he seek to know who you were and what your world was like? Perhaps he could name your favorite color or baseball player or the girl who had a crush on you. Recall specific moments.

4. How much *nurture* did I receive from my father?

Can you remember hearing the words "I love you"? Can you still feel your dad's hand on your shoulder? Maybe he listened to you when you needed to talk, or he encouraged you when you were uncertain. He might have created an environment where you could be uniquely you, or he might have tried to shape you in someone else's image. Again, try to think of specific examples.

In some cases, it's possible for a father to *try too hard*. An overly involved father, for example, is overattached. An overly consistent dad is rigid. An overly aware father is intrusive. And an overly nurturing dad can be smothering. Was this your experience? Once again, try to think about specific incidents.

As you work through these questions, you may become troubled. It is almost as if you had more than one father—say, a creative, powerful, involved father in your early school years, and an overly busy, distant, controlling dad when you were a teenager. This is not unusual. As a son, you went through different stages where you grew and changed and moved on. But did your father grow and change and move with you? Or were there certain periods of your life where he bailed out or abandoned you totally?

To properly answer these questions you will need to think back (or for the early years have someone help you think back) through major periods of your life: your very first memories, your early school-age years, your teenage years, your first years on your own, and the birth of your first child. Try looking at some snapshots or mementos as pieces of a jigsaw puzzle. You will want to try to uncover some specific memories and examples from each period, which will help you answer this question: "How close or how distant do you remember being with your father during each of these periods?"

You may want to start by writing a summary paragraph on each one of these periods in your life. If your thoughts begin to spill out about one particular time frame, keep writing. Possibly something has been dammed up. And when it flows out, new freedom is possible.

Like Father, Like Son

After completing these two inventories, it will be easier to see how your father's influence affects your thoughts and actions today. In the exercise below, answer questions about your father's legacy to you.

My Father's Impact

1. *How has my dad affected the way I show affection to my children? Do I show affection the same way he did?*
2. *How did my father discipline me? Do I use the same methods? Is my attitude or tone when I'm correcting my children the same?*
3. *How did my dad communicate his values and principles to me? Which ones took root and why? How am I doing this with my own children?*
4. *Did my father teach me about sexuality? How? Were we able to talk about other facts of life—dishonesty, racism, jealousy? Do I talk naturally to my children about these same kinds of concerns?*

Living with the Lack

Each month, our bank sends a long, itemized statement to my house and I sit down and reconcile the bank's records with our checkbook—or at least check to make sure the online download of the statement matches my records. The goal is accuracy—to know exactly where the Canfield family stands. If it turns out that we don't have as much in the checking account as we thought we did, then we force ourselves to live the next month under the newly discovered constraints. "Sorry, kids. We have to cut back on eating out this month." Likewise, if we have more money, then we plan accordingly.

If you've spent some time answering questions about your father as a man and a dad, and you have worked through how you are both *like* him and *different* from him, you are now in a position to begin to understand how those balances affect your life.

This will be tough and often painful work. It can be like a man waking up in the morning with only a little sleep; sometimes you just don't have the heart to look into the mirror. When you look deeply into your relationship with your father, it often serves as a mirror into some very hidden areas. They reveal certain things about you and how you feel about how you were fathered. You can look in that mirror, turn away, and immediately forget what you see. Or you can pause long enough to face the fact that your face is dirty, your beard is scraggly, and your eyes are bloodshot.

But it is vital that we face the facts. Claim ownership of your feelings. Avoid denying that your father had some pretty profound effects on who you are and how you feel. Until we can face ourselves in the mirror, and make some necessary changes, we have little hope of ever walking with confidence in the merciless light of day.

Speak the Truth

One of the best ways to face the facts is to speak the truth. If you've identified a deficient account in your relationship with your father, write it down on paper or tell your wife, a family member, or a trusted friend. Get it out in the open where it is on record.

Your words open a door that can lead into freedom and healing and a firm foundation for your children. If your relationship with your father is damaged, "healing can only occur to the extent that the loss and pain can be described."[4] Basically, I am asking you to find the courage to "live with the loss," to live with the ambiguity of a relationship with your father that wasn't all you wanted it to be—to finally admit that some dreams die, and they die hard. You need to grieve.

In processing our past, we need to admit that something very real and important—what we wanted from our fathers—has died. The loss of what you expected—and even needed—from your father is much like a death in the family. Your father, in one sense, has died in his role as guardian, protector, and counselor. Grief is the natural response to such a loss. Grief is the means by which we heal loss. The biblical beatitude rings true: Blessed are those who mourn. Many of us are familiar with Dr. Elisabeth Kubler-Ross's early research of the five stages of the grieving process: denial, anger, bargaining, depression, and finally acceptance.[5] Some men, in grieving their father's "death," get stuck in the anger stage. They focus on the list of grievances against their dads instead of letting themselves grieve further. But I'm afraid most men get stuck in the denial stage. "Nobody—," writes Gordon Dalbey, "neither men nor women—wants to face the painful father-wound."[6]

The Faces of Denial

Denial can assume a thousand different faces. Some young inner-city men who grieve their absent fathers try to fill the void through gang membership, sexual exploits, and violence. Young suburban men may choose workaholism or promiscuity or pornography. Other older rural men lose themselves in routine or resignation.

Behavior resulting from our frantic attempt to deny our father-hunger is essentially "deficit spending." We are like those people who pay off their MasterCard bill by getting a cash advance on their Visa card. We are like those people who realistically can't afford to maintain their present lifestyle, but do so by taking out loans they can't afford to repay. We are living on credit, dangerously denying what we know to be true: that all our compensating and compulsive behavior may cost us dearly when the bills come due. We overspend as men and persons, but I am even more concerned about the deficit spending we do as fathers. What do we do if we lack something in our sonship? Typically, we exact it from our children in our fathering. We make them pay. We pass the debt on to our children.

For example, say your father never said, "I love you." It would be possible—and common—to react to this deficit in one of two extremes—either by also withholding affection from your children, providing an identification *with* your father, or by overcompensating and smothering your children with affection in a reaction against your dad. You either demand affection from your children that you really wish your father had given, or else you become permissive in a false attempt to create an atmosphere of nurturance. Either way, you manage to temporarily avoid having to face your father-wound by having your children pay the deficit instead.

And the cycle goes on.

But it doesn't have to be this way. As you admit ways in which your father may have fallen short, you can also make this commitment: "The deficit spending stops here. I won't willfully pass these cycles on to my children."

Many men now recognize the deficits with their dads. A National Center for Fathering/Gallup survey found that a majority of men agree that "most people have unresolved problems with their fathers." In addition, one of every four men said that they struggle to talk openly with their fathers. See Father Fact #1 on the next page for specific results of this survey (and see appendix 3 for other key findings).

The process of recognition is an ongoing one. Because the father-son relationship is so critical and powerful, there will be new issues arising along the way. As you deal with one issue, others will spring up. What is important, for the time being, is to begin to prioritize what you have learned from working through the questions in this chapter. You (and your friend) will have to determine what things are the most significant. I'd suggest using two questions as your criteria:

- What one issue, if it were resolved, would do the most to reestablish or strengthen your relationship with your father?
- What one issue in your own life hinders you the most from having a healthy, functioning relationship with your kids?

I suspect you won't have to think long on these questions. The issues should pop to the surface fairly rapidly. Again, your big task will be in accepting their significance. If sexual deviancy is an issue, admit it. If anger or workaholism is an issue, admit it. Your temptation will be to focus on the smaller, even nitpicky things, when larger issues are pressing.

With those issues firmly in hand, you are ready to move on to the next step of processing the past: resolution. The cracks in your fathering foundation have all been identified. It's time to begin to patch them up.

FATHER FACT #1
The Father Problem

The National Center for Fathering/Gallup Poll on the Role of Fathering in America measured attitudes toward fathering. By a large majority, Americans agreed that the most significant social problem facing America is the physical absence of the father from the home.

1. The most significant family or social problem facing America is the physical absence of the father from the home.

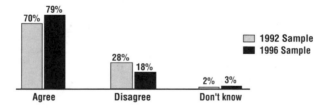

Thus four of every five respondents agreed that the father's physical absence is the most significant social problem in America. This 79 percent agreement is an increase of 9 percentage points from a similar NCF/Gallup poll conducted four years earlier.

2. Most people have unresolved problems with their fathers.

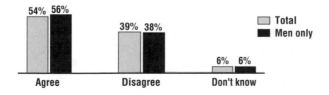

Notice that among men the level of agreement is 56 percent. This suggests that men continue to struggle as adults with the relationship to their fathers. Significantly, the generation that has borne the brunt of father neglect, 18- to 34-year-olds, displayed the highest level of agreement with the statement, 61 percent.

Three items in the survey measured the level of tension that adults feel toward their fathers. Although it is difficult to admit any estrangement from a parent, men and women are recognizing a tension in their relationships with their fathers, according to the results. Between a quarter and a third of adults acknowledged an impaired relationship with their fathers. Only 26 percent of men were strongly confident they could talk freely with their fathers.

3. I can talk freely with my father.

RESULTS FOR MEN AND WOMEN:

	Men	Women
Strongly agree	26%	31%
Agree	50%	38%
Disagree	17%	22%
Strongly disagree	4%	6%
Don't know	1%	1%
Not applicable	2%	1%

The results offer an interesting contrast between men and women—women were less likely to feel free to talk with their father, but more women than men knew what their fathers felt toward them during their childhood.

4. As a child you knew what your father felt about you.

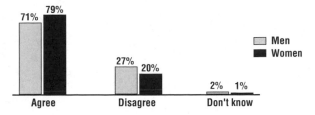

Certainly there is room for men to resolve their feelings for their fathers, as shown by male response to the following statement:

5. I feel at peace with my father.

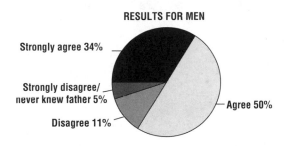

Significantly, only one-third of the men surveyed could say with assurance that they felt at peace with their fathers.

RESOLVE YOUR PAST

Bob's dad was an alcoholic. Bob could count on his dad coming home every Friday night to get cleaned up so he could go get drunk. When his father wasn't drunk and tried to deal with the real world, he often verbally abused Bob, hurling names and epithets Bob's way; telling Bob, "You can't do anything right!" and dishing out sarcasm at the dinner table. His dad also would get physical with Bob's mother, sometimes slapping her at the end of an argument, sometimes shoving her against a counter.

One Friday evening, when Bob was ten, he climbed up into a tree as his father left the house. Perched between two branches, he watched his father enter their blue '55 Buick. As his dad turned the key and began to pull away toward the liquor store, Bob yelled, "I hate you! I wish you were dead! *I wish you were dead!*"

The little boy got his wish. Two hours later, Bob's father was in a car accident that ended his life. The last scene of Bob and his dad together—the '55 Buick and Bob's cutting last words—haunted Bob throughout his life.

Like his great-grandfather, grandfather, and father before him, Bob too became an alcoholic. Sometimes it almost seemed as if he were acting out a script. Eventually, Bob realized there had to be something more to this life, and he began a pilgrimage that led him into a deep spiritual faith. He stopped drinking. But it wasn't until Bob began to come to terms with his childhood that he began to finally heal in his damaged heart.

The Dream and the Miracle

One night, he had a vivid dream. The same images that had haunted him his entire life returned: sitting in a tree, looking out over the driveway, watching his father get into the '55 Buick. But this time the event did not repeat itself. In the strange and rapid transition of dream scenery, Bob found himself beside the car, looking into the driver's side window. As the man behind the wheel turned his face, Bob saw that it was not his father. It was Jesus. Rolling down the window, he looked at Bob and then said, "Get in, Bob. It's OK. You can ride with me."

That night was a turning point. The words of Jesus carried an invitation for relationship and started the process that would lead him to forgive his dad. For so long, Bob had been carrying around the baggage of guilt, anger, and many other deep emotional rags of a torn relationship. It was time to let go, accept forgiveness, and move on. Through a long process, Bob has been able to forgive himself and his father. By allowing himself to grieve, he has overcome the deep pain of his childhood. The four-generation cycle of alcoholism in his family has been broken. Hopefully, his own children will never know the pain of such blatant abuse and neglect.

As fathers, many of us need to reach a point of resolution in our feelings toward our fathers. For Bob and David Meece (chapter 1) the issue was an alcoholic dad. Your father and you may have struggles in a different area; yet the feelings will be similar. Whether your feelings are anger, envy, loss, estrangement, or even hatred, you must deal with them. Only then can you be a healthy, strong father for your own children.

A Time to Resolve a Relationship

In the previous chapter, you learned to recognize ways in which your father affected you for good and for bad. I asked you to take a long and probably painful look inside, to see how you are like your father and how you are different. I suggested that you look at the way your father reared you to see if any patterns emerged from your father's fathering. If you found many deficient accounts, I asked you to accept and grieve the loss. Indeed, I asked you a great deal.

Confess . . . and Forgive

Now, for many of you, I will ask of you what may seem impossible— to attempt to resolve the relationship with your father by extending forgiveness. I will suggest you create an event with your father that acts as a signpost for a new direction. Either face-to-face with him, or visiting his grave site, or through an objective third party, express your feelings to him, sharing with him what you've learned in the first step of recognition. If you need to *confess* anything as a son, be bold and own up to it. But more critical, if you need to *forgive* him for any words or actions, be bold and extend him forgiveness. All along, honor your father and state your commitment to a renewed relationship with him.

This, I know, is a frightening step. But it is necessary. What is the use of dredging up emotions, patterns, and psychological and spiritual damage if we do not intend to resolve these stirred-up feelings and wounds? It would be like walking into a field of beehives without knowledge of the pathway out. If you don't move on to the next step, with the goal of a new relationship with your father, you are likely to be left feeling stung by regret or anger. If, however, you move ahead, you can create a landmark that will send you confidently on your way as you father your own kids, and that will be large enough to be visible as you pass by it going on toward the future struggles of your children's adolescence and adulthood.

By resolving your feelings toward your father—and hopefully establishing some guidelines for a renewed relationship—you will finally find freedom from repeating the mistakes of your father's fathering.

The Pull of Our Fathers

Those who use a compass to navigate must learn to contend with "magnetic pull." There are magnetic lines of force that extend through the earth, but they do not converge at the North Pole. Instead, they converge somewhere in the Arctic Circle. Your compass takes a reading off this point. Thus a compass does not automatically point to true north. Instead, it points to "magnetic north." If you stand precisely at a certain longitude—from Lake Superior to Alabama's Gulf Coast—then your compass pointing to magnetic north would also happen to be pointing to true north. But if you go west of this line, your compass will veer east as well as north. Similarly, if you take your compass east of the magnetic line, the needle would point a little toward the northwest.

A father's power is like "magnetic pull." We cannot escape his influence on our lives, even as adults. When you were a child, you were a mapmaker, trying to make sense of this strange world. Not surprisingly, like any mapmaker, you sought reference points to chart your discoveries—your parents, and, for most boys, your father in particular. "What does it mean to be a man?" you asked, and then you likely consulted your father's model to find out, just like a hiker consults his compass. "What does it mean to go out into the world and work a job?" "What does it mean to be a father?" As we saw in the first step of recognition, your father has a great deal of pull; he has magnetic pull.

We cannot, and should not, deny the pull of our fathers. They have given us direction and are important to our identities. But for each of us, our fathers are not really true north. Your father is a human being who falls short of the original design for fathers. Some fathers fall far short. Absent fathers, abusive fathers, critical fathers—they all fall far short. If you try to take your bearings from these men, you may wind up lost in the wilderness. The research proves that many sons of such fathers do. For example, psychologist and author Jane Drew points out that children of abusive fathers are at high risk of being abusive themselves.[1] But *all* fathers veer a few degrees from true north.

Finding True North:
How to Adjust Your Compass

This is a pretty desperate dilemma if you are relying on your compass to keep you from getting lost. But the wise backpacker knows about "magnetic north" and makes the necessary adjustments to find his way accurately through the woods. Good maps tell you the degree of difference between magnetic north and true north. It's called *compass declination,* and it helps you adjust your compass reading. For example, a topographical map of the Grand Canyon gives a compass declination of 15 degrees east. That means if you were hiking at the Grand Canyon and you wanted to head north, you would find north on your compass, but then mentally move the compass reading 15 degrees to the west. That would point you to true north. You could then take off confidently, assured that you will reach the campfire before dark.

Moving Toward Resolution

Likewise, the step of resolution bridges the difference between magnetic north and true north. You meet with your father in one form or another, but then take what you've learned through the process of resolution. In this process, you *express your feelings, confess,* and (where necessary) *forgive,* and *honor your father.* When you take these steps and make a commitment to a renewed relationship, it's like you are adding the degrees of compass declination to your compass reading. You have now plotted true north —what fathering is supposed to be. Where once you had been ordering your life according to a false reading, now you choose a new and sure landmark, and you follow it into healing, into confidence, into the effective fathering of your children.

I can hear the objections: *But why do I need to go to my father? Why can't I simply learn correct directions from other men and wise books?* Or, *The guy has been dead twenty years. I never really knew him.* One struggling man in California summed up what many feel: "But I can't talk to my father—besides, what good would it do?" The answer is simple—when you leave your feelings about your father unresolved, you invite trouble. Recognizing that your father is magnetic north and not true north is only part of the process; you then must be able to compensate without overreacting.

Tim grew up with a father who rarely let him help with a project. If his father was driving nails, for instance, and Tim took up a hammer and tried to drive one too, his father would inevitably take the hammer from him, saying, "No, no, you're doing it all wrong; let me show you." Then, he would finish the job for his son. "I never felt I did anything well enough for my father," Tim recalls bitterly. As an adult, Tim is now a consummate perfectionist.

I believe you cannot truly be a healed father until you have resolved yourself as a son.

Resolution with My Own Father

With my own father, I came to understand that our relationship had been damaged and needed to be resolved. When I was growing up in Wichita, my father worked as a technician for Beech Aircraft. I never really respected what my father did for a living; he had never completed his college education because he was too busy paying the bills for our family of six. Later I realized he was highly skilled and valued by the company. But in my teenage mind, Dad was just an hourly paid factory worker.

In high school I began to run with a crowd from the other side of the tracks—the "better" side. I think now it intimidated my father to see me come home in my friend's Mercedes-Benz. One day I arrived home from a long weekend with my rich friends. Dad was eating a bowl of ice cream; I sat down at the table, and our conversation quickly disintegrated into an argument. Finally he said, "I bet you think I'm just a dumb factory worker." I turned to him, stared him in the eyes, and with all my teenage insolence, I told him, "That's right, you're just a dumb factory worker."

He turned away. And remained away.

Over the next two decades, I forgot the incident. Meanwhile, changes were occurring my life. I married my wife, Dee. We had one child, then two, then three, and four. Soon I was the father of five children—and a concerned father, not only for my own sake, but also for the sake of all fathers out there. Suddenly, this man who did so little to honor his own dad had founded the National Center for Fathering.

My dad never asked about what I did for a living. And although my family (including five of his grandkids) lived just three hours north of Wichita, Dad had only visited us twice in nine years.

I asked my dad for a visit; I knew we had to talk. I needed to resolve what I had done wrong and ask for forgiveness, as well as express my feelings about my relationship with him. There were far too many issues unresolved. My commitment to dealing with issues was the spark of the process of resolution.

The Process of Resolution

There is no one magic method for resolving your relationship with your father. The methods are many and varied. However, I do believe that the process will include all or parts of the following five elements:

1. An exchange between the two of you
2. An expression of your feelings about the past
3. A time of confession (and restitution if needed)
4. A time of forgiveness (if necessary)
5. A commitment to a new relationship

1. Meet to Exchange Your Thoughts

For a resolution to occur, you must first open a formal dialogue with your father; you must be ready for an honest exchange of ideas and thoughts. The element of "exchange" in my resolution was a face-to-face visit with my dad; we talked in the car. My friend Jeff flew home one Christmas. On one slow evening, he invited his dad out for a walk. They made it only as far as the railroad-tie fence in the front yard before sitting down to talk. You may choose to call your dad, swing by his house, make a pot of coffee, and talk.

I will grant that there are two big obstacles to arranging for this exchange. One is fear. When Philadelphia screenwriter and playwright Dick Goldberg got married, his father took him for a walk. His father tried to tell Dick how much he meant to him. "I changed the subject," recalls Goldberg. "I wasn't ready to hear that. I couldn't handle it."[2]

Two decades later, Goldberg worked up the courage to tell his seventy-nine-year-old father how much he admired and cared about him. "My father was moved," says Goldberg. "Once you've done it, it becomes easier. You get over the threshold of anxiety about what the response will be. You know what it will be: reinforcement and joy."

Second, such an exchange for most adult men represents a deep conversation, something they can hardly imagine with their fathers, much less accomplish. After extensive research, author Ralph Keyes wrote, "I've discovered that many other men have felt the same difficulty [that I have] communicating with their fathers. There was always a stiffness in the air between us, as if we were both guests at a party, and the host had gone off without introducing us."[3]

Yet despite the distance, we must also be aware that we are powerfully drawn to our fathers. Some psychoanalysts were studying the dreams of men who were about to become fathers. Amazingly, often the expectant father's father would appear in a dream. This led Luis Zayas to comment, "The specific presence of the men's fathers in their dreams supports previous psychoanalytic reports of a process of reworking, perhaps resolution, in a man's relationship to his father as he begins to consolidate his own paternal identity."[4]

More than likely, you will have to take the initiative for setting up a face-to-face exchange with your father. With so much on the line, it is not wrong to hope for the best. But there are no guarantees. Your father may not welcome such an open exchange. You may be shut down by such remarks as, "You shouldn't say those things. . . . You always asked for too much. . . . You're just trying to blame me for your problems."

During this critical exchange with your father, you must always remember to concentrate on elements of resolution that are under your control. Your immediate goal, remember, is to resolve your feelings, attitudes, and actions as a son. You can accomplish this even in the face of your father's opposition.

But what if your father is no longer available to meet with you? Maybe you never knew your dad, or he refuses to see you, or you cannot locate him, or he is deceased. Samuel Osherson, author of *Finding Our Fathers,* writes, "In such cases one is deprived of the actual emotional healing that comes from reaching common ground with one's father, hearing and seeing a new bond forged between generations."[5]

But the process of resolution I've outlined need not always involve a face-to-face meeting with your father. If your father has passed away and you still feel the pain of his presence, go to the cemetery and attempt to resolve your feelings. This forces you to come to terms with whatever inheritance he has left you, and provides a quiet place where you can bury the pain, resentment, and bitterness that may have bound you.

An exchange can also involve an objective third party, such as a friend, a support group, or a small group. Hugh, a big Texan who had a statewide reputation as a cold and calculating trial attorney, came one evening to where a group of men had gathered to discuss the subject of fathering. Hugh was concerned about his relationship with his three daughters. As the meeting began, we discussed the need to resolve our feelings about our fathers. Because it was a small group, we went around and gave each man the opportunity to tell his story. Hugh's turn came . . . and the merciless trial attorney broke down weeping. When he began to groan and weep uncontrollably, it made everyone, particularly those who knew him, sit up and listen closely. Finally, he cleared his throat. "I have never told anyone my feelings about my father," he said.

As the story unfolded, his father was committed to long-term psychiatric care when Hugh was just a young child. Hugh occasionally saw his dad but was kept from any prolonged exposure, and soon he grew embarrassed of his mentally ill father. Hugh's father was a diabetic, and one night after he escaped from the hospital he died from a lack of insulin. He was on his way home; Hugh believes it was to see him.

What happened the night Hugh shared his story with us was as miraculous as his father's death was tragic. He had longed to be resolved to his father and to be held in his arms, but it never happened. Hugh's father died more than thirty-five years ago, but that evening this group of men listened, affirmed, and hugged Hugh. They listened to the things he wanted to say to his father and helped him through the process of resolution.

2. Express Your Feelings

A face-to-face exchange, of course, requires an exchange. You must be willing to disclose your feelings, and you must know what you need to communicate. Marvin Allen, director of Texas Men's Institute in San Antonio, recommends you begin the conversation by asking, "What was your childhood like, Dad?" or "What was your father like?" Invariably, Allen claims, the father will describe a man much like himself. At that point, the son has an opportunity to say, "Dad, I know how you felt, because I had a father just like that."[6]

With such words, a meaningful conversation begins.

As you enter into the dialogue, you can choose to focus on your grievances or your grieving. In other words, you can emphasize your list of what your father did wrong, or you can instead talk about how you felt about what your father did wrong. The latter is the best approach. Focusing on your feelings allows you to release them.

For most sons, their feelings have been bottled up over the years, building enormous pressure. I suspect many men would ask, "Why in the world would I want to deal with these emotions?" It's easier just to forget we have such sloppy things. But the fact is we can no more stop having emotions than we can stop thinking thoughts or making decisions. Emotions are part of who we are as human beings, even the male half of the species.

Because men often have not been taught about emotions, we've missed out on learning the great lesson that there are appropriate, self-controlled, gracious, even masculine ways of expressing what we feel. If we do not learn to use such ways of expressing our emotions, I believe one or two things can occur. First, our emotions might find inappropriate and uncontrolled means of expression. We may turn pain into anger, and anger can result in violent behavior, possibly even abuse toward our own children. Or we may feel abandoned and sink like sediment into a case of depression. A second possibility is we may allow our emotions to collect inside us, petrify, and weigh us down like weights around our ankles so that we can't find the freedom to express emotions when we want to. As a father, I don't doubt that deep inside you, you long to love and laugh with your children, to hold them in your arms and tell them how deeply you care for them. Some of you may not be able to freely express such sentiments. They are trapped behind the emotions for your father.

When you express your feelings toward your father, you must commit yourself to the manner in which you release them. It should be a slow, carefully controlled release of emotion, not an explosion. This is critical. You should seek to avoid shaming your father with blame and highly charged accusations. The entire process of seeking to build a new relationship with your father must always be bathed in honor and respect for the office of father.

The process of resolution offers us that opportunity. I suggest you verbally thank your father for what he did give you that was good. "Dad, I remember the time you drove all the way to Kansas City just to see me play in that basketball game. You were the only father there, and I was proud that you came. Thank you." Or, "Dad, you were always gentle and kind with Mom. That made me feel good and taught me a lot about how to treat my wife. Thank you." Some of you may have to stretch to an infinite degree to find something to thank your father for, but stretch until you find something. Don't initiate an exchange with your dad until you have something in mind to honor him with, even if it is, "Dad, thank you for sending that postcard, letting me know where you were," or "Dad, thank you for giving me life."

You have a need to honor your father. Elva McAllaster, a retired college professor, writes, "In deep subliminal ways, we want to honor a father, admire him, respect him, be praised and valued by him."[7] I have met too many men—and I was one of them in my teenage years—who rush into a confrontation with their fathers. They heaped on him page after page of what he did wrong. In essence, what sons like this do is reverse roles with their fathers. Now they are the dads, angrily lecturing their sons who are forced to sit mutely on the edge of their beds.

These combative sons are not breaking cycles, they are continuing in them—directing their emotion this time toward their father as they might also do toward their wives, children, and friends. Admittedly, there is a greater thrill of power in being the prosecutor, throwing out your accusations, recommending a sentence. But when you talk about your feelings, you give your dad an opportunity to hear you and fulfill one of the greatest roles of a father—that of the sympathetic listener. In a sense, you have granted him a second chance. As he listens to you and your pain, you paint a picture of the problem in such a way that he does not have to solve a puzzle—as he has often done in the past—to meet your need. Meeting your need, in this moment, is simple: "I love you and I'm proud of you, Son."

Now, all of this is not to say that a confrontation should not take place, if that is precisely what is needed. But let the facts confront your father, and not your harsh words.

Some people believe that confronting a father's behavior, or rebuking him, is never warranted. I disagree. Honoring our fathers means not ignoring the dishonorable as much as it means recognizing that which is honorable. For the sake of the relationship, we willingly engage our fathers in a discussion of right and wrong. The apostle Paul, in a letter to his protégé and spiritual son, Timothy, tells him, "Do not be harsh with or strike at an older man, but appeal to him, and urge him as if he were your father."[8] Confrontation, as long as it is done in a gentle manner, is not only permitted but encouraged.

FATHER FACT #2
Tips for a Reconciling Exchange

In his fine article "If Only I Could Say 'I Love You, Dad,'" Ralph Keyes offers seven suggestions for sons who want to reach out to their fathers.[9] I heartily recommend these steps:

Take the initiative. Sons are in a better position to do this than fathers. If sons don't begin talking to their dads, the conversation may never take place.

Don't begin conversation with grievances, no matter how justified. Ease into a discussion of your feelings about your father with more general conversation about his childhood and yours.

Listen to what your father has to say. Don't butt in, argue, or mentally compose a response as he's talking. Look for dimensions of your father that you didn't know existed.

Search for common ground. Are you experiencing some of the same things he went through? Do you have fond memories of time you spent together? Say so.

Keep in mind that your father is a son, too.

Remember, it's as important for your father to hear that you care for him as it is for you to hear this from your dad.

Tell him. Soon. Next year may be too late—or next week, or even tomorrow. The best day to tell your father that you love him may be today.

3. Confess Your Faults

Where we have dishonored our fathers we confess that to them. We must be careful here. Sometimes, we seek forgiveness where none is needed. Research indicates children have a tendency to blame themselves for their parents' divorce: "If I had only been a better kid, then Mom and Dad wouldn't be upset, and Dad wouldn't have left." In an even greater leap of logic, children also occasionally blame themselves for their father's death.[10] If you are a fatherless child, you are not responsible for your fatherlessness.

In my resolution, however, I had some genuine issues to confess. I remember Dad and I were parked in front of my house. I asked him if he remembered when I called him a "dumb factory worker." He stared out his side of the window and mumbled, "Not really," in such a way that it was clear—yes, he did.

"Dad," I said, "I know I caused you a lot of pain back then. I saw it in your face. And I want you to know that I'm sorry I did that. I'm really sorry."

He still didn't look back at me. "Oh, that's OK," he said. "That's water under the bridge. We just have to forget about those things."

"I know, Dad. But do you forgive me?"

"Well . . . I guess," he muttered. "Sure."

We talked some more, and the conversation on the subject slowly died out. We decided to go inside. His hand went to get the keys, his gaze fixed ahead, but then he slowly turned to me, looked me straight in the eyes, and asked me, "By the way, what do you do?"

I could barely answer him. This man who had never expressed any curiosity in my vocation had just asked me what I do.

I was forgiven.

Confession is a means by which we claim ownership of the relationship. We admit that just as our father influenced us, so we influenced him. We, too, have done things to cause him pain. In our exchange, we are doing more than just reconciling our feelings; we are reconciling our actions as well. The way to reconcile the actions of the past is to confess those actions that harmed the relationship. One definition of the word "reconcile" reads: "to remove all enmity and leave no impediment to unity and peace."[11]

4. Forgive Your Father

The companion of confession is forgiveness. Forgiving our fathers is the other action under our control. Actually, forgiveness is probably a more looming issue than confession. Some of us carry some very deep wounds inflicted by the men who were entrusted with our care. And I understand the outcry of those of you who might say, "Forgive him? No way! Don't you know how badly he hurt me? I'll never forgive him for what he did to me (or to my mother)."

But understand that in asking you to forgive your father, I am not asking you to condone his behavior or nonchalantly pretend like nothing happened. Forgiveness resolutely faces the facts (with all their pain) and then consciously decides not to hold those actions against him.

Maybe once, after a big mistake that you made, your father told you he was ashamed to be your dad. How do you react if the pain is still great? You could send your bitterness out like a collection agency thug to pound on your father's door and exact payment, but what good would that do? It would probably only force your father to barricade himself farther inside his house, away from you. When you forgive him, you move on with your life and devote your energy to more pressing matters—like raising your own children. You no longer demand that he give you what he has proven he is incapable, or unwilling, to give.

Forgiveness is not dependent on your father's repentance or response. In *Making Peace with Your Father,* David Stoop writes, "Our father may be dead. He may still pose a danger to our well-being so that we cannot approach him for resolution. He may simply be unwilling to resolve. This does not, however, mean we cannot forgive him. Forgiveness is something we do on our own initiative with or without his cooperation." And he adds, "If our aim is truly to make peace with our father and to move on in a life of joyful wholeness, we have no choice but to forgive him."[12]

You may have to allow yourself some time to truly forgive your father. Don't necessarily expect that in one face-to-face meeting with your father you will be able to so quickly forgive him, as if it were no more than turning on a light switch. Give yourself some space, but, at the same time, commit yourself to the discipline of forgiveness. It may take many meetings with your dad to genuinely forgive him.

5. Commit to the Relationship

Expressing your feelings resolves your emotions. Confessing, forgiving, and honoring resolves your actions. In so doing, the door has been opened for the new relationship with your father.

You must commit yourself to such a direction. "Dad, I know some things have not been very good between us, but with the years that you and I have left together, I'm going to do my part to make things better. I'll always be your son, and you'll always be my father."

Now is the time. If you have not already done so, and if you are able, you need to speak the three words that are rarely spoken between father and son.

"I love you."

"Dad, I love you."

It is a landmark. Authors Robert Bly and Gordon Dalbey have led us in thinking about rites of passage—the moment when a boy changes into a man.[13] We recognize that there is something substantially different between manhood and boyhood, but when does the transition occur? As Dalbey has pointed out, American culture has few recognizable rites of passage, unlike

African cultures for example, where an elaborate ceremony calls a boy out to join the men of the tribe and learn the male ways.

I believe there is a similar passage between sonship and fatherhood, and that the act of resolution can act as a rite of passage. This doesn't mean we ever stop being sons, or that a true man wholly abandons certain boyish qualities. However, such actions as making a woman pregnant and seeing the child come to term do not make a man a true father.

Some time ago, I was sitting next to a tall, lean youth on a plane. He was a high school all-American basketball player who was being flown in for a college recruiting effort. I told him what I did at the National Center for Fathering, which got us talking about his fatherless childhood, as well as his young friends who already had children. "Anyone can make a baby," this young man told me, "but it takes a man to be a father." This athlete expressed wisdom beyond his years. We live in a nation of male baby-makers; how many fathers do we really have?

Resolution can be an event that serves as a rite of passage between sonship and fatherhood. Essentially you tell your father, "Dad, up until now my energies and my emotions have been spent following you, even attempting to please you. Who I've been and what I've done have been because I am your son. But now, I have children of my own and I must take those energies and emotions and devote them to their lives."

As a result of resolving your feelings, you achieve a degree of closure on your sonship. You have grasped the baton; the next leg of the race is yours to run.

RELATE TO YOUR FATHER

Marvin grew up in the American heartland, on a family farm in Kansas. The second of seven children, he was nurtured with a steady diet of solid value, work ethic, and religious principles. In many ways, Marvin had many advantages. He was part of a family that had bonded together in purpose—feeding pigs, cleaning manure, baling hay. Though quite ordinary, the daily duties of running a family farm brought Marvin unity with his parents and siblings. With each moment, he was taught the value of hard work, cooperation, and frugality. He learned the Golden Rule, to treat others as he wanted to be treated. These would be values that would serve him well into his adult life; they were, in fact, the foundations on which he would build a successful practice as a family surgeon.

If Marvin had a doubt or longing growing up—a sudden and inexplicable feeling something was slightly out of kilter—it was quickly swallowed in the press of doing things. Marvin could never forget how well he was provided for. But when Marvin left the farm to go to college, something changed. He began to feel a void. For a while, it remained undefined, elusive, fluttering like a moth in deep fog. As he read and studied, however, this void began to take the shape of a simple sentence: *I love you.* That was the sentence, he realized, that he and his father had never spoken to each other.

Although Marvin knew that his father loved him, he longed to hear the words. His father's love was understood, but not felt. Cloaked behind this emotional distance was a subtle twisting of Marvin's perception of love. It was something to be earned, like respect, and rested on his contribution, the successful completion of day-to-day chores.

Marvin began to long for more. As he heard and read of better and deeper relationships, he resolved to attempt to break through the emotional distance with his father. On a break from college, Marvin chose to speak the three words that had never been shared between them: *I love you.* The only response was silence. Then he hugged his father. But his father remained cold yet compliant, not sure what to do with his own emotions. Marvin's dad answered with the learned and controlled expression of a farmer who had unexpectedly stepped into something disagreeable. "It felt like hugging a fence post," Marvin recalls.

But Marvin was not so easily put off. During the next six months, he repeated the scene. "I love you, Dad," he said, and he embraced his father as he said the words. The response to the words and hugs was always the same—a calculated and seemingly unbreakable distance. Marvin's intentionality was fierce and tender; he resolved to continue to show love to his father, no matter how he responded.

Finally, after the tenth time of being told he was loved, Marvin's father looked his son in the eyes and said, "Son, I love you too."

It was a turning point in the relationship between father and son. "It opened up unexplored territory in our relationship," Marvin says. Over time, Marvin and his father were able to share each other's dreams, failures, and joys. For the first time in either of their lives, they began to understand one another on the level of heart-to-heart.

Connecting in a Disconnected Culture

By learning to express their emotions to each other, Marvin and his father realized a primal and often hidden force: a man's desire to be in close relationship. Even in a culture where many of our heroes are still strong, silent, and solo types, every man has within him a heart that needs to be connected to others. No man is an island. We all have a desire to be known and to know others intimately. Not only do healthy relationships bring a sense of worth and esteem to individuals, they also become reference points from which the world can be deciphered and understood. Relationships are the lifeblood of human experience.

In the first two steps of processing your past, you have worked at recognizing your father's influence on you and resolving your feelings, attitudes, and actions as a son. Once recognition and resolution take place, you can begin to develop a new relationship with your father (or, if he is either unwilling or incapable, with a father figure).

Connecting the Past with the Present

The desire for relationship powerfully seeks to connect your past with your present and future. You intimately hold your wife, longing to be one with her in the present. You love and nurture your children, a vibrant and elemental connection with the future. You also, maybe without knowing it, long to connect with your past, especially when it comes to knowing your father. I've mentioned the term "father-hunger." It is, in its simplest and most profound sense, a desire to be connected with one's past. Writes author Robert Bly, "Somewhere around forty or forty-five a movement toward the father takes place naturally—a desire to see him more clearly and to draw closer to him. This happens inexplicably, almost as if on a biological timetable."[1]

Why is it so important that you learn to relate in new ways with your father? I can hear the objections. *Isn't it enough I have resolved my feelings with my father? Haven't I essentially "buried the past," so I can get on with the future? Shouldn't I be devoting my energies to fathering my own children, rather than developing a relationship that has always been difficult? Aren't I just setting myself up for more disappointment and heartache?*

I can sympathize with your reservations and fears. I have been there too. Yet, at the same time, I would emphasize: *The heart of a father, once heated, must find deeply significant ways to reconnect itself with the past.* The present and future are critically related to the past. By relating in new and healthy ways to your father, you anchor yourself in the past and provide a crucial bridge of perspective for your children. You connect them through vital and living relationships to history, tradition, and legacy.

We are losing our sense of connection in this country. One European woman made this remark about life in the United States: "After four years here, I still feel more of a foreigner than in any other place in the world I have been. There is no contact between the various households; we rarely see the neighbors and certainly do not know any of them."[2] The woman recalled evenings in Luxembourg, where she could amble with family down to the local cafe for several hours of lively interaction with the townsfolk.

The disconnections have ripped a hole in the way values are transmitted. In the words of former U.S. education secretary William Bennett, "We now ask prisons to do what fathers once did and ask the entire criminal justice system to do what parents, schools and neighborhoods once did."[3]

Harry and His Dad

The feelings of disconnection are overwhelming and often affect fathers deeply. Harry is a man in his midthirties who has a deep passion to be a good father to his young son. But he has a lot to overcome. His own father left when Harry was two, and since then they had spent only a few days together, when Harry was eight. His dad taught him how to swim at that time, but never reappeared in his life. Thanks to other father figures, Harry never really felt the void in his life—that is, until he had a son of his own, when suddenly his dad's absence became huge. As you might expect, for years he has had to fight back waves of resentment.

Recently, Harry's grandparents—his father's parents—celebrated their golden wedding anniversary. Several days beforehand, Harry found out his dad would be coming, and all the emotions he had long repressed started flooding back. The weekend, however, came off more smoothly than he expected. Harry and his two older brothers, Dennis and Matt, were able to spend some extended time with their dad just hanging out, working on the car, and talking.

On Sunday evening, the four of them were together at Harry's house, drinking sodas and relaxing in white wicker chairs on his sunporch. After some casual conversation, Harry's father asked them, "Do you want to hear the story of what happened when you guys were young?" It was clear to Harry that his dad had been carrying a burden, and now was his chance, after many years of anxiety, to unload. As he talked about his marriage to their mother and the years he had been faithful with child support, a shocking revelation surfaced. "I'm not even sure if I'm the father of each one of you."

Harry looked at his brothers. Everyone carefully searched each other's faces—the curve of an ear, the thickness of a nose, the stitch in a furrowed brow. Harry noticed that Dennis, the oldest, didn't resemble their father nearly as much as he and Matt did. But who could know for sure? The three of them were shell-shocked. Their father—or the man they had thought was their father—was also astonished, for he had long assumed that their mother had told them everything.

When I talked to Harry several days later, he was still reeling. "I never knew what kind of impact it would have on me to not know what my identity was. In some ways, I'm still looking for direction."

The Generation Bridge

When you maintain or reestablish a relationship with your father, you can build a generational bridge between your children, your father, and through him, to your father's father and beyond. You preserve the gift of identity: *I am part of a long-established line of people who bore the same name that I do, and who worked so that I might be here.* A sense of history also provides your family with a sense of purpose: *We are not merely trying to survive together; we have a destiny—to perpetuate (or recover) the good name we've been given.*

Yet there looms even a larger issue, which is critical to why you should do everything in your power to build a new and healthy relationship with your father. And it is this simple fact: The most important thing families do is relate. Healthy families work at their relationships—accepting one another, affirming one another, esteeming one another; unhealthy families are often content to let their relationships degenerate. When your children see you in relationship with your father, and see you making an effort to maintain and strengthen that relationship, then when they ask the question (as they are sure to do), "What is it that families do?" they know the answer: Families relate.

This is not easy work. The bridge between the generations, if it is to be a real one, must have at its foundation unconditional love. By resolving your issues as a son, you have cleared the obstacles that might have prevented you from loving your father unconditionally. The emotional baggage from your childhood—those issues connected with pain and self-esteem—have been identified and grieved over. You are now free to begin a new relationship with your father based on what you *desire,* not what you need.

Dream Weaver

Remember the story of Marvin at the beginning of this chapter? He resolved to over and over tell his father he loved him, regardless of whether he responded or not. He was finally free to love his father unconditionally. His need to hear his father say that he loved him too no longer held him in bondage. Though his father could not respond for a time, Marvin resolved to continue in declaring his love. Stripped from suffocating need, buoyed by a spirit of forgiveness, he was able to rise to new levels of communication. He could hear what his father was saying. He entered into his dreams.

Unlike Marvin, you may have had a terribly abusive or painfully distant father, but I assure you he did not stand there at his wedding ceremony thinking, "I intend to do all I can to make life as miserable as possible for this woman and the children she gives me." In fact, it is very likely that he told himself, "I am not going to be like my father. I'm going to try to give to my children what I never got for myself." He had dreams. He had plans. Unfortunately, unlike you, he apparently never learned how cycles could be broken, and he fell into them as easily as his own father did.

Your father's dreams, passed through the inheritance from his father, are important to you. They are part of your inheritance. If you have the opportunity, ask him, "Dad, if you could wish anything for your grandchildren, what would it be?"

There is a dream specifically appropriate for you and your family that is different from the dream appropriate to your brother's or sister's family. Your father may very well have the key to that dream. By entering into a new relationship, you build a connection from the heart of a father to the heart of a father to the heart of your child. A restored relationship with one's father can lead to the lasting link of dreams.

Moving Out of Dark Places

If you love your father unconditionally, and he responds to you, your relationship—like Marvin's with his father—will take you places you had never dreamed were possible.

If your father opens up, you will begin to understand not only what your father did, but why. If your relationship with him growing up was basically a healthy one, then you will benefit from the wisdom in an old African proverb: "Everybody has been young before, but not everybody has been old before." Among those astute enough to learn from experience, age brings wisdom.

In any case, we need to learn from our father's experiences, even if they were mostly negative. If you're able to come to an understanding of why your father was the way he was, you will be able not only to avoid the mistakes he made, but to free yourself from perhaps the most haunting question of your life: Can *anyone* be a good dad? Without actually investigating your own father and discovering why he is as he is, you run the risk of falling into a fearful hopelessness, having fully accepted the generic, diminished idea of father. "I am the son of defective male material, and I'll probably be the same as he is." That's why you need to *know* your dad—who he is, what makes him tick. It's why you need to develop a relationship with him. Unless his identity is exposed to the light of understanding, the overwhelming temptation is to give up, collapse, and live with the dark and numb places inside yourself.

Your Father's Knowledge of Fathering

In addition to the added confidence that fathering can be done, our fathers can also provide us the knowledge of how fathering *should* be done. Admittedly, building a new relationship with your father does not automatically make your dad a fathering expert. You may need to seek out other men —those who have succeeded with their kids—to give you the advice you need to raise your children.

But there is one kind of knowledge that all older fathers possess (provided they remained in the home as their children grew): knowledge of "what comes next." As your children grow, each new stage of development takes you into uncharted territory. At the very least, your dad can inform you of what to expect as your children grow.

Your father, if he is willing, grandfathers your children. In grandfathering, he fills in some of the gaps of your fathering. Some of these may be physical gaps, such as watching your children while you take your wife out on a date. Other more serious gaps may be filled in through your father's objective distance. Since your father does not feel the immediate burden of parenting his grandchildren, he is able to step back to see some areas where you might be blinded. Yet, at the same time, he is still concerned and involved enough to be able to point them out to you.

Working diligently to reestablish or maintain a relationship with your father also models for your children the importance of relating to *their* father, who just happens to be a pretty decent and likable guy. The Golden Rule states: "Do to others as you want them to do to you." As you do to your father, your children will do to you. Your children are learning about this world and what are appropriate thoughts and actions. In particular, they are watching their father for cues. "How should a man treat a woman?" your sons wonder, and then they watch the way you treat your wife. But they also ask this question: "How should a child relate to his father?" And again they look to you as an object lesson. "How does Dad relate to his dad?"

If You Build It . . .

The climactic scene of the classic movie *Field of Dreams* remains a vivid metaphor of the powerful possibilities of a new relationship between son and father. Twilight has set in, but on a baseball diamond built in a cornfield, the lights are shining brightly. The main character, Ray Kinsella (Kevin Costner), is playing catch with his father on the infield grass. With each dusty pop of the ball into a leather glove, you know they have been reconciled. It is a strange scene, because they are engaging in a traditional father-son ritual: playing catch. And yet, Ray is no longer a child. He has skillfully built the ball diamond that has made it possible for his father to be there, and he has proven himself worthy to receive this moment through his self-sacrifice. He has just introduced his dad to his granddaughter, but in fact, through the magical machinations of the plot, the father is not even an old man, but Ray's age. They are two adults, yet father and son. They are playing catch. They are relating. It's a new thing.

David Stoop, author and psychologist, describes the benefits of such a relationship:

An interesting thing often happens inside people once they finally put their father issues to rest: All of a sudden, they feel grown up. . . . By dealing with our father issues, we free ourselves to finish growing up emotionally. We look back on a recent trip back home and realize that for the first time we didn't feel like a kid anymore in our father's house.[4]

In relating anew to your father, you are trying to recapture the original design for fathers and sons, but doing so in the context of what is true now, not what should have been true then. You are an adult, a competent adult. Previously, you may have felt that "pleasing your father" was somehow your main task in life, but now you must devote yourself to your wife and children. And of course, having worked through the processing of your past, you have discovered some things about your dad (and yourself) that you perhaps never allowed yourself to admit. Your new relationship will have to make allowances for these factors.

The Shape of a New Relationship

So, what will your new relationship with your father look like? The two of you will determine that yourselves. We've warned against "formula fathering"—the attempt to govern how you father your children through a prescribed set of rules—but perhaps we also need to warn against "formula sonship." As you relate to your father, relax. The relationship will define itself.

James Cunningham and his father provide a vivid example. Cunningham, like Ray Kinsella, also had a father who played baseball. As a small boy he remembers watching his dad hit a ball into a cornfield beyond the ballpark. After the game, they would share an Orange Crush and a Moon Pie.

Although James says he loved his father very much, he put off telling him so. Then his father developed terminal cancer. He didn't want to die in a hospital, so James decided to remodel an office in his clinic. There his dad spent his final days chatting with patients, watching ball games, and being tended to by his son and daughter-in-law. "You know that we love you very much," James told him one night. "It shows," murmured his father before drifting off to sleep. He died the next morning. "I still miss him," says Cunningham, "but I don't feel like we had any unfinished business."

Before Mr. Cunningham died, his son and he watched ball games together on television in the back room James had built for his father. The two of them sat beside each other, discussing batting averages. Instead of receiving an Orange Crush from his dad after the game, now James provided for his father, even feeding him by hand in the later stages of the cancer. It was a new relationship with new roles, which Cunningham and his father discovered together in an atmosphere of love.[5]

The relationships between Cunningham and his father, as well as Marvin and his father, share some common elements. We would do well to learn from them as we seek to develop a closer connection with our own fathers.

1. Initiate the Process and Stick with It

First, and maybe most importantly, both Marvin and James not only took the initiative to relate anew with their fathers, they stuck at it. The new relationships didn't just happen by accident; there was a resolve in the hearts of the sons to know the hearts of the fathers. Marvin, if you remember, repeatedly told his father that he loved him before his dad ever responded. Both James and Martin were careful to view their new relationships as a process, rather than a series of disconnected events. They both consciously made an effort to increase both the quality and quantity of their communication.

If you have made the effort to resolve issues with your father, you must remember that this is just a starting point. In order to really know your father, you must spend time with him. You've already had one chat with your dad; have another, and another. Of course, don't feel that you need to match the emotional intensity of your reconciliation exchange. You can think of that event as squirting lighter fluid on the campfire: It helped start the fire but can result in burnout and singed eyebrows. Instead, you and your dad have hopefully found the freedom to pull up a log next to the delicately dancing flames, sit down next to each other, and tell each other your stories.

But don't count on it. Like James and Marvin, you will probably have to be the one to take the initiative. Fathers who were uninvolved with their children while growing up often labor under a sense that they "missed out"—and they have. But they often make the assumption they'll never have another chance to connect with their children. Isolation can be a self-imposed punishment. And all fathers remember the pressures of an early career and a young family. Your dad may feel reluctant to impose upon you for a visit.

So it's up to you.

2. Share New Experiences

If you paid close attention to the stories of James and Marvin, you would have noticed that each son sought to bring a new element into the relationship—which, not coincidentally, was a desire to speak three words, "I love you." For many fathers and sons, growing up in a culture where men are often taught to swallow their emotion, this is a turning point in their relationships. As Marvin said, "It opened up unexplored territory for us."

Spending time with your father is not enough. We need to look for ways to engage the best and deepest parts of our fathers. A good start is to spend some one-on-one time together. Shared interests—tuning up a car, attending a basketball game, remodeling the house—can provide a common bond, which may, in turn, lead to a sense of togetherness. From there, anything is likely to happen.

Fathers, too, need to sense a connection with the generations. Not only should you spend some private time with your father, but you need to invite him to participate in your family life. Our culture has so few events that encourage intergenerational interaction. Grandpa breezes into town for his granddaughter's wedding but then tries to stay out of the way of the busy hosts. We dash off to a funeral for the death of a grandparent. As a family, we need to find more opportunities—other than Christmas and Thanksgiving—to reconnect.

Exploring traditions and family rituals provides a rich opportunity for coming together, as well as a possible moment in the sun for your father. Sometime, when you are gathered together as a family, ask your dad what family characters or traditions he remembers from his childhood. Each family has more than its share of fascinating people, and, by allowing your father the spokesman role, you provide a valuable service to your dad, yourself, and your children. The generations can connect. Let your dad show your kids an old family photo album and tell stories from years gone by. Or ask him to write a letter of advice to your child at a milestone birthday, like the twelfth or sixteenth or eighteenth.

3. Express Your Love

Finally, it is critical you express your love for your father. Both James and Marvin found this to be at the very hub of their new relationships with their fathers. Make it a point to regularly communicate your love. You've said the words once; now you can say them again: "Dad, I love you." A healthy and honoring relationship with your father is an affirming relationship. You'll discover that processing your past is a lifelong pursuit. You never quit remembering and reflecting on what has happened in your life. In fact, the longer you live, the more past you'll have to process. But, this doesn't mean you keep reliving the pain or repeating the grieving process (that's called chronic depression). You are now freed up to discover the positive things that your father did for you as a child, and second, you may be graced with discovering the healthy purpose of some of the pain you experienced in your life. You can now say, without pretense, need, or demand, that you love your father. And you should. Often.

This type of unconditional love is how Marvin and James expressed their feelings and actions toward their fathers. In a sense, they wanted to express thanks to their fathers for what they did *well*—providing for them in their childhood—by bringing something new to the relationship. In their motivation and action, they chose to focus on their fathers' good qualities, not the negative, no matter how bad. Marvin's gift was to close the emotional distance with his father; for James, the gift extended much further—to show his love by caring for his dad during his last days.

One of the greatest ways you can demonstrate love to your father—and mother—in their later years is to care for physical needs. Though our culture has a social "safety net" and your mother and dad may seem independent or financially secure, your parents probably will need you in special ways during their final years.

One of these days we are going to be parenting our parents. We'll be asked to care for them in the same way they cared for us. Someday, you may find yourself lifting the spoon up to your father's lips, in the same way that he once fed you. You may find yourself driving him to his events, just like he did for you back in junior high.

Although this will often become burdensome, I hope it will never be a burden. Instead, it is the "honor of sons" to care for their parents in their old age. In a culture that provides nursing homes and Social Security checks, you will be able to provide your father what he truly needs and desires—relationship. And you, as the son, have the opportunity to experience, as James did with his dying father, the joy of giving selflessly. On the night before his father died, James told him that he loved him; his father responded, "It shows." May those words be the last ones on the lips of each of our fathers.

If Your Father Refuses

But what if, for whatever reason, a renewed relationship with your father is not possible? Some of you may have fathers who have died; others might be separated by distance, either physical or emotional, which makes it impossible to connect on a deeper level. Or   and this is where processing your past may get very painful—many of you may have successfully gone through the process of resolving your feelings, attitudes, and actions as a son, but your father did not respond positively. Relationship, by its very definition, is two-way, and without your father's participation, the ultimate goal of resolution will not always be possible.

If your father didn't respond, it leaves you with another painful event to process, probably as hard a blow as any you suffered in your childhood. You will need to grieve the event in the same way you grieved through your other disappointments. But, as you do, realize this: You are free! You have fulfilled your obligations as a son, and you have resolved your feelings, attitudes, and actions as a son. You are free to move on.

But move on where? How can you do the next step of relating if your father is not available or willing to relate to you? The answer is to find a "father figure" and relate to him instead.

Finding a Father Figure

We have a choice. We can be haunted by the ghouls of our fathers, those ghostly creatures who are powerless to help us and who, when we try to embrace them, disappear into thin air. Or, we can find other men who will act as live, flesh-and-blood, readily available *goels*. *Goel* is a Hebrew term that is translated as "kinsman-redeemer." Back in ancient times, if a Jewish woman became a widow or a child an orphan, the society would provide that person with a protector, normally the closest relative—for example, a brother to the husband and father who died. The *goel* provided for the family, and essentially took the upbringing of the child upon himself. He was a redeemer of sorts—he "bought" the child out of a lifetime of fatherlessness.

The ancient Hebrew culture understood that the need for a father is a constant. In the same way, each of us who is fatherless—by abandonment, death, or distance—must also seek out a father figure, a *goel*.

A *goel* is any person who fulfills a father's role in your life. As I have told you, when I was growing up, I couldn't call my dad. Oh, he was still alive, but I was an insolent teenager and he was a distant father. One day I skipped my high school classes and took my Corvair out for a drive in the country. I wasn't watching where I was going, and soon found myself sliding off the road and into a muddy ditch. I tried what I could to get out, but I got farther and farther stuck, to the point where water was actually seeping into my car through the bottom of the doors. I was helpless.

I walked to a neighboring farmhouse to make a phone call. No way was I going to call my father; after all, I was skipping school at the time. I called my grandfather; he was my kinsman-redeemer.

Granddad came and pulled me out, but he did one other thing that proved how much of a father's role he was playing. "I think you better tell your dad," he advised me.

"You going to tell him?" I asked.

"No, I think you should tell him."

Most likely your *goel* will be an older man, like Norm Wallace, one of my confidants. If you had a fatherless childhood, your *goel* will probably be a true kinsman-redeemer, like a grandfather, an uncle, or an older brother. Whether the man is a relative or a kindly older friend, your father figure will offer you wise, thoughtful advice as well as a welcomed hand, as my grandfather did.

Children, I have noticed, have an uncanny ability to seek out father figures. I've seen it in my neighborhood. I've tried to be an involved and nurturing dad. A whole platoon of children traipse through my living room on a daily basis. A couple of times, kids have come across the street from the park and demanded that I come out and play football. We carry this same father search into adulthood. And the union with a father figure is encouraged by the fact that most older men find themselves in the stage of life where they are both capable and willing to give advice. We honor them when we seek them out.

Father figures are not hard to find. Make a conscious choice to search out a man who models effective fathering (and grandfathering) and who would be willing to invest himself in you. Formally commit to some time together—say, a lunch every Wednesday. Even if you have a wonderful, ongoing relationship with your dad, father figures can supplement what your father gives you. For many men, this is necessary because of distance. My dad, for example, lives three hours away in Wichita. We talk on the phone and I visit on occasion, but I still need the interaction of a Norm Wallace, someone with whom I could set up a lunch appointment for that same day.

By developing a relationship with a father figure, you can see life through another perspective, often much wiser and more objective than your own. Norm, for example, often picks up on things that I would have missed through his own experience of fathering.

Norm often advises me through the history of his own kids. Once I brought the kids by, and he remarked (in his affirming way) how well they're growing. "Your daughter's going to be driving pretty quick," he informed me. "I remember when Anna started to drive. Now, you make sure to get Hannah a big car, like we did for Anna. It's too easy for kids to get killed in one of those little cars."

Many of the suggestions I have made to develop a new relationship with your father can also be applied to a father figure. If you find yourself fatherless, I believe it is imperative that you begin to cultivate at least one solid relationship with a father figure. If you were unlucky enough to have a ghoul for a father, you just may be fortunate enough to bond with a *goel*. And although he will not be able to fulfill all of the purposes and roles that your biological father could have, he can serve as a centering point for your fathering. You will not be alone.

THE FOUR "I CANS" OF FATHERING

BUILDING
A HOUSE

One day many years ago, my wife, Dee, called my office to tell me our five-year-old son, Micah, had cut a hole in his great aunt's quilt. If that wasn't bad enough, he then lied about it. I told Dee I'd be home for lunch.

Part of my fathering inheritance is an extreme hatred of lying. My dad once took me to my grade school after hours, convinced the janitor to let us in, and then rummaged through my desk to find an unfinished home-work assignment that I had lied about losing. Sometimes when I catch my kids lying, my backside still tingles with my father's "inheritance."

This was Micah's first premeditated, willful lie, and I wanted to be sure he didn't start a bad habit. When we stepped into his bedroom, he was so ready to confess that I didn't even have to pull my KGB routine. "Micah," I said, "did you lie to your mom about cutting that quilt?"

"Yes," he burst forth in a sputter of tears.

"Micah, you shouldn't lie, you know that."

"I know." More wailing.

I wanted to teach him how horrible lying is. "Micah, do you know who the father of lies is?" (In the Bible, the devil is called the father of lies.)

"Yes," he said.

"Who? Who is the father of lies?"

Micah took a deep breath. His lower lip quivered. "Saddam Hussein," he muttered.

Do you know what a challenge it is to discipline your child when you want to laugh hysterically and hug him instead? Being a good dad has its challenges, and proper discipline is only one of them. Fortunately, there are some light moments along the way. Back in the 1800s, Wilhelm Busch wrote, "Becoming a father is easy enough, but being one can be tough."[1] And Mr. Busch never had to deal with rampant drug abuse, the teenage sexual revolution, or many of the other dragons that we fathers of today are called to slay.

In part 1, I asked you to consider the shape of your heart as you think about your relationship with your father and his influence on the way you father your children. A strong heart is very important for the marathon race we'll discuss in part 3.

Here in part 2, the best word picture is that of a house. In particular, we are interested in the four load-bearing walls that enclose the home. They will become the four main practices of the effective father: involvement, consistency, awareness, and nurturance.

Your relationship with and your feelings toward your father are like the foundation, essential in building a safe and secure house. If you've worked diligently at reconciling your relationship with your father, then you have a firm foundation from which to begin parenting your own children. Even the most painstakingly repaired foundation is just a slab of concrete.

In part 2, we'll put the walls in place.

Walls may have negative connotations when applied to parenting. Don't box your children in; avoid rigid absolutes; allow for free thinking. But walls do more than confine. They also protect, keeping out burglars, harsh sounds, and bad weather.

Walls also help to define. A father who practices the principles of effective fathering will help a child always know where "home" is, no matter how far that child might wander. For all the things that effective fathers do, they also set appropriate boundaries, like a father who puts a gate at the top of the stairs so that his playing, growing toddler doesn't happen to tumble down them.

When I first began researching what makes an effective father, I was overwhelmed at the number of resources available for mothers—books, community seminars, mothering organizations, wise friends.

"Do you have anything for dads?" I would ask, again and again.

"What?" was the answer I almost always received, accompanied by a blank stare.

I learned there was only a smattering of material to help a man become a better dad. Some thought men didn't read, others that men weren't interested in knowing such things. But I sensed that many men were awakening to the importance of our fathering role. It was my own heart's desire, and I heard the same from thousands of other men. We want to do it well and are simply seeking a few tips, some handles on fathering. Give us something simple and basic, something with broad application. (Maybe you feel the same way, and that's why you're reading this book.)

So my colleagues and I began our own research. We studied the historical literature, we surveyed the scholarly literature back to 1940, and then, in order to get to the heart of the matter, we began to interview men. Beginning in December of 1987, we have surveyed more than 10,000 fathers. We have formulated over 600 questions about their fathering practices and ideals. (Some of those questions, expressed as statements, are excerpted in appendix 1.) In the process, we identified forty-eight different aspects of fathering and/or factors that influence how a man fathers. But we weren't satisfied; the results seemed too complex to be of much help. Eventually, though, some patterns began to emerge. We found that these forty-eight aspects of fathering could fit under one of four functions of a father: involvement, consistency, awareness, and nurturance (I CAN). We called these functions the "I CANs" of fathering, as in "I can be an effective father."

These four items are not a formula for fathering—a rigid step-by-step program with a glib guarantee for success. Fathering instruction that attempts to manipulate children along preconceived lines is bound to fail. However, the four "I CANs" provide a framework for what a child needs—a certain latitude for self-discovery, trial and error, and the freedom to fail. This framework is better than what fathers sometimes want—performance and peace at all costs.

These "I CAN" functions—involvement, consistency, awareness, and nurturance—are flexible enough to meet the changing needs of children. Involvement, for example, will differ for a man who has two small kids as compared to a man who has two children who've grown and left home. As a result, the "I CANs" are a framework for thinking about our fathering, for evaluating how we are doing as dads. They give us concepts and directions.

The "I CANs" represent the general functions at the heart of being a father. As parents, we cannot control our children by only making demands and rules. As much as we might wish it at times, children do not operate with remote controls. Our children are their own persons, who make their own decisions. As infants, they crawl about the house and decide when to cry and to wake up in the middle of the night. Later, as teenagers, they'll decide which clothes to buy, which friends to have, and which colleges to attend. Our children run themselves.

The best we can do is provide an environment of security, instruction, and nurturance. We give them an atmosphere of love in which to grow up, and occasionally we act as walls for them to bounce against.

The challenge of the present is rising to the occasion—and you can do that. You have been uniquely placed in the role of father of your children. Your wife may mother them, their teachers may mentor them, their coaches may train them, the government may foster them, but good *fathering* is needed in its own right.

You possess the same power—father power—that your dad possessed. Through the use of the I CANs, you can ensure that your father power is used to benefit your children.

When you are involved, consistent, aware, and nurturing toward your children, they will grow up strong and possibly marry and have their own children, all with a positive view of what a father is. And your efforts to become that positive fathering model will be a daily testimony of honor to the position of father.

Now let's go build a house.

FATHER INVENTORY #3
The I CANs Profile

This self-scoring fathering inventory is based on the research described in this section, "The Four 'I CANs' of Fathering." It is designed to give you the benefit of accurate feedback, to help you answer the question "Where do I stand?" for each of the four fathering functions. More importantly, it will help you identify specific areas where you may need to focus your efforts. As you read the next four chapters you will calculate your scores for each of the I CANs. Later you will complete an overall summary of your profile on page 156.

INSTRUCTIONS:

Decide how accurate the following statements are concerning your fathering practices. Circle the appropriate answer in front of each profile statement (PS). If your children are no longer living in your home, respond as you remember when they were at home. If your children are very young, think ahead to what you will do based on the experience you've already had with your children.

1=Mostly False 2=Somewhat False 3=Undecided 4=Somewhat True 5=Mostly True

1 2 3 4 5   P S 1   My child and I often do things together.
1 2 3 4 5   P S 2   I do not have major shifts in my mood.
1 2 3 4 5   P S 3   I have a good handle on how my child's needs change as he/she grows up.
1 2 3 4 5   P S 4   It is easy for me to encourage my children.
1 2 3 4 5   P S 5   My children accompany me on errands.
1 2 3 4 5   P S 6   I try not to vary much in the way that I deal with my children.
1 2 3 4 5   P S 7   I know what encourages my child the most.
1 2 3 4 5   P S 8   I praise my children for things they do well.
1 2 3 4 5   P S 9   I frequently read stories with my child.

1 2 3 4 5   P S 10   I do not change much in the way that I deal with my children.

1 2 3 4 5   P S 11   I know what motivates my child.

1 2 3 4 5   P S 12   I express affection to my children.

1 2 3 4 5   P S 13   I often work together with my child on a project.

1 2 3 4 5   P S 14   I am unchanging in my personality characteristics.

1 2 3 4 5   P S 15   I know when my child is embarrassed.

1 2 3 4 5   P S 16   I constantly tell my children that I love them.

1 2 3 4 5   P S 17   My child and I often have fun together.

1 2 3 4 5   P S 18   I tend to be somewhat unchanging in the way I practice fathering responsibilities.

1 2 3 4 5   P S 19   I could identify most of my child's recent disappointing experiences.

1 2 3 4 5   P S 20   I show my children that I care when they share a problem with me.

1 2 3 4 5   P S 21   My child and I spend a lot of time together.

1 2 3 4 5   P S 22   My moods are pretty much the same from day to day.

1 2 3 4 5   P S 23   I know how my child's emotional needs change over time.

1 2 3 4 5   P S 24   I tell my children that they are special to me.

1 2 3 4 5   P S 25   I often involve my child in working with me.

1 2 3 4 5   P S 26   I feel that the way I deal with my children does not change much from day to day.

1 2 3 4 5   P S 27   I know what is reasonable to expect from my children for their age.

1 2 3 4 5   P S 28   When my children are upset, I usually try to listen to them.

1 2 3 4 5   P S 29   I spend time playing with my child a couple times a week.

1 2 3 4 5   P S 30   I am predictable in the way I relate to my children.

1 2 3 4 5   P S 31   I know what my child needs in order to grow into a mature, responsible person.

1 2 3 4 5   P S 32   I point out qualities in my children that I like about them.

INVOLVEMENT

How much is a dad's involvement worth to his children? Can you put a number on it in dollars and cents?

In an unusual court case years ago, the figure was $16 million. That's how much the daughters of then Major League Baseball manager Tony La Russa asked for in a court of law for his not being around to help raise them. The two women were separated from their dad at an early age, and La Russa gradually disappeared from their lives. Then, at ages twenty-seven and twenty-five, they claimed that they had tried to contact him, but he rejected them.

I don't know the details of that situation. Maybe these women just wanted a chunk of their dad's money, or maybe they sincerely hoped to establish a meaningful relationship. Whatever their motives, they set the price for their trauma and pain at a cool $16 million. Even by today's standards, with our society's growing affinity for lawsuits, that's still a pretty high price for a dad.

Another well-known father promised his son they would do something together on the boy's birthday. They made plans in advance, and the son counted down the days. But then, several weeks before the big day, the dad got an important speaking opportunity for that same day that would pay an honorarium of $1,000. Besides the money, this event had great potential to further his career. Still, he felt bad about breaking the date with his son, so he sat the boy down and tried to cut a deal. "Tell you what, Son," he said, "I'll go speak at this event, and since you'll be missing out on our day together, I'll give you the thousand dollars."

The boy thought it over for a few seconds, then looked at his dad and said, "No, that's OK. I'd rather have the time with you."

Dad, slice it however you want: $16 million for twenty years or a thousand for a day. Our children place great value on our time and our presence—our involvement. Let's be sure we don't shortchange them.

The first wall that an effective father constructs in his home is the wall of Involvement—the first of the four fathering dimensions. The first wall is always critical because part of it rests on the cornerstone, from which the other three walls take their bearings. The entire building will be plumb—or else out of alignment—based on the accuracy of the cornerstone and the first wall.

In the same way, involvement determines much about the other three fathering dimensions. It's impossible to be consistent, aware, and nurturing regarding your children unless you are also somehow involved with them. As the "I" in our "I CANs" of effective fathering, involvement provides the vital environment to meet our children's needs, allowing them to grow and be healthy.

Benefits of Being Involved

Studies have conclusively shown that children who receive higher levels of attention and interaction with their parents are healthier and better adjusted than children with uninvolved parents. A 2003 study by the National Center on Addiction and Substance Abuse found that if teens don't feel close to a parent, they are 50 percent more likely to smoke, drink, and use illegal drugs than teens who do feel close to a parent. The same is true for youth who are often bored in comparison with those who do not classify themselves as often bored.[1] According to findings at the University of Florida, children with highly involved fathers have:

- higher scores on cognitive tests,
- lower rates of violence, delinquency, and other problems with the law,
- increased chances for high school graduation and college or vocational study (regardless of the fathers' educational level),
- more career success,
- more evident positive characteristics such as empathy, self-esteem, self-control, psychological well-being, social competence, and life skills.[2]

Most of us will not be greatly surprised by these findings. It doesn't take a brain surgeon to understand that involvement is critical. Asked for a quick answer on how to improve a father's relationship with his children, any reasonable man will almost certainly say, "Spend more time with them." The simple, instinctive reaction of a committed father is to be involved in the lives of his children. Involvement is so basic that you can't even be an average dad, let alone a good or highly effective one, without it.

Yet, if involvement is so obvious, so critical, why are so few of us spending enough time with our children? According to longtime fathering researcher Henry Biller, the average daily amount of one-to-one father/child contact in the United States is less than thirty minutes.[3]

Obviously, there is a discrepancy between what we know to be right and what we actually do. In this chapter we will look at some benefits and strategies of involvement. Equally important, we will look at some underlying issues that might be keeping many of us from being—and staying—involved with our children.

A Father's Unique Contributions

A father's involvement with his children is unique. We could, of course, also compose a list of the benefits of mother involvement. But we would be mistaken if we believed those lists of benefits would be the same. Even if you could arrange for your wife to be with your children 168 hours a week, even if you could afford to hire a couple of private teachers and coaches and clergymen, and even if you were allowed to lavish your children with the best educational tools and self-esteem strategies, you could never accomplish what the results of these studies reveal.

A father's role in the lives of his children is unique; a mother cannot do what he does.

Research bears out the unique role of the father: Father love is actually a better predictor than mother love for certain outcomes, including delinquency and conduct problems, substance abuse, and overall mental health and well-being.[4]

In fact, the evidence is increasing that there is no such thing as a generic "parent." Instead there is a mother, who brings unique parenting skills, and a father, who brings other unique skills. According to Yale Child Study Center psychiatrist Kyle Pruett, "It is through the father that the baby first learns about comings and goings, transitions, separations, and non-mother nurturing." An involved father initiates his children into "a world of objects, activities and people outside the mother's sphere . . . [which] expands the child's horizons and stimulates his thinking processes."[5] Norma Radin, professor of social work at the University of Michigan, amplifies: "Fathers tend to be playful and physical, initiating unusual, exciting forms of rough-and-tumble play."[6] This approach, she adds, "complements Mom's more verbal, soothing style."

Even children recognize the difference. Pediatrician and author T. Berry Brazelton notes that at three weeks a baby will show different reactions to his mother as compared with his father: When his father approaches, the baby will hunch his shoulders and lift his eyebrows as though in anticipation of playtime.[7]

Children need a parenting team—male and female. Traditionally, that team has often been defined too much along the line of one-dimensional roles: The father provides; the mother cares. Increasingly, evidence indicates such definitions are too narrow for the children's needs. Children need their fathers' hearts—not just their dads' wallets—to grow into healthy adults.

Significantly, healthy involvement also brings some important benefits into our lives as well. Several studies indicate that highly involved fathers feel more important to their kids, have happier marriages, and go just as far in their careers as fathers who are less involved with their kids.[8]

How Do You Spell Love?

Nothing can replace a father spending time with his children. Earlier, I described the critical need children have to hear their fathers say, "I love you." But in addition to our words, we need to also *show* our children that we love them. We do that most effectively by spending time with them.

Spell Love T-I-M-E

My colleague Judd Swihart wrote a book some years ago entitled, *How Do You Say "I Love You"?* His premise is that there are different ways of showing love to the people we care about, and it's easy to get our signals crossed. A common example is the husband who works sixty hours a week so he can buy his wife nice things, but she'd trade it all for some physical displays of affection on a daily basis, because that's what makes her feel loved. These ways of communicating love vary from one adult to another, but I'm convinced that children, at least until their midteens, largely operate on the same frequency when it comes to love. You may buy them balloons that say "I Love You," you may make sure they get the hugs they need each day, and you may bend over backward making sacrifices. Even though such practices are positive and are meant to build their confidence and security, your children probably don't make those connections. Why? To them, love means much more when it's spelled differently: T-I-M-E.

Once when I was speaking in Seattle, I got a note from a young woman who was in the audience. "My father is a millionaire," she wrote. "He gets paid 100 dollars an hour. If I had 100 dollars, I would buy an hour of his time."

Clark Smith, a friend of ours at the National Center for Fathering, describes to parents and teachers a brilliant word picture that illustrates the point: "Fathering is a pasture fenced with time. The size of the fence determines the size of the relationship. Increase your parenting time even a little and the relationship grows greatly. Nip a foot or two out of the fence and watch the pasture shrink."

What Children Say

Again and again, I have seen this truth fleshed out, for good or bad, in the lives of children. The size of their relationship with their father can be measured by the amount of time he spends with them. Each year, the National Center for Fathering sponsors an essay contest for children. Most often, the children write about T-I-M-E. Often, I have found myself skimming over their letters, looking for the most heartwarming expressions, but gradually I have come to realize that the little details of their relationship with their fathers are most important to them. It says that he loves them. Here are three examples.

Timmy: "My daddy loves me. He plays with me. He takes me to the park. He takes me for ice cream. He takes me swimming. Daddy helps me with my homework. He likes to listen to me read my reading books. He plays baseball with me. He takes me on walks with my dog. He tickles me a lot."

Bethany: "He chases me. He tucks me in bed at night and prays with me. When we go to the beach I get on his back and he swims."

Leigh: "One time, my daddy took me up in a big, big tree. He tied a big rope around his waist and tied the other end of the rope around my waist. We both climbed all the way to the top of the tree. He also taught me how to wash the dishes. He taught me how to use hot, hot water so that all the germs will come off the dishes."

FATHER FACT #3
Nurture Versus Nature

Among sociologists and criminologists, the debate continues between nature and nurture. Some say criminals have a bent toward evil, a desire to cut corners and gain an advantage—it's their nature. Others say criminals become that way because of the negative influence at home, including absent or indifferent fathers—it's how they were nurtured. Though we cannot say improper nurturing will create criminals, healthy nurturance clearly contributes to feelings of self-worth and confidence. (See chapter 7 for an in-depth discussion of nurturance.)

The National Center for Fathering conducts seminars in a variety of settings, including correctional facilities. One prisoner wrote this letter as an exercise to work through his feelings about his dad.[9]

Hello Slime for brains,
    I'm writing this letter to you for one reason. That is because I'm trying to be a better father than you were. That should be easy. You're basically an idiot, and I'm not. At least I'm trying not to be. I want to tell you how I feel about my childhood. I really didn't enjoy it too much because of one simple fact: I didn't have you there when I needed you. For example, for all the sports I played in. All the questions I needed to ask. I really don't know what else to write because I blocked out most of my childhood for one simple fact: it wasn't nice.

Each of these letters has one thing in common: the commonplace. Swimming, ice cream, praying, tickling, doing the dishes, climbing trees, answering questions. Nick Stinnett, a professor and researcher of human development and the family, writes:

> People's fondest memories of family life are typically nothing really complicated or expensive activities. They remember such things as eating meals together, going to an uncle's house together or enjoying dad pulling them in a sled. The common thread is simply doing some things together that are enjoyable. The activities they remember are not all entertainment; they include work too. We have some evidence that when people work together toward a goal that is important to them, it tends to bring them closer together.[10]

Quality Versus Quantity Time

You have heard the issue raised before; maybe you were even the one who posed the idea: It's not so much how much time I spend with my children, but the quality of the time together. I will say it up front: I have some problems with this theory. First, the reference point is an adult perspective; it has in it the adult belief that intensity can fix nearly everything. We may not be able to take a walk with our children once a day, but we can fly to Disney World. And what is better: a walk in the woods or a ride down Space Mountain?

But children, as we have seen from the letters, don't reason that way. They take joy in the small details, for it is in the everyday, commonplace activities that they know that their fathers love them moment to moment. They seek more the presence of their father, not their presents.

But there is an even greater problem with this idea, one that is exposed in the very way it is phrased: quantity versus quality. It sounds like quality and quantity are opposed to one another, as far disconnected as, say, communism and capitalism. Nothing could be further from the truth. It would be like going up to a farmer and asking him, "What is a better use of your time—planting or harvesting?" Clearly, it is a comical question, for the one depends upon the other, and it is all part of a process.

In the same way, the quantity time versus quality time debate is moot. We will never experience quality time unless we've first put in the hours. Those moments of high quality in fathering are moments of "harvest" for us dads, where father and child alike experience satisfaction in the relationship. But a father who tries to harvest all the time—picking only the quality fruit of relationship—will quickly discover himself in a desert. Quantity time is a prerequisite to quality time. It takes quantity time to build a relationship of mutual trust, and trust is absolutely necessary for real quality time.

We too often think of involvement with our children as a one-way street—it allows a father to get to know his children better. But, we have to remember, the opposite is also equally true and important: It allows children to know their father—his values, what makes him laugh, how he drums his fingers at a traffic light. In short, involvement allows children to get to see inside the heart of a father. In this, there is connection, and connection, if it runs its proper course, leads to a healthy imitation.

Strategies of Involvement

My friend Paul is an involved father. He works forty hours each week, and in fact chose a job that allows him to be home each night and each weekend. At home, he likes spending time with his daughter Susan. They play Chutes and Ladders on the living room floor, and he reads her a story before bed. Cindy is a bit older. With her, involvement means driving her to gymnastics and cheering at her meets. It means sitting down next to her at the kitchen table when she lays out her math homework.

Sometimes Paul has his own work to do, his own errands to run. "I'm going to the hardware store," he announces. "Anyone want to come along?" Occasionally Cindy or Susan will join him. The youngest child is Jacob. Among all the things that involvement means for this toddler, it also means changing diapers. Paul participates in the daily activities of his kids.

In many ways, involvement is a simple concept. In discussing different types and strategies of involvement, I hesitate. I do not want to complicate what needs to remain simple. In general terms, an involved father is one who is engaged in the life of his child.

Michael Lamb, a longtime researcher in the U.S. Department of Health and Human Services, offers this description: "Fathers carry out their involvement in three basic ways—engagement, accessibility, and responsibility."[11]

1. Engage the Child

When a father and his child are doing something together, where the purpose of the activity (on the father's part, at least) is to be with his child, then he is engaged with that child. Dad enlists his teenage son to help change a tire; he steps in for Mom and goes shopping for school clothes with his daughter; he suggests a walk down the street for ice cream or yogurt; he attends his children's choir performances and basketball games.

My children yearn for my engagement. They will often plan their evenings around my availability and willingness to engage them. And if I don't show interest in them, other things will—like surfing the Internet, TV, neighbors, and friends.

Maybe you're accomplishing some task together, or maybe you're just out to have a good time and make sure your child does the same. The important thing is that you are building strong relationships with your children and making memories that will last for years.

2. Give Access

In contrast, accessibility is unstructured time—being in the vicinity of the child without necessarily doing an activity together. You can be attentive to your child and enjoy his or her presence even while you are focused on something else. Accessibility also enhances the child's sense of your availability even when you're not physically together: You could, for example, give your child your work phone number and say, "Feel free to call any time you need me." And the child knows you mean it.

3. Accept Responsibilities

Responsibility means that fathers help with the care of their children during the daily routines—feeding mouths, wiping noses, giving allowances, changing diapers, driving them to lessons and games. We are there to meet our children's needs, no matter where those needs fall in the range of trivial to life-threatening.

On one wall in our offices, I have a print reproduction of a painting that for me epitomizes the responsibility aspect of involvement. It is a Victorian-period print entitled "Worn Out." It was painted as plagues swept through Great Britain and families clung to each other for strength. In this painting, a curly-haired boy, ill with the plague, sleeps in the room's only bed. In the chair next to the bed, the child's father leans his head back, eyes closed, his legs slanting down and crossing near his heavy boots. I imagine he's been there all night tending the child, perhaps even fighting for the child's life. There's no indication that the father knows anything about medicine, but there's a small bowl below his chair. Perhaps he used it to feed the child broth, or put water in it to dampen the child's forehead with a sponge. There is an open book at his feet.

The most poignant detail of the painting, however, is the child's tiny hand—it is grasping tightly to his father's shirtsleeve just above the elbow. He is drawing strength from father power. He has survived another night.

This painting also sums up the other two aspects of involvement. I imagine that the dad was, at times, actively engaged with his child—reading a story or whispering comforting words to him while he cooled the child's forehead. The dad was also accessible. I like to think that the child knew, even in the heat of the deepest fever, that his daddy was right there beside him, ready to talk with him, ready to help. And he was also responsible—taking care of his sick son. What he actually did was very simple, yet, at the same time, incredibly difficult.

The painting also says this to me: Loving involvement means self-sacrifice. No matter what time of day or night, the father was there, responsible and involved. And it is here, I believe, that we begin to understand why so few of us are spending enough time with our children. When we are truly involved, we must give extra of ourselves.

Factors Affecting Our Involvement

Obstacles exist to our involvement. That may seem surprising, since we noted that involvement is a simple thing. We spend time with our children. Yet, on closer reflection, becoming involved with our children may mean overcoming a number of deep-seated obstacles. Effective fathering, more than anything else, involves a responsive heart. A responsive heart consists of underlying values, motivations, and priorities—all crucial to a father's success. Without them a father will be finished before he even starts.

Lamb identifies four factors that determine how involved a father will be in the lives of his children: skills, supports, institutional (workplace) factors, and motivation.[12] In each of these areas, as a father you must know your heart and be willing to give of yourself.

Our Skills

My childhood friend Doug was phenomenal on the basketball court. He was quick and graceful, knowing exactly where to be at all times, sinking double-pump scoop shots. Watching him play, you think of him as intelligent and gifted. But then I remember watching Doug out on water skis. Suddenly he seemed awkward, and a slow learner, especially since we'd just seen the boy whose father owned the boat do a one-ski slalom run. Doug's entire demeanor drooped in that environment, and the next time he didn't want to come along unless we played basketball.

I think that's how many fathers are when it comes to parenting skills. Although it may be true that some people are more naturally gifted for fathering—with temperaments and personalities more suited to children—most often the necessary skills come with experience and confidence. Maybe we never had the opportunity to be around children much, and never learned how to do things "right." We get uncomfortable, then self-conscious, and give the child back to our wives. It isn't that we're any less capable than our wives; we're just less practiced, and we prefer to stick with the more comfortable roles. As one father, complaining of his lack of fathering skills, told me, "I just don't really like to be around children."

As a result, many fathers feel inadequate for fathering. They lack confidence, so they hand the child back to their wife. The first thing that such hesitant fathers must do is process their past, as we have described in the

first section of this book. As we have attempted to show, there is a direct
and powerful connection between fathering of the past and fathering of the
present. Second, fathers unsure about their skills should also immerse
themselves in fathering resources—books, seminars, and, most importantly,
the support of others.

Support

The most important resource is the support of others: other dads who
are dealing with the same issues, older men with the wisdom of experience, and your children's mother. But even with support, we must be dis-
cerning. Lamb writes, "High paternal involvement is unlikely to occur unless significant others—mothers, relatives, friends, work mates—approve
of this behavior."[13] Probably the most significant other is your wife. In fact,
as we survey thousands of fathers across the country and ask the question
"Who has most influenced you in your fathering?" the most popular answer
by far has been "My wife."

Our wives' encouragement gives us strength to persevere when we
make mistakes, or when the teenage years come and the rewards of fathering aren't nearly as apparent. But wives can also inhibit us as fathers. If a
wife wants little Timmy dressed "just so," then her husband will only fail
once or twice before giving up altogether. She has unknowingly discouraged him from being involved in that part of his fathering role. Or maybe
she criticizes the way he disciplines the child, throwing up another barrier
to his well-meaning efforts. As Michael J. Diamond, associate professor of
psychiatry at UCLA, points out, "The mother is the gatekeeper of fatherhood. She may allow it or obstruct it."[14]

We also receive a mixed bag of support and discouragement from other
sources. Many men, often deeply insecure, believe fathering to be somehow less than masculine. When a father goes home to his family instead of
going to a football game, he may often be teased: "Going home to change
the diapers?" Many parenting events may also make many fathers feel out of
place: PTA meetings, doctors' appointments, childbirth classes, and so on.

Influence of the Workplace

The workplace, however, is often where the father meets the most resistance to his fathering commitment. Seldom is the dimension of fathering taken seriously in the business world: Most of our bosses aren't likely to suggest that we take more time off to tend to family matters. The pressure, more times than not, is to perform and to perform well, regardless of the hours or number of cross-country business trips it takes to "prove yourself." Taking time off for the children, in fact, may signal a weakness to many employers. Ellen Galinsky of the Families and Work Institute suggests that a man who takes paternity leave "is not seen as a young lion. He's not seen as serious and committed."[15]

I suspect I don't need to convince you of the tension we fathers feel at times between our work and our families. At its simplest, it is merely a question of priorities. Yet, at the same time, those priorities are often organized around a set of complex values issues. Many men excuse themselves from more of a fathering role because they must do what is expected of them on the job. They are, after all, the providers for their children. Yet, in many cases, it is not so much a case of *must* as it is *want*.

In our culture, it is often easier for men to seek their identity in the workplace, rather than the home. Much of this is due to the sense of disconnection we discussed in chapter 3. A man often does not recognize the connection between his public history (work) and his private (family); he chooses to give the immediate rewards of work an unbalanced importance. The workplace, even though it demands a great deal of a person, also offers fairly quick rewards, such as bonuses, raises, and new titles. In addition to the extra money, such rewards also fulfill deeper needs for power, recognition, achievement, and identity.

In short, the business world can offer fast food for a starving ego. In comparison, fathering is much less immediate in terms of rewards. How many times, for example, have your children said "thank you" in the past year? And when did an important, valued person in society tell you what a good person you were for driving your child to soccer practice?

Motivation: Investing for the Future

When it comes to motivation, fathers need a long-range perspective—one that can see past the immediate temptations of recognition, power, and achievement that the business world offers us. Remember the father's unique contribution. It's true. Only a father can fulfill all the roles—affection, care, training—that fathers perform. You are the only person who can truly be a child's father. A child needs her father in unique and dynamic ways throughout her entire life.

A good father needs to invest himself in the lives of his children. And such an investment requires an unconditional love and a willingness to sacrifice. It is hard work over the long haul with few "immediate" rewards. Most financial advisors will tell you that saving money is not a miraculous growing process, like planting a tree and then coming back twenty years to find a massive, towering structure. You don't put $100 into a bank account and expect to have a fortune in five years. Instead, saving becomes a way of life: You invest a little bit every month, and it grows accordingly—and surprisingly.

Investing is a good analogy for fathering, because our time and energy are also very limited, and involvement consists of these daily investments in our kids. Listening attentively as your five-year-old tells the same story for the tenth time is a small deposit in his life. When your daughter is nervous about volleyball tryouts, taking her down to the gym for an hour of setting and hitting is a small deposit. The fascinating thing is, our children mature at a much higher rate of interest than any mutual fund, and you'll be amazed at what they will accomplish when they are given the small, consistent deposits of our time and effort.

Involvement is the first wall to be raised and secured in place, and it will have a striking effect on the strength of the other three walls of consistency, awareness, and nurturance.

The old adage says, "The hand that rocks the cradle rules the world." As fathers, we are building the protective houses that are sheltering the leaders of the coming generation. Are we neglecting our duty by placing our children in so many windup contraptions that rock them off to sleep? Perhaps we should turn off the DVD player we turned on to keep our kids occupied and quiet. It's time to cradle them in our arms and rock them; it's time to put down the paper and the report and dive headlong into the challenging, thrilling world of our children.

FATHER INVENTORY #4
Involvement

INSTRUCTIONS:

Take your responses from the statements on pages 91 and 92 and place them next to the corresponding items below. Total the scores for the items under each of the I CANs and plot the appropriate score on the graph on page 156.

P S 1	My child and I often do things together.	Score	_____
P S 5	My children accompany me on errands.	Score	_____
P S 9	I frequently read stories with my child.	Score	_____
P S 13	I often work together with my child on a project.	Score	_____
P S 17	My child and I often have fun together.	Score	_____
P S 21	My child and I spend a lot of time together.	Score	_____
P S 25	I often involve my child in working with me.	Score	_____
P S 29	I spend time playing with my child a couple times a week.	Score	_____
		TOTAL	_____

Plot your score below and on page 156.

8	10	12	14	16	18	20	22	24	26	28	30	32	34	36	38	40

Chapter Five

CONSISTENCY

Michelle, a sixth grader, had her new friend Holly over on Saturday, and they spent the day talking and giggling over every little thing. Michelle began to think she'd found a "new best friend." But then on Monday she heard that Holly had been making fun of her with some other girls, and she wondered, *Is this how relationships work?*

William tried out for the football team as a sophomore. During the late-summer two-a-day practices, Coach Nelson kept telling him, "With your size and skills, you're going to be our starting tight end this year." But now that school has started, the coach doesn't even remember his name. William is puzzled: *Is it something I did, or is this how I should expect to be treated by older men?*

Both Michelle and William will look to the examples of their fathers as they try to answer questions about relationships, and many other questions as well. And the questions will never end. Children are natural explorers; they need to discover. Toddlers discover objects by putting them in their mouths. In grade school, they discover crushes and what is fair at recess. As teenagers, they explore the bigger issues—self-identity, faith, the opposite sex.

Stable and Secure

I like to think of the wall of Involvement (described in the previous chapter) as a wall made of wooden boards. The father and kids worked on building the wall together. The dad started some of the nails that fastened the boards to the frame, and the little boy got to pound them the rest of the way in. Then the whole family painted the house, slopping it on thick, occasionally stopping to have a playful paintbrush "fight."

The wall of Consistency, however, is made of brick. Your kids look at it and think, *Wow, is that ever solid. I bet nothing could make that wall crumble.* The bricks themselves are laid evenly in their well-ordered rows, with just the right amount of mortar between them.

Like a Baseball Umpire

Such stability is what every child wants: a dad who has a fixed position from which he does not waver, which gives the child a place from which he can explore his world and make decisions about who he is and who he will become. To understand a child's (and for that matter an adult's) need for consistency, let's think a minute about the role of a baseball umpire. He needs flawless eyesight, confidence, and decisiveness, even the ability to resolve conflict. But if you asked the players, I'll bet the quality at the top of their list would be something children also need from their fathers—consistency.

Hitters depend upon a consistent strike zone. It doesn't matter so much if the umpire calls high or low strikes, or even gives the pitcher a few extra inches around the plate. If the umpire is consistent, the batter can adjust his thinking and step up to the plate with confidence. But if the umpire is unpredictable, the hitter will be confused and more likely to fail. He steps into the box nervously and is ready to start screaming when things don't go his way. The pitcher also depends on a consistent strike zone. If the umpire is giving him the slider low and away, he'll throw it there all day with good success. But if the umpire calls one pitch just below the knees a strike, then calls the next one in the same location a ball, the pitcher has to be wondering, "What do I have to do to please this guy?"

What happens when an umpire is inconsistent? Both pitchers and hitters get angry and confused. Clearly, pitchers and hitters depend on a consistent umpire to do their jobs effectively. Similarly, children depend on their fathers to be predictable and reliable so they can grow up (that's their job) with confidence and security.

Feeling Secure and Less Anxious

Let's suppose that John takes his five-year-old son on a walk. Young Bobby begins hand in hand with his father, walking down the sidewalk. Pretty soon, though, Bobby sees a rather large, colorful rock in someone's yard, and off he goes to look at it. Then, all of a sudden the thought hits him—maybe I shouldn't be doing this. Where is the first place that a five-year-old looks? At his father, of course. His father has stopped walking, and when Bobby looks to him, Dad gives three or four firm shakes of his head, side to side. The boy dashes back toward the sidewalk and his father. A few seconds later, Bobby once again is off on the path of discovery, chasing a butterfly into a neighbor's yard. Bobby chases it behind a bush and it disappears. The boy stands up and tries to find his bearings. Yes, right there on the sidewalk, not far from where he left him, is his father.

Let's suppose, however, that instead of staying on the sidewalk, John changed his course. Bobby returns from his paths of discovery and Dad is gone. The child is, all of a sudden, lost in a large and frightening world. Obviously, no father would take his five-year-old son on a walk and desert him. Yet, when we are inconsistent as fathers, we run the risk of abandoning our children. If a reference point is unreliable, our children will often become hesitant or even fearful of following new paths of discovery. Their sense of confidence and safety can be severely shaken.

More than anything, consistency is a reflection of your underlying values. Our standards of conduct for ourselves and our children are based on our system of beliefs—so are our dreams, and priorities. Yet, even with a belief system and a set pattern of standards, remaining consistent as a father will be difficult. Discipline will be required to be consistent in both external realities (our behavior and how we use our time) and internal realities (our character and emotional control).

How to Show Consistency

Several studies suggest specific areas in which children need consistent fathers. Through our research data we have identified six categories that correlate highly with consistency. The top three deal with external realities—what our children see us doing. Interestingly, they are related to how we spend our time. They are being consistent in (1) our presence, (2) our schedule, and (3) our free time.

1. Our Presence

For too many fathers, home is merely the place where they eat, sleep, and do their best to keep the noise level down. They leave the daily workings of the household to their wives, and when they're out of the house, they're not responsible for what happens there. Yet the presence of a dad is crucial, no matter how hard many fathers try to downplay their role in the family.

Consistent fathers make the best use of that presence, being active and valuable parts of their families. They can "be there" whether they're at home or across the country. Every day there are decisions to be made, crises to handle, and wounded egos to soothe. Obviously, you can't take care of a skinned knee when you're in a board meeting or halfway across the country. But you can still call to check in and talk with your wife and children about problems that need solving and decisions that need to be made. Such a presence reassures a child that Daddy knows about the situation and will do whatever he can to help. It's also helpful on longer trips to leave your family an itinerary so that even when you're not near a phone they know exactly where you are and exactly what you're doing.

This issue of being there becomes much more complicated when the father is divorced and trying to maintain his presence exclusively through occasional visitation and long-distance phone calls. Divorce brings certain insecurities to the children and limits the ways a dad can express his consistency. If you are a divorced dad, you can still be reliable in the ways you relate to the children. Send regular letters and make phone calls consistently; be dependable with child support as well as with your behavior during the times you are able to see the children.

When our presence in the family is consistent, we establish expected patterns that help to build memories and can become traditions. Whether it's a monthly lunch out with each child, a birthday treat, weekend card games that last into the night, or a family drive to see Christmas lights, traditions give children something to look forward to, and become almost necessary occurrences in their lives. You might hear one say, "It's just not a birthday without that special dinner at a Mexican restaurant," or "It doesn't seem like Christmas without our tree-trimming evening."

2. Our Schedule

Part of the power of a dad's presence is in the child's perception of his availability. Being regular and predictable in your schedule and habits helps create a sense of security for your children. It can be a great source of comfort to a child to know, at any time of the day, exactly where her father is. Sally can measure her day by her dad's coming and going. She wakes up at 7:30 in the morning. *Those are Daddy's footsteps moving around in the kitchen.* In the evening she hears the garage-door opener and looks at the clock. *It must be 5:20. He's home!*

"Canfield, you're asking too much," you may be saying. "Such consistency is only possible for fathers who have cushy jobs where emergencies never come up, and for guys who never work overtime." It's true that our increasingly complicated lifestyles can be a major barrier to our efforts to keep a consistent daily schedule. For some of us, there's no way to predict what will happen at work tomorrow, much less what time we'll be home from work.

But there are still ways of meeting the need of your children to feel secure in knowing where you are, that you can be reached if necessary, and that you are coming home in the near future. The telephone is one way, whether a mobile phone in your car or briefcase, or your office phone in the middle of a busy day. When my wife first gave me a cell phone as a gift, I fought it at first—as I do almost all new technology. But I have come to realize what a valuable fathering tool it is. Because I spend a lot of time on the highway or in spontaneously planned lunch meetings, a cell phone provides my children with the assurance that they can always get in touch with me.

Here are several ways you can be accessible:

1. Give your child your work number, with permission to call during a set lunch hour or break time.

2. Drive your child to school once a week, if you start late morning or have an afternoon or night job.

3. Drop a note in your child's lunch sack one morning before you leave, telling him you will be thinking about him at work today and inviting him to call at a set time (then be ready to answer the phone when he calls).

4. In the evenings, swing by his or her room or place of work just to say hi.

5. Volunteer to be the taxi driver for an evening activity. You'll be surprised at what you learn.

A father should always seek to be available to his children. Some of this may seem like a large hassle for a few results, but these efforts to be consistent provide a large measure of security for your loved ones.

3. Our Free Time

Consistency is not just how we spend our time with our children and at the office, but also how we use our free time. As men, we all have areas of our lives into which we escape from time to time. We don't have to answer to anyone, and no one tells us what to do. And we need these escapes, to be sure.

But our children need us to be consistent in all aspects of our lives. Earlier I described children as natural explorers, and we all know men who could be described as "overgrown children," because they're still exploring as well. We call it recreation, and it's necessary. But so is consistency.

One weekend Roger accepted an invitation to go fly-fishing with a friend from his office, and Roger took to the sport immediately. He bought all the equipment and started learning to tie his own flies. For several months he walked around the house talking about where the big fish like to feed in a creek, and even how they "think." He practiced casting in the backyard. In a few months, however, he tired of fishing. Next, he set his sights on personal computing, investing several thousands of dollars in hardware and software. Through the winter, he spent his evenings discovering the world of information on the Internet. And then came the NCAA basketball tournament, and "March Madness" deleted his interest in computers. Then, he took up stamp collecting. And so on.

The children noticed. With each new hobby they thought, *There goes Dad, off on another of his seasonal kicks.* Even though they're only describing his recreational habits, they're also receiving the message that Dad regularly changes his mind—*you never know what Dad's going to do next.* I know fathers who are really like Roger—responsible, committed men whose inconsistency in this one corner of their lives contradicts other things they have tried to model for their children.

In one of our essay contests, Allison, a fourth grader, wrote this about her father: "He has so many ideas that I can't name them all. Almost every day he has a new idea . . . once in a while he has too many ideas."

A Consistent Character

Your children will also be looking for consistency in your internal realities, those issues that display your character. Are you consistently emotionally stable, able to keep a promise, and displaying moral standards?

Emotional Control

As a father you create a unique emotional atmosphere in the home. It is part of your presence; you may not always realize it, but it happens nevertheless. The emotions you show in your daily lifestyle determine whether your household will be one of comfort and acceptance or a place of uneasiness and foreboding.

Being consistent with your mood swings does not mean you keep yourself from any display of emotion or limit yourself to emotions that are peaceful and unobtrusive. In fact, your children do need to see that you can be angry and yet not lose control of your words and actions, or that you can be elated about something and still not go overboard in celebration. The issue is: Do your children know what to expect from you emotionally? More than one adult child has said to his therapist, "When I approached my dad, I never knew whether he was going to hug me or belt me."

Inconsistent fathers have their children always on edge. They wonder, *How will Dad react when he walks in the door after work? Yesterday he was quietly depressed about his situation at work, and he sat on the couch staring at the wall. The day before, he slammed the door and exploded with a verbal barrage about his boss. Today he's talking about moving to Florida and finding a new job.* Such a father has set the emotional tone for his household: unpredictable and, for his children, very insecure.

Can your child approach you at any time to talk about something, or does he have to "feel you out" first to see what kind of mood you're in? Does your daughter know what to expect the next time she accidentally spills her milk or breaks a dish? I've found it common that fathers who struggle with consistency in their mood swings have not had the benefit of a man who modeled reliable expression of emotion. If the reference point in your memory is an inconsistent one, you can relate it with a positive one, but it takes some effort.

Keeping Promises

At least as equally damaging as an unpredictable mood is a broken promise. We live in a society that no longer places a strong emphasis on keeping our word. "My word is my bond," people used to say, and it was as good as done; nowadays, that statement means little. In fact, it is spoken more often as a sarcastic joke, with a wry smile and a raised eyebrow, than as a statement of sincere intentions. Even our signed contracts, which we use in place of our word, have loopholes if you can find a skilled enough lawyer.

Because of the erosion of the importance of our word (or even our signatures), we live in a culture low on trust. Our children desperately need a father whom they can count on to keep his promises.

Jeff promised his eleven-year-old son, Dustin, he would be home from work early on Friday, take him to lunch, and then spend the afternoon playing football with him. All week long, the boy counted down the days when he could have some special one-on-one time with his father. *I'll run a down-and-out, Dad will hit me on the fly for a 70-yard touchdown. Wow!* Dustin thought. He could imagine Dad tackling him on a fourth-and-one. They would lie in a pile, laughing.

At 11:30 a.m. Friday, the boy was sitting outside on the front porch steps, football in lap, waiting for his father. At 12:30 p.m., a half hour after his father was supposed to pick him up, he was still waiting on the steps. Jeff, who unexpectedly had urgent business come up at the office, called home at 1:00. "I haven't forgotten you, buddy; I'll be there in a little bit." Jeff's business stretched out until 2:00 and then 3:00, and, finally, well past supper. He would call every hour or so, promising his son that "he would be there shortly." Dustin believed his father and walked around the house tossing the football in anticipation of the time with his father.

His father finally came home at 10:00 p.m. and found his son asleep on the couch, the football cradled in his arms. As he was carrying him into bed, his son awoke. "I'm sorry, Son," his father told him. "I just couldn't get away." His son, only half awake, whispered back, "That's OK, Dad; I had fun thinking about it."

Jeff at least thought enough to call, not once but several times, to remind his son he hoped to be there. Yet not coming still dashed the boy's dreams. To our children, our promises are large, no matter how small they may seem to us.

As fathers, we need to guard our words. If you are coming up on a busy season at work, then you should think twice about promising to help your son for thirty minutes every day with his chemistry set. Be very careful before making a promise. Too often good intentions can cloud reality.

Regardless of how hard we try, broken promises will still happen. How you handle those broken promises can do a lot to restore your child's confidence in you. If you say, "Grow up, Son! People don't always mean what they say," or if you try to make up for it with another promise, he'll quickly learn that your promises aren't even worth listening to. Instead, ask your child's forgiveness and recognize that a promise is still a binding thing. If you can't fulfill it, be sure to provide a sincere and satisfactory explanation and not an excuse.

FATHER FACT #4
The Paradox of Consistency

This chapter emphasizes that fathers need to be consistent. Yet an effective father changes over time, adapting to the changing needs of his children.

At the heart of a loving and living consistency lies a paradox: Fathers need to be consistent, while they also need to change. It goes much further than being spontaneous and creative. A healthy consistency will be one that is solid enough to communicate values, but flexible enough to meet the needs of the children.

The fact is, your child is changing, slowly yet surely. In the final part of this book, we will look at the six stages of the fathering life course and learn how an effective father adapts as his children change.

You may have established a pattern of consistency that meets the needs of your sixth grader, but if you hold fast to the same behaviors for three more years, your high school freshman will wonder why you're so embarrassing to him.

We need not only be responsive to the different stages of development, but also to a child's individual personality. Even when we perform our fathering duties faithfully and lovingly, it's almost a guarantee that different children will understand and interpret our actions differently. One child is embarrassed whenever you say his name in a public place; another thrives on the attention. One child likes physical, outdoor games like kick ball, while the other would rather stay inside and read. Our children are unique individuals, and as fathers we need to make adjustments so we can relate to them accordingly.

Consistency in Moral and Ethical Behavior

In seeking consistency in their father's internal realities, children are seeking a moral center, a place to anchor themselves. If they do not perceive a moral center, they too will drift. In a classic study, researchers Alan Acock and V. L. Bengston compared the values of parents to those of their children. They concluded that "it is not what parents think, but what their children think they think, that best predicts their offspring's attitudes."[1] We try to teach our children right from wrong, and they get a somewhat accurate picture of what we mean. But what happens when a child learns something about her father that completely contradicts what he has taught her?

Few things damage our children's respect for us more than when we spout moral absolutes and then live out a different standard. A child will rarely respect such inconsistent values. Harry punishes his daughter for lying, and then as he's doing his taxes, he "forgets" to report the extra $200 he made one weekend. Or, there's the son who listens to his father's interminable lectures concerning sexual purity, until one day the son finds his dad's adult magazine collection in the bottom of a drawer.

It often takes just one such inconsistency for our children to label our entire belief system as faulty. Our children will eventually learn that we are flawed (and we can teach them a lot by being vulnerable about our mistakes), but if they come to think of us as a fraud, they may disregard the good with the bad and start looking for another reference point on which to build their value system.

A father I know was wrestling with what some may consider an "insignificant" matter—wearing his seat belt. For years, he had only bothered wearing it when traveling several hours or on busy freeways. But then something significant—and scary—happened. His oldest child, his daughter, began driver's education classes at school. That's when he started wearing his seat belt every time he got in the car, recognizing that no matter what he *tells* his children, the life he *lives* communicates what he really believes. His desire to send a consistent message to his children was important enough that he decided to make permanent lifestyle changes.

Perhaps the most common expression of this mode of consistency is in your practice of discipline. When you model behavior you expect from your children, the limits and expectations you place on their behavior make more sense to them. They know when you lay out certain rules for them to follow that you also follow those rules. They also know you'll be monitoring their actions, and that there are negative or even painful consequences when they step out of line.

My Rachel, as is often the case, serves as a good case in point. She's strong-willed, and fortunately, allows Dee and me to live in the same house with her. When she was a toddler, I remember driving home on the freeway with Dee, our two sons, and Rachel, and I discovered that she'd learned a phrase we don't allow in our household. It isn't obscene, but we're trying to teach our kids that it's disrespectful and demeaning to others.

At first, I thought I heard Micah say, "Shhh, shut up," and I turned around and said, "Son, I don't want you saying what I thought I heard you say." About three minutes later, we heard a faint voice from the back of the van, saying, "Shut up, Daddy. Shut up, Mommy." It was sweet, little Rachel, trying to get a reaction out of us. I turned around again and said, "Rachel, we don't talk that way. You will get in trouble if you talk that way." A moment later she tested the waters again: "Daddy, shut up!" Well, the giggling in the backseat from her brothers was nearly shaking the car off the road, and even Dee was giggling next to me. What was Dad going to do? I couldn't get off the freeway, so I said, "Rachel, we're going to have a talk when we get home."

And after that talk, she got the message. Rachel has continued to test our limits, but I also know that she feels good about finding the boundary points. What Daddy says, he means.

Remember, limits don't box children in; they give children the freedom to express themselves within safe boundaries. That's why most children are looking for consistency in discipline. Similarly, if a violation of rules results in a spanking one time and a halfhearted warning the next, children will be confused as to what is really wrong or right. Children want their boundaries clearly defined.

Time After Time

Consistency is a misunderstood word. In our freewheeling, often centerless culture, consistency is frequently misinterpreted as a synonym for *boring, regular,* or *predictable.* And nothing, it would seem, sends off a whiff of un-coolness like that which even hints of repetition, liturgy, or tradition.

Yet consistency is a vital aspect of fathering. It is by being consistent that we show our love, time and time again, to our children. Through consistency, we drive our children to their soccer practices every Tuesday and Thursday. Through consistency, we discipline our children fairly and according to well-established rules, so that they grow up understanding right and wrong. Through consistency, we set aside time specifically for our children so that they will know us and we will know them. Through consistency, avenues of trust and respect develop that allow connections between the heart of the father and the heart of his children. Through consistency, the children know who their father is, who he *really* is.

Consistency, by its very definition, means time after time after time. In our day and age, we've become accustomed to the instant and easy: shopping online, downloadable music, cell phones. Consistency doesn't work that way. If you have resolved to break some of your harmful habits and be a better father, don't expect your children to come around in a few days, or weeks, or months, or maybe even years. Consistency is one of the most important gifts you can give your children, but you can't acquire it immediately. You have to establish and prove your consistency—and it takes time.

Watch Out for Walls and Ruts

Often—and many times without our being aware of it—fathers will hide behind defensive walls of consistencies. In the name of consistency, we do not allow our children to see us for who we are. So we hide our emotions; we hide behind the wall, fearful our children will think we are weak for having different emotions.

Ironically our emotional and spiritual expressions are among the most important qualities a father can model. Few men are comfortable showing emotion, but children need to see how to handle emotions responsibly. Whether they see you cry over a loss, maintain control during anger, or celebrate an achievement, they need to see the feeling part of you; after all, it's a vital part of who you are.

In addition, watch out for ruts. Once we find something that seems to work with our kids, or at least something that doesn't do any damage, we tend to stick to it. We develop patterns that work, and before long the things we do are motivated by the pattern rather than the reason we started the pattern in the first place. It's like when we use clichés in language. It's easier to merely repeat an old, familiar saying that fits the situation than it is to come up with something fresh and truly meaningful. Being consistent means avoiding the ruts.

I remember the morning Micah and I were sitting at the breakfast table, and soon we were joined by my daughter Sarah and one of her friends, who had spent the night. The girls were still in their pajamas. My sweet, seven-year-old Micah, who noticed every detail, took one look at Sarah's friend and uttered one short sentence that sent both of the girls shrieking out of the room in embarrassment. Without my going into detail, Micah had noticed the developing features of Sarah's friend, and saw fit to comment quite plainly and frankly.

I still couldn't believe he'd said it, so I asked him, "Micah, what did you mean by that?" Sure enough, he was only making an observation, and he meant exactly what he said. Maybe he thought he was giving her a compliment. So I took Micah aside for a little father-to-son talk. No big deal, he just hadn't quite figured out which topics are—and aren't—appropriate to talk about openly.

Dads who go too far with consistency might reprimand or even discipline their kids because of some harmless, embarrassing action or statement.

Other fathers go overboard and let fun-loving spontaneity drown out their good judgment. Our children will say and do things that are inappropriate and embarrassing. We can make the best of them by laughing when they're funny, exercising discipline only when necessary, and, most of all, turning them into teachable moments with our children.

The consistent and steadfast father sets a high standard for himself and for his children; the goal of these standards is relationship. Despite the changing circumstances, his behavior patterns and his interactions with his children do not vary. He will perform his fathering role diligently, even when hardships arise or he is called upon to make sacrifices.

FATHER INVENTORY #5
Consistency

INSTRUCTIONS:

Take your responses from the statements on pages 91 and 92 and place them next to the corresponding items below. Total the scores for the items under each of the I CANs and plot the appropriate score on the graph on page 156.

P S 2	I do not have major shifts in my moods.	Score	_____
P S 6	I try not to vary much in the way that I deal with my children.	Score	_____
P S 10	I do not change much in the way that I deal with my children.	Score	_____
P S 14	I am unchanging in my personality characteristics.	Score	_____
P S 18	I tend to be somewhat unchanging in the way I practice fathering responsibilities.	Score	_____
P S 22	My moods are pretty much the same from day to day.	Score	_____
P S 26	I feel that the way I deal with my children does not change much from day to day.	Score	_____
P S 30	I am predictable in the way I relate to my children.	Score	_____
		TOTAL	_____

Plot your score below and on page 156.

8	10	12	14	16	18	20	22	24	26	28	30	32	34	36	38	40

AWARENESS

Nikki longed to be known. Her mother gave birth to Nikki at age seventeen and subsequently ran away from home often, leaving Nikki's grandmother to care for her. Nikki's father, who did not marry her mother until many years later, was hardly ever around.

In an essay about her father, Nikki wrote:

If he would just try to get to know me, my father would like me because I'm not a bad person, but he won't even try. So, I get tired of being good because nobody cares anyway and then I get in trouble in school. Last time I got in trouble they couldn't reach my mom so they called my father. He drove 70 miles, and when he got here, I was standing outside with a bunch of kids, and I was so proud because my daddy was coming to see me. Then he went up to some other girl and hugged her. He didn't even know who I was.[1]

"He didn't even know who I was." These are words that should strike fear into the heart of every father. You may be able to pick your daughter out of a crowd, but it's still possible you do not know who she really is. What's she like on the inside? What are her aspirations and fears? What kind of woman is she developing into? And what about those friends who are surrounding her?

The third fathering function is Awareness—the extent to which a father knows his children and their world. The aware father knows his children's characteristics, growth needs, and daily experiences. He knows what events are happening in their lives, but he is also aware of how his children will think and feel, and how they'll react to those events.

Awareness is a wall with windows—windows that let us look into our child's soul and out into his world.

A father may do his best to be involved and consistent but fail miserably at awareness. Bob was such a father. A high-profile leader in the community, he discovered early in his career that he was not giving enough attention to his two sons, who were still in grade school. With determination and good motivation, Bob purposively cut back his schedule. He began to attend fathering seminars and read books. He set aside time to build into his children's lives; he took them on camping trips, attended all of their sporting events, set up one-on-one lunchtimes. And he was, in his fathering, as consistent as a sunrise. Day after day and year after year, Bob showed dedication and commitment to his children. He invested into their lives his principles, time, and energy.

Yet, somehow, Bob was unaware of his children's needs. I met his younger son, James, when he was twenty-six. What he told me startled me. When he was thirteen—for a period spanning a few months—he was sexually abused by his older brother, who was sixteen at the time. Neither of his parents had had any awareness of the abuse.

His father, although consistent and involved with his two sons, did not know this. Why? Bob had made little effort to connect to their innermost lives. In all their activities he felt somehow emotionally distant. He did not inquire about their hopes and fears nor share his feelings with them. And the boys did not feel free to volunteer their feelings.

Together but Alone

The unraveling story of Bob and his two sons can teach us a great deal about what contributes (and what doesn't) to the level of awareness we have about our children. James eventually talked to his brother and father about the abuse in his childhood. At first, his brother dismissed it as a few innocent incidents; his father was angry and deeply hurt. "I did all that I could to be a good father and look what happened!" As James worked his way through counseling, he eventually became aware of the emotional distance with his father.

As they discussed James's childhood together, his father came to a startling revelation. Bob had never worked through his past with his own father. His father had abandoned his family and disappeared from their lives—no visits, no phone calls, no child support. Bob, like his father, had never learned how to emotionally connect with his children. His own father left the family when Bob was thirteen—the same age of James when he was molested by his brother.

"The realization hit me that I, too, had abandoned my children emotionally," Bob confessed.

Because Bob never resolved his issues as a son, he passed on the same damage to his own sons. His past impinged on and crippled all of his efforts in the present. His involvement lacked emotional connection; his consistency was more of a lecture than a two-way conversation. The strong values he hoped to pass on, he pressed on his children, not *impressed*. Because he couldn't connect heart-to-heart with his sons, he focused more on mechanical repetition rather than relationship. "You did all the right things, except one," said James. "You never showed us your love." Because of the emotional distance, there was never a sense of understanding, of awareness, between father and sons.

From Knowing About to Knowing Children

In his involvement and consistency, Bob collected information. In doing so, he knew things about them, but he didn't know them. As we read through this chapter on awareness, we will be well served to learn from Bob's mistake: Awareness must inform the heart as well as the head. But before we are too critical with Bob, we should realize this: Most of us, as fathers, never even get as far as Bob did.

An aware father who examines his role will find that he has a unique opportunity to help his children resist temptation and develop healthy self-images. Vice president of The Heritage Foundation Rebecca Hagelin encourages:

What America needs perhaps more than anything else is fathers who will father. I'm the mother of two teenage boys, and believe me, I am well acquainted with the behaviors that have led to the popular phrase "boys will be boys." But I am also blessed to know what it means to my sons' development and character for them to have a father who holds them accountable, is engaged in their lives, and is intimately familiar with their strengths, weaknesses, personalities and individual needs.[2]

This kind of father seems to be a rare breed. Maybe it starts when our first child is born. Our wives have learned much more about young children, so they're automatically the "experts" while we're at an immediate disadvantage. Maybe we feel like we're being forced to serve "under" our wives, who seem more able to nurture and talk to the baby. Our pride is hurt, and we wait until our children get older, when we think we can relate to them more easily. But even then, too many of us fathers limit our knowledge of our children. We tend to emphasize only those aspects of their lives with which we are comfortable, such as their schoolwork and future education, and minimize "less important" aspects like getting along in peer groups.[3]

Unlike Bob, many of us have little information about our children. In contrast, consider some of the things we do have knowledge about—maybe the batting averages of the Atlanta Braves, the specifications of next year's Corvette, or the titles of all the John Wayne movies. Or maybe it's knowledge that's less trivial, knowledge that might make a difference in your life: the key views of your state representative, the current prime interest rate, the cost of housing in your neighborhood, the *Consumer Reports* best buy among used cars, and so on. It's apparent that we do keep tabs on what's going on around us in our society. In fact, I could easily do an hour-long lecture on some of these topics.

But how many of us could even answer simple questions about our children, who are as important to us as anyone or anything in our lives? Because the answers to questions about your child's interests and activities can reveal his desires, needs, and goals, you may want to complete Father Inventory #6, "Knowing My Child," on the next page.

Although Bob fell short of a genuine awareness of his children, at least he made the attempt. With good intentions and strong commitment, he started down the road of awareness, even if his final destination was far from where he wanted to be. Bob's overwhelming disadvantage was that he did not process his relationship with his own father before attempting to become aware about his children. Hopefully, as we have moved through part 1 of this book, we have dealt with those issues. Now, let's consider some fundamentals of awareness.

Two Kinds of Awareness

I divide awareness into two categories—and both are vital if you want to be an effective father.

General Awareness

This first kind of awareness consists of the kind of information you would learn in a college class called "Knowing Children 101." It's the basics, yet it's crucial information: (1) the basic needs of children, (2) the ways they will likely change as they grow and mature, and (3) their physical and intellectual capacities at particular ages and levels of development. It's the overarching knowledge necessary for rearing children, much as auto mechanics must have basic knowledge of a vehicle's operation—how engines and cars fit together, and what's likely to happen to cars as the mileage increases.

FATHER INVENTORY #6
Knowing My Child

How many of the following questions can you correctly answer about your child? The more you answer, the better you know his interests, fears, and even goals in his young life. If you have several children, complete a separate inventory for each one.

Meet with your child to discuss your answers; let him fill in the blanks where you didn't answer and correct you where you are wrong. It could lead to a great discussion of who he is and hopes to become.

1. Who is my child's all-time hero?
2. What is my child's most prized possession?
3. Who is my child's closest friend?
4. What causes the most stress for my child?
5. What were my child's greatest achievement and greatest disappointment in the last year?
6. What is my child's favorite meal?
7. What would my child like to do when he or she grows up?
8. If my child had $40 to spend, what would he or she buy?
9. What does my child most like to do with me?
10. What is the most important thing I need to discuss with my child in the next six months?

As concerned fathers, we should seek to be informed about children. We should seek out magazines, books, fathering seminars, and basic psychology texts. We would be wise, too, if we imitated how our wives learn about children: New mothers almost always consult their own mothers. Our children's mothers (our wives), much more than we do, see the need to sit down with their mothers and say, "I never learned all this. Have you got a minute?" They also talk to one another, as I'm sure you've noticed. And along with whatever else they may discuss, the children become a major topic, and the women share information. It will not ostensibly be a teaching session where one of them says, "Let me tell you how to break Sammy of his thumb-sucking." Instead, the information will be passed because of their friendship, where one of them lives through the problem, sharing her concerns all the while. When the problem is finally solved, it is only natural to reveal the remedy as part of their next conversation.

When it comes to knowing how children grow and change, your parents are valuable resources. That includes your father. In part 1, we discussed how you might be able to include your father in the lives of your children. And even if your father, for whatever reason, is not a credible source of information, you can seek out a father figure. One way or the other, it is critical to get the input of an older father, who has "been there, done that."

Another valuable source is your children's mother. She's the one who spent many evenings babysitting other people's kids as a teenager. She's the one who actually read all those child-care books when she was pregnant—

some of them twice! She may be reading one now. She usually is in tune with the stages of your child's life, which bring something new for the child to explore: new emotions, new experiences, new knowledge, new abilities.[4]

This general awareness is important enough that it is the basic premise behind the entire third section of this book, where we will explore the changes you can expect—from your children and from yourself—as you pass through the fathering life cycle. General awareness provides an overview— a road map—of your child's development.

Specific Awareness

If general awareness is "Knowing Children 101," then we'd call specific awareness "Knowing Your Child, 102 through 990." This is the practicum you enroll in every semester until you graduate from your fathering role (that is, until you die). A general understanding of our children must ulti- mately be tested, specifically, on our own children. We need to take into account the unique and changing level of maturity, emotional makeup, intellectual capacity, and individual needs of each of our children.

Craig and Carol have two young daughters. Kate is four—and she'll be quick to add "and-a-half!" All her life, Kate has smiled easily and befriended everyone who came near. She was always ahead of her peers in her verbal skills, and Craig took pride in her ability. When she was just starting to talk, he would sit with her for hours asking her to repeat things: "Say 'avocado.'" "Av-a-caaa-do," she would articulate. "Say 'Michael Jordan.'" "Mik-a- jooord-en." They'd go on for hours. As she grew, Kate learned to solve problems using her verbal skills, trying to talk Grandma into giving her what she wanted and telling Daddy "white lies" when she needed to.

Brenda, who came along two years after Kate, didn't learn to talk as fast. Until recently, she only allowed a select few people to pick her up and hold her. She turned her intellectual energies toward all the things she could pick up and manipulate with her hands, and quickly became very action-oriented. At two-and-a-half, Brenda can nearly outrun her sister. When Craig tries to get her to say "Aardvark," she just looks at him, wrin- kles her brow, and shakes her head. When she wants something, her natu- ral inclination is to just go get it.

Craig has two distinct children, and he has realized that he will need to handle them differently as they continue to grow. Both of them need to feel loved and secure, but maybe Kate will want to be told more that she is loved, while Brenda may just want to be held. When Kate has done something wrong, a stern look may put her in tears, while Craig may need to discipline Brenda in some more physical way.

An effective father knows a child's strengths and weaknesses, what motivates, embarrasses, encourages, and hurts each child. As children get older, their lives become more complicated, and so does the task of keeping up with them. They go to school, play Little League sports, and have more friends. It's easy to see how a father could lose track of his kids—but that doesn't excuse us from seeking to understand more and more about our children.

Chances are, very few of you have had books published about your son or daughter, so you have to rely on other methods to increase your specific awareness.

We have already discussed the number one way of knowing your children: *involvement.* Spending time with your children gives them the opportunity to reveal themselves to you more fully. As you share experiences with your children, you will learn the answers to questions—both spoken and unspoken—concerning what they enjoy, what makes them anxious, and how they approach life.

Second, *as you take part in their activities, be sure to praise their accomplishments.* Many times you learn about your child by responding to something he or she has done, and your praise makes a more powerful impression. You could say to your daughter, "Wow, I sure was proud when you sang that solo tonight. I never knew you had such a lovely voice." From her response, you learn how your daughter feels. She might, for example, respond: "Thanks, Dad, I was hoping I could pull it off." If you are listening closely, you have made a discovery: She enjoys singing but also needs more confidence. Or, she might say something entirely different: "It's no big deal. Mrs. Wilkins made me do it since no one else volunteered. I'd really rather be playing my clarinet." Either way, you've learned if your ears were in tune.

Third, *seek out the perspectives of others.* There are other people who see and interact with your children in situations where you cannot be. So talk to their teachers and coaches, and get to know their friends. It could be that your children react differently in the classroom or gymnasium than they do at home, and their teachers and coaches may notice qualities in them that haven't occurred to you. When you look at your child, you look at him from certain preconceived notions. Other people, who look at your child from another perspective, see something different.

Finally, *ask your child's mother*. Mothers are typically more tuned in to their children's feelings than fathers are. Dee has come up to me and said something like, "You may not have noticed, but when you told Joel to clean up his room, he thought you were angry with him." She's usually right; there are things I just don't notice. But I'm learning over and over that wise fathers take advantage of the unique sensibilities that their wives bring to the teamwork of marriage.

Awareness Before Success

Awareness is more than just a word; it's critical to the success of your fathering. When you are aware of each child—what he or she thinks and feels—you can focus. You no longer have to simply make guesses, or draw shaky conclusions based on what other parents have done or what may have worked for so-and-so's children. You are able to evaluate any advice or experience in light of your child's unique needs at her particular stage of development.

The unaware father might say, "Things are tense with my teenager, and I have no idea what to do. I'm willing to try anything at this point." He's shooting in the dark, hoping he'll stumble upon some response that can make things better, even if it's only for a short time. Awareness allows you to work from a position of strength, where you know what stifles your children and what makes each of them thrive, and with that knowledge you lovingly act to meet their needs.

You also understand each child's particular strengths and weaknesses, gifts and liabilities. My daughter Sarah, for example, was always our family paramedic. I realize that fathers normally fulfill that role, but I'm actually not the one in our family who was best cut out for it—I still remember hitting the floor after watching blood being taken from one of my children. But Sarah thrived, you might say, on such crisis. She used to watch TV shows like *911* and *ER* closely, and she always thought through possible emergency scenarios. She was fearless in situations where I hesitated. She is the one who sprang into action when Rachel, my youngest, put something "foreign" into her mouth or when Micah needed help cleaning up after his latest bicycle crash. She is gifted in this area, and I could depend on her to do the right thing. I also tried to encourage her by allowing her to assume an appropriate role.

In a like manner, we fathers need also to be aware of our children's potential weaknesses, which are also specific to our individual child's personality and stage of development. As a father who has a general awareness, you know, for instance, that thirteen-year-old sons experience strong peer pressure. Furthermore, in terms of specific awareness, you know that your own thirteen-year-old son often says that he'd "give anything" to have that $1,000 mountain bike. Armed with general and specific awareness, you might consider talking to your son about the dangers of materialism or volunteering together to help the less fortunate.

It is true for everyone: Our greatest strengths can turn into our greatest weaknesses. Maybe your child is very outgoing but is too trusting of strangers, or is getting mixed up with friends who drink. Maybe your fourteen-year-old daughter is naturally affectionate, but she's acting very "serious" about her latest boyfriend. There are land mines waiting to explode when our children take a few steps to the left or right, and when we are unaware of what is happening in their lives and the particular personality traits that make them susceptible to certain dangers, we're only asking for disaster.

Aware fathers never assume that their children are immune to trouble. Even a cursory general awareness of the world in which our children are growing up alerts a father to an alarming potential for danger. Children under the age of twenty-one drink 25 percent of the alcohol consumed in the U.S. More than 5 million high school students (31.5 percent) admit to binge drinking at least once a month.[5] At least 8.7 million teens had tried marijuana; and in the new category of substance abuse, 37 percent of teens say they have close friends who have abused prescription painkillers like Vicodin, OxyContin, and Tylox.[6] It's equally distressing when it comes to sexual activity. Recent studies report that among teens eighteen and nineteen years of age, 69 percent of females and 64 percent of males have had premarital sex.[7]

A specific awareness of your children will allow you to both anticipate problem areas as well as diagnose core issues when your child does go astray. Is your child interested in—or actually involved with—drugs? Maybe he's looking for an escape. Is your daughter getting dangerously involved with her boyfriend? There's a good chance she's not getting enough physical and verbal affection from the other man in her life—you. Is your son experimenting with alcohol? Maybe the parties he's going to help to boost his low self-esteem.

Great (and Small) Expectations

If you have a seven-year-old daughter, you should probably not take her to a symphony orchestra concerto. A general awareness of children would make that clear. On the other hand, what if she is a budding cellist? She might just be fascinated enough to sit through the performance, if her father takes a walk with her during intermissions. Only an aware father can make such judgment call.

An awareness of our children tempers and molds our expectations. We are less likely to make the mistake of molding them into someone else's image. I can't tell you the number of times I've heard comments like these from grown sons and daughters:

- "My brother was an all-state quarterback, and since I played tennis, my dad was never happy with anything I did."
- "I made a consistent B average in school, but Daddy was never happy with anything but A's."
- "I've never been able to really talk to my father after I decided to leave the family business."

Too many of us fathers communicate expectations that our children either can't or don't want to live up to. One of the great dangers of fathering is molding your children into your own image. Either you desire your children to be like you, or to cast a favorable image on the family. Is this merely a matter of selfishness? Possibly. But I believe more of us are merely unaware of who our children really are and the dreams they have for their own lives.

Many other fathers are absentminded and just don't stop and consider what's reasonable to expect from their children at a particular age. When Hannah and Sarah were three and one-and-a-half years old, respectively, I left them alone in our house so I could run to the market two blocks away for chocolate chips. Dee was out with friends, Sarah was asleep in bed, and, in my own defense, my intentions were great. I was looking forward to some quality time on a project with Hannah: baking several dozen choco-late chip cookies.

When I came back, however, Hannah was gone. Apparently she had wandered outside and began calling for me. One of our neighbors was just coming out to rescue her. I got to learn my lesson twice that night—once from the neighbor and again when Dee returned home—that three-year olds are a little young to be babysitters.

Gaining Confidence and Joy

Awareness not only benefits children, but also their daddy. A man who gains awareness gains confidence, a rare and precious commodity when it comes to fathering. We've seen the news reports; we've been warned by parenting experts—it's a dangerous world out there for a child, and it's only going to get worse. Sometimes I feel like curling up into the fetal posi-tion and waiting until my kids are all grown. But when I am aware of who my child is, what he is experiencing, and how he perceives the world around him, I begin to see some solutions and not just problems. When I realize—even to a limited extent—that I can be the father that my children need, my spine straightens up a bit, my shoulders relax. "I will be that father."

When we help our children develop and mature, there is accom-plishment. Tell me: How do you feel when your child—in ways unique to his or her own gifts and personality—finishes his first Mozart piece at the school recital? Or when your fearful child, with the careful and gentle encouragement of his daddy, finally goes down the big slide at the park? Or when your son, who has struck out with two on and one run behind in the bottom of the ninth, takes refuge in an ice-cream sundae with you, his father, after the game? Admit it: just plain proud. And that's OK—father-ing is meant to be joyful and it will be, more times than not, when you are aware.

Our Motives and Methods

At the heart of a father's ability to be aware of his children is the ques-tion of motivation. Are we, like Bob with his two sons, just going through the motions, remaining emotionally disconnected with our children? Or, even worse, are we aware of our children because we want to "spy" on their activities, measuring them against a rigid performance mentality? The motivation behind awareness must be *to open heart-to-heart connections with our children.* In the next chapter, we will talk about the critical issue of a father's nurturance. Awareness, like the system of veins and arteries, allows the heart of a father avenues to nurture his children.

Unless the motivation is pure, it is easy for awareness to become intrusive. The intrusive father wants to know about every aspect of his child's life, so much that he isn't allowing his child a life of her own. For him, knowledge is power: "That girl will never pull one over on me!" he might say to himself, and even as he says it, his daughter is scheming to deceive him again. His motivation for learning about his child is to "find out what she's up to" so he can then reel her back in with his strong hand of authority. He believes he can keep his child out of trouble by controlling her, by making all her choices for her.

The intrusive father might listen in on his son's phone conversation and read his daughter's diary—both without permission. Whatever the dad says, to the child, it's obvious he doesn't care about her thoughts and feelings; he's only keeping tabs on her, poking into her privacy, trying to squash her individualism. The daughter is a suspect, being tracked by the FBI, the Fathering Bureau of Investigation.

An aware father, on the other hand, gains an understanding of his child and her situation as a way of communicating concern for her. His approach might sound like this: "I can see you and Tommy have grown pretty close in these last few months, and I just want to talk with you to make sure you understand situations that may come up, because I want to be sure you know what you're getting yourself into." Where the intrusive father is always suspicious, an aware father is more supportive. "How are things going at school?" asks the aware father. "Is there anything I can do to help you? I know you're faced with a lot of challenges, and I just want you to know I'm here and ready to be of help."

But even though we may have good intentions, the way in which we handle the awareness that we gain can be another thing altogether. It can be easy for us to get pieces of information but put the puzzle together incorrectly. We run the risk of pigeonholing our children. Maybe Willie is a very detail-oriented person. Math comes easy for him, and he's able to sit for hours working on it. It doesn't take long for Nick, Willie's father, to pick up on this, and so he goes out and buys Willie expensive computer equipment and calculus textbooks. He starts talking to Willie about getting admitted to MIT, even though Willie's just fourteen. Nick is using his awareness to encourage his son's strengths, but he's also focusing too narrowly. Willie would also like to learn to play the piano or join the debate team. Unfortunately, his father continues to push him to make the most of his mathematical skills, and his other interests and skills keep getting shoved aside.

We also may be tempted to generalize. After learning one aspect about a child, we can translate it into all areas of her life, burdening her with high expectations. Your teenage daughter has invested several hundred dollars in camera equipment, and you're actually surprised at how well her pictures turn out. She always seems to catch people at just the right moment. So one day you say to her, "Honey, we're putting together a new brochure at work, and when Mr. Hawkins asked who we could get to take some pictures of our new building and the countryside around the city, I volunteered you. I thought you might like to make a little money." Your daughter looks at you as if she's about to cry. "I wish you wouldn't have done that," she says. "I don't know the first thing about outdoor scenes and landscapes. I like taking pictures of people."

Awareness is vital to fathering, but it's often difficult because we have to find a delicate balance. We should use what we know about our children to encourage them and meet their needs. In the choppy seas of childhood and adolescence, we need to learn more about them in order to guide them through the storms to the harbor of adulthood. The good news is, along the way, you and your child will find the moments of smooth water that offer a deep sense of serenity. Enjoy those moments—and enjoy your children.

FATHER INVENTORY #7
Awareness

INSTRUCTIONS:

Take your responses from the statements on pages 91 and 92 and place them next to the corresponding items below. Total the scores for the items under each of the I CANs and plot the appropriate score on the graph on page 156.

P S 3   I have a good handle on how my child's   Score _____
needs change as he/she grows up.

P S 7   I know what encourages my child the most.   Score _____

P S 11   I know what motivates my child.   Score _____

P S 15   I know when my child is embarrassed.   Score _____

P S 19   I could identify most of my child's recent   Score _____
disappointing experiences.

P S 23   I know how my child's emotional needs   Score _____
change over time.

P S 27   I know what is reasonable to expect from my   Score _____
children for their age.

P S 31   I know what my child needs in order to grow   Score _____
into a mature, responsible person.

                                            TOTAL _____

Plot your score below and on page 156.

| 8 | 10 | 12 | 14 | 16 | 18 | 20 | 22 | 24 | 26 | 28 | 30 | 32 | 34 | 36 | 38 | 40 |

NURTURANCE

If a father is to succeed in rearing his children, he must create a nurturing environment for them. Nurturance, the fourth "I CAN" of effective fathering, is nothing less than critical. In the last chapter, we saw how awareness informs our fathering role—it tells us what needs to be done. Through awareness we learn about our children's developmental needs and their unique personality traits, but we also learn how to read them emotionally. The way we follow through and meet those emotional needs is through nurturance.

Like the first three walls to be set into place, the final wall of Nurturance provides strong support for the house. But more than that, this wall encloses the structure, turns the four walls into a house, the house into a home.

A Subtle Form of Fatherlessness

When most adults think of fatherlessness, they see children raised without fathers due to divorce, abandonment, or premature death of the father. Indeed, some 24 million children in America—34 percent—are growing up without their biological fathers.[1]

That is a tragic and devastating figure. But I wonder: How high would that figure be if it included children whose fathers are physically present, but emotionally distant or absent?

Those statistics would surely include Jane, whose father failed to show her love and respect. The emotional gulf between Jane and her father, Brad, left her virtually fatherless. When she was growing up, Jane was often the subject of her father's disappointment and ridicule. She could never do anything well enough for her father. If Jane received a B in science, her father would point out that Sharon, the pretty girl down the street, always got A's. When Jane became a teenager, she developed a bad case of acne. Her father responded by making jokes about her "Pizza Face."

Needless to say, Jane developed a low self-image and a desperate need for male attention—her father had failed to nurture her in these areas. She gave herself to the first man that happened to enter her life who showed her emotional and physical attention. "I was hungry for a man to hug me, to say a kind word to me," she says. After learning of his daughter's pregnancy, Brad showered blame and contempt on his child. "I always knew this would happen to you," he would lash out at her.

When Jane revealed that the baby's father had been recently sentenced to prison, her father and her grandparents insisted that she "get rid of this child." Their concern was not what was best for the baby or for Jane, but their own reputations. Even though they claimed to be opposed to abortion, they encouraged Jane to terminate her baby's life. She refused. She put the baby up for adoption instead. After giving her daughter a name, Elizabeth, she gave her child away.

Fatherhood Regained

But Jane's story doesn't end like most, continuing disastrously through the generations. Little Elizabeth was adopted into a caring, nurturing family. Jerry and Stacy, a couple in their midforties, were content with three boys of their own. Stacy went so far as to make the choice of another child no longer a choice, having a tubal ligation. Then, one night, Jerry had a dream: he was to rear a daughter. During the course of the next several weeks, Jerry and Stacy discussed the possibility of adoption, which led them to put in an application. A few months later, they adopted a little baby girl, Elizabeth, the child of an unwed teenage mother named Jane.

Ironically, Jerry, though not Elizabeth's biological father, has become a true father, rescuing her from a continuing cycle of emotional fatherlessness. Unlike Jane, Elizabeth is nurtured. Where Jane was called "Pizza Face" by her father, Elizabeth's daddy showers her with such titles as "The Most Beautiful Little Girl in All of the World." And he means it. Where Jane was seldom held or touched or comforted in her family, Elizabeth receives a steady diet of touches from the boys, especially the two youngest ones, ages eight and five. "From the moment Elizabeth gets up until the moment she goes to bed, she is getting loving touches," Jerry says. Where Jane was expected to live up to her daddy's expectations—to feed his ego—Elizabeth is perfect in her father's eyes, no matter what she does.

The Cycle of Nurturance

We learn to love by being loved. Love is not a magic trick that we learn from a back alley magician or commit to memory from a self-help book. Love is something we experience first, and then communicate to others.

It's difficult to nurture others unless we too have been nurtured. In fact, nurturance follows a cycle, being passed down from previous generations, grandfather to son to grandson, and so on. Nonnurturance works the same way; for example, I come from a long line of nonnurturing men. My father, grandfather, and great-grandfather did not consider physical and verbal affirmation to be an important part of their lives. We were men of few gestures and even fewer words. I cannot remember hugging or any extended periods of touching besides an occasional handshake. Back rubs were taboo. They didn't say "I love you" or "I'm proud of you." They didn't want their sons to "get big heads," so they remained quiet. Since I didn't see a man display these nurturing qualities, it's been a struggle for me as well.

Before we look at how to nurture our children, let's remember two vital truths. First, *your ability to nurture your children depends a good deal upon how you were nurtured by your father.* Once again we see that effective fathering means dealing with past issues involving your life as a son. Second, *you need to examine your primary motivation behind your own fathering.* Is it more like Brad's, hoping to feed a starved ego through his child's performance, or is it more like Jerry's, unconditionally meeting the needs of his children for affirmation, encouragement, and loving connection?

How to Nurture Our Children

Nurturance is the means through which we form intimate bonds with our children, the way we respond to their emotional needs. Babies as young as three months old can tell the difference between their mother and father.[2] They can tell by the way each speaks to them and holds them, and by their different smells. Our nurturance is shown through our actions of comforting, encouraging, affirming, and listening to our children. We can do this several ways.

1. Through a Touch

Nurturance often begins with a touch. A classic UCLA study found that people need eight to ten touches a day for good emotional health.[3] How many do you receive in a day? How many do you give to your children? To your wife?

A touch is no small thing. It can be a matter of life and death. In the thirteenth century, Frederick II, the emperor of the Holy Roman Empire, unknowingly conducted an early experiment in the power of touch. His goal was to see what language patterns a child would develop if he never had a parent to prattle, coo, or talk to him. The emperor's question was whether the child's first words would be Hebrew, Greek, Latin, Arabic, or perhaps the vernacular language of his parents.

So Frederick instructed a group of wet nurses to feed and tend a group of infants, but not to speak a word in their presence, nor coo affectionately. The nurses also were told not to cuddle the babies. Frederick awaited the results of his experiment. Unfortunately, the results never came. Every single child died.[4] What had started out to be a simple test in linguistics ended up a profound and tragic lesson for the ages: Children need to be nurtured through word and touch.

In another study, a Kansas State University professor concluded that children of a nurturing father are more likely to be empathetic adults who are able to care about and share the feelings of others. Children who have a warm relationship with their father are likely to be more secure in the world, more vocal, and more eager to play than children who do not.[5]

Something about physical touch makes us feel better, both physio-logically and psychologically. In *The Blessing,* marriage and family specialists Gary Smalley and John Trent cite two interesting studies on physical touch.[6] A professor of nursing at New York University found that when one person touches another with his hand, the hemoglobin levels in both peo-ple go up, which means body tissues are receiving more oxygen, making us feel energized or, if we are sick, speeding our recovery. In another study at Purdue University, researchers asked the library circulation staff to alter-nately touch and then not touch the students' hands as they handed back their library cards. After interviewing the students, the researchers found that those who were touched had more positive experiences in the library than those who were not.

Despite the obvious power in touch, research indicates that few parents do so on an ongoing basis. Most parents touch their children only when necessity demands it, as when helping them to dress, undress, or get into the car. And this amount of touch usually decreases as our children get older.

For many fathers, physical affection comes much easier when it is asso-ciated with play. Dad takes little Julie and flips her up over his head, hold-ing on to her only by her ankle. Mom puts her hand on her heart, takes a deep breath, and goes into the other room, but Julie shrieks with delight and says, "Do it again, Daddy!" As the children mature, the play continues but changes. Daddy will pull the kids off the couch and shout, "It's time for a . . . dog pile!" and he'll wrestle around on the floor with them. Not only does such "roughhousing" reveal that dad has a playful side, but it also pro-vides a critical form of nurturance. Through this rough-and-tumble play, our children learn about risk taking and problem solving. Kevin MacDonald, an associate professor of psychology at California State University at Long Beach, has found that shy and introverted children tend to come from homes in which there is little or no healthy roughhousing.[7]

Everyday gestures of affection through play are a natural way to show affection. You're outside shooting baskets with your teenage child, and you hug-foul him as he fakes and drives to the hoop. In between baskets, you tousle his hair, pat his back, and put an arm around the shoulder after your semi-intentional foul. These displays give children a sense of comfort and security.

But your children also need more. You must search for moments that your physical affection can be appropriately and intentionally expressed. Such times of often "wordless" action can have a powerful effect on the lives of your children. Consider these three real-life examples:

- Larry was in his military uniform, ready to board a plane. He was leaving home. While Larry's mother and sisters took turns hugging him, his father stood by watching. Finally, the father approached his son. Placing his hands firmly on the boy's shoulders, he gave him a couple squeezes before standing back. Beaming, he stared at his son for several seconds. Finally, he reached up and took his son's hat off, leaned close, and kissed him on the forehead. He then replaced his hat.
- Garth had growing pains in his knees during his early teens. The pain was so bad that, night after night, he could not sleep. Often, he would retreat to the bathroom and fight back his tears. And, night after night, his father would hear him in the bathroom. He would come in, kneel next to his son, and rub his legs and knees until his son's pain subsided.
- Terry grew up with a father who almost never touched him, unless he'd done something wrong. Now Terry has four children of his own, and his father is in a nursing home. Being the oldest child, Terry has taken on the responsibility of caring for his father in his old age, and he drives to see him almost every weekend. As he has become familiar with the staff at the nursing home, Terry has taken over some of their tasks on the days when he's there.

  This has given him the opportunity to touch his father in ways that he never had before. Terry takes his father's hand to help him stand up and puts his arm around him to help him into the bathroom. Terry also shaves his father: his own hands tenderly lathering his father's face, then carefully running the blade around his father's chin, and mouth, and Adam's apple. It was all new and uncomfortable for both of them at first, but now it's the most rewarding part of Terry's visits. He can now be close to his dad in ways that were never allowed before. And the times with his father have influenced Terry's physical affection with his own children. Such purposeful and loving touch creates bonds and connections between father and son in ways that nothing else could.

2. Through a Word

For men, words often seem like wimpy, little creatures. Weighing no more than air, they quickly disappear and are soon forgotten. Yet when it comes to nurturing our children, words are powerful.

As a father, you must pay careful attention to words. As we have seen, it is critical to let your children know, in words, that you love them. Like Marvin and James (in chapter 3), Kyle's father never told him he loved him while he was growing up. They were words he longed to hear, as well as express, to his father. As an adult, he was determined to tell his father he loved him. On a visit to the hospital after his father had had a stroke, he decided to tell his father. But just before he could, his father beat him to the punch. "I love you, Son," he said.

Kyle later told me his reaction to hearing those three words:

I felt my face flush, and I'm sure he felt awkward about it too, but I don't think anyone will ever say anything that will mean more to me. When I got in my car and gripped the steering wheel, it was like a weight had been lifted off my shoulders. And now, whenever I talk to him on the phone, it's like he can't wait to say that he loves me.

So many children grow up like Kyle, never hearing the words "I love you" from their fathers. Our children need to be constantly reminded of what makes them special.

As a researcher, I've learned never to pass up an opportunity to collect data. That's what I did years ago at my daughter Sarah's twelfth birthday party—a sleepover. For me, this was not just a bunch of giggling preteens, but a potential wealth of information.

Armed with paper, pens, and a bagful of M&Ms, I bravely ventured where no man had gone before. Try to picture the scene: a room with a dozen twelve-year-olds all riding late-night sugar highs and me, a forty-year-old father. "Girls," I said as I walked in, "how would you like to help me with some research?" I waved the bag of M&Ms to let them know they would be compensated. They agreed and I proceeded. My question was simple: "How does your father make you feel special?" Here are some of the responses they wrote down:

"I feel special when my dad compliments me on something I've done well."

"I feel special when my dad says he appreciates me."

"I feel special when Dad tells me I am beautiful."

These responses point out the necessity of communicating how precious our children are *in words*. If you don't say it, it will not be truly captured in your child's heart. For boys, such verbal interaction may actually be even more important than for girls. Research shows that boys have a much more difficult time vocalizing—a vast majority of children who receive speech therapy are boys. And those boys become men and fathers, just like you and me. As their model, we need to overcome discomfort and impediments, and verbalize our true feelings about them.

Often, however, our words have strings attached. Much of the "love" expressed is conditional and takes the form of high expectations: "If you keep practicing, maybe next year you'll win the entire competition." Instead of saying, "Nice going. That class was hard, and I know you worked for that C," a dad says, "I'd really like to see you get all B's next semester." Maybe these fathers are actually proud of their children, but they just can't express it. Their children can't see their father's pride and they feel, no matter what they accomplish, that they are never quite good enough.

We ought to strive to sincerely affirm our children even when they don't succeed. How we react to our child's failures is often very revealing as to our true fathering motivation. If your son strikes out in the ninth inning and with his team down by one with two runners in scoring position, you could react in one of two ways. One is tied to your own ego: "Oh, Son, you struck out; how could you let your team down?" What your child hears is, "I'm embarrassed to be your father," and believe me, it will affect the relationship in many ways and for a long time. The other is to love him unconditionally, regardless of how he performs. In either case, your habits of affirming or criticizing your child will have long-lasting effects on your relationship and your child's outlook on life.

The late Dave Simmons told of a situation where he was able to swallow his own pride and bless his son. Dave inherited from his father the knack for putting high expectations on his children. One night after Dave had watched his son Brandon quarterback his high school football team through a humiliating loss, he took his son for their customary postgame frozen yogurt. They drove in silence; Brandon's head was down, expecting a detailed critique. But instead, Dave was able to give his son words of blessing that changed their relationship: "Well, Son . . ." Dave said, "I just want you to know that I love you just as you are. I love you whether you're the football hero or whether you play terrible. I love you because you're Brandon and not because you're number ten on the football squad."[8]

3. Through Listening

In addition to speaking a word that nurtures, we must also listen to the words of our children. Our children want us to know who they are. They want to tell us what's wrong, so we can comfort them. They want to talk about what's important, so we can understand them. All those things require that we listen to *their* words.

It's unfortunate that many children often have to compete for their father's attention. We must never become so busy that we have no time for the words of our children. When we don't make the time to listen to our children, we are "saying" a great deal to them.

You're driving your family to the local amusement park for a fun-filled Saturday. In the backseat, your four-year-old son is looking forward to the experience. "Hey, Dad," he says, "are we gonna ride that really big roller coaster?"

"As much as you want to," you reply.

"I mean that really high one with the loops and curves," he continues.

"That's the one."

"But, Dad, what if there's a long line? What if we have to wait?"

"Then it will only make the ride better once we get there," you reply.

"If that happens, Dad, do you think we should try the bumper boats for a while until the line goes down? Or the tilt-a-whirl?"

Now at this point, you could understandably say something like, "OK, Son. That's enough. We'll be there in a few minutes." You'd be perfectly justified—after all, the kid was starting to annoy the whole family.

But what is your child really saying? Something like, "I'm excited about today, and I want to share my excitement with my dad! This is gonna be great!"

Sometimes the value in your child's words is not so much in what is being said, but the saying of it. Sometimes our patient listening shows that our children are worth hearing. They are special enough to deserve our attention when they are talking. They are worthy to be known and under-stood.

I'm not advocating giving your child free rein over your time for what-ever whim may come up. There will be instances where you really can't be a good listener at the moment; and when that happens, be careful not to dismiss your child's concern. Let her know that what she has to say *is* important to you, and make a date for a later time when your mind will be clearer.

Our children will learn very quickly whether or not we are willing to listen to them. If we continually push them away with their "minor" con-cerns, they may not come to us with a bigger issue. Imagine that your teenage daughter is considering whether she should go to a party. Someone said there may be drugs there. She could use your point of view, and this is just the kind of situation you've always encouraged her to talk to you about. But you've never really been around to listen to her in the past (or when you have been around, you've been preoccupied with something else), so she calls her best friend instead. She ends up going to the party just to see what happens; she may have even lied to you about where she'd be that night. And you . . . well, you sit at home worrying about other things, obliv-ious that something pivotal could be happening in your daughter's life, because you never made the time to listen.

Nurturance: Boys and Girls

Although physical affection and verbal affirmation are the building blocks of nurturance, research indicates that boys and girls need both from their fathers. One study found that the strongest predictors of self-esteem were "physical affection" for girls and "sustained physical contact" for boys. Interestingly, touch, in different forms, was crucial to fostering a sense of personal value for both girls and boys.[9]

Dads, too, have different natural tendencies in fathering. We tend to show more physical affection to our daughters, and we have a more natural companionship with our sons since we share more of the same interests (after all, we were once boys ourselves).

What Boys Need: A Model

With our sons, however, companionship does not always give fruit to affection. As a teenager, I spent several summers working with my father, but we never talked in any deep way, and he wasn't comfortable hugging me. There are too many fathers who only touch their sons when they're punishing them, who never initiate meaningful, affirming conversations with their boys.

Norma Radin, a professor of social work at the University of Michigan, reports that sons of sensitive, affectionate fathers score higher on intelligence tests and do better at school than children of colder, authoritarian fathers.[10] Fathers also influence their sons' sex-role development not so much by their characteristics (such as masculinity) as by the warmth and closeness of their relationships with their sons.[11]

Much of what a son learns about relationships, he learns by watching his father. We need to trash the "Tough-guy" model and show our children it's perfectly natural to express emotions, physically and verbally. From a father, a boy learns how a man relates to his world.

Jeff had an older sister who started dating several years before him. He watched as his father, just before her first date, sat his sister down and gave her the you-be-careful lecture. Years later, on the night of Jeff's first date, his father tossed him the car keys, winked at him, and said, "Good luck, Son."

The effective father wouldn't have perpetuated the double standard under which many teenage boys operate when it comes to sexual activity. This father would have sent his son out knowing that, if something unexpected comes up and he has questions, he'll be able to bring them to his father without being lectured or judged. And the father would have modeled proper treatment of women with his actions toward his wife and daughter.

I cannot overemphasize the importance of *modeling* for our sons' maturity and responsibility in relationships. Carlos watches his father scream at his mother and then walk out, not coming home for several hours. To Carlos, a man can get angry and walk away from the conflicts in his life. If something isn't going the way he wants, he can "blow it off" and let other people worry about it. On the other hand, what if his father had been able to resist the urge to walk out? What if he went back, admitted he was wrong, and asked for his wife's forgiveness? Carlos would get an entirely different view of manhood.

Sons are looking to their fathers to be healthy models of what it means to be a boy, a man, and a father. It's the greatest gift a nurturing father can give his sons.

What Girls Need: Proper Affection

All little children are cute, yet most parents seem to pick up and hold daughters more often than they do their sons. Although it may seem natural to cuddle little girls, soon little girls have become big girls, and this presents a father with a dilemma. His daughter is more than cute; she's beginning to look more like a woman than a little girl. Being cautious not to overstep his boundaries, a father may take the opposite extreme and avoid any affection that could be misinterpreted in any way.

Yet our daughters still need our attention, healthy physical affection, and affirmation. Indeed, fathers must continue to demonstrate physical affection through their daughters' adolescent years. Counseling centers across the country are filled with adult women who condemn their fathers for never showing affection. It's common for these same women to have a string of dissatisfying or completely untrusting relationships with men.

As your daughter changes from girl to young woman, she is particularly vulnerable. She needs a great deal of nurturing support from her father. Because this is an awkward time for dads, many men often attempt to make light of the situation by making jokes or laughing. Others, such as Brad, even ridicule their daughters with teasing names for any physical flaws. But even lighthearted joking is seldom harmless. Your daughter will always wonder what you really meant, and she may develop an attitude of anxiety concerning her appearance. In a worst-case scenario, you could be setting up a pattern that could lead her into an eating disorder.

The other, more common reaction to the discomfort is to withdraw completely. You're actually just being careful, but your daughter thinks you don't care, or that something's wrong with her. She's trying to figure out men, and you're her closest and best example of one. What is and isn't appropriate when men are present? How will men respond when she "flirts" for attention? As her father, you act as a kind of first boyfriend, and you play a large role in showing her what a proper, respectful response sounds and feels like. If you fail to affirm your daughter's femininity by showing her physical and verbal affection, she may very likely discover it on her own, in unhealthy relationships with the men in her life.

So fall all over yourself and gush with pride when she walks down in her new dress, or when she does something that is especially charming. But make it clear that she has won your heart not with her looks and feminine charms, but because she is a fascinating and worthwhile person. You'll show her that there *are* men who are consistent, trustworthy, and unafraid to show their emotions. With you as her positive reference point, she'll learn what to expect from men she meets. You can bet she'll meet plenty of men who are irresponsible, chauvinistic, and dishonest, and she'll be able to see through them right from the start.

Your daughter needs to hear your ideas and feelings about relationships, and even about sexuality. A positive atmosphere concerning sex will assure her that you have a satisfying sexual relationship with your wife, and will make it easier for her to share her ideas about men, her own femininity, and sexuality. She'll be more likely to look to you for a male perspective.

Often you can use humor and word pictures to give the male perspective and ease the tension. Author and popular seminar speaker Gary Smalley did both once when his teenage daughter was getting ready to go swimming with the boy she was seeing at the time. Gary saw her walk through in her latest, most flattering and revealing swimsuit, and he figured it was time to have a talk. He sat her down, swallowed hard, and said, "Honey, I'm not sure you realize what goes through a boy's mind when he sees a woman in a swimsuit like this. Let me describe what it's like. Imagine if you took his favorite candy bar and smeared the chocolate all over his lips and around his mouth. Then, just as you're finishing, you say to him, 'Now stand over there and don't lick your lips.' That's a lot like what happens when you wear that swimsuit." With Gary's help, she quickly got the picture.[12]

More and more research indicates that "a woman's sense of worth as a woman, as a person, is rooted in her experience with her father."[13] A girl's desire to be nurtured by her father never leaves her. Several years ago I passed a female acquaintance of mine, probably in her midthirties, on the street. She was absolutely beaming. I had to stop her. "What's going on?" I asked. "You look like you just got engaged to the man of your dreams." She was carrying a very small envelope in her hand, swinging it as she walked, which she lifted and waved in my face as she walked by. "A little while ago I got a big bouquet of flowers," she said, "from my father."

Discipline As Nurturance

For both boys and girls, discipline is a critical nutrient. We give our children defined guidelines to follow, and there are consequences when they step outside those guidelines. In doing so, we are nurturing our children into confident, well-adjusted, and responsible people.

Ultimately, discipline is about relationship. We need to banish the idea that it is an event—a one-shot act of *punishment*—and view it instead as a *process*. It's part of the way we relate to our children every day, whenever we're together. Sure, there is conflict; that's a necessary part of shaping your child's character. But it's how we carry out discipline that makes all the difference.

When we try to exercise behavioral control without love, the results are harmful at best and barbaric at worst. The focus shifts from the child's disobedience to the tense emotions, and we lose whatever opportunity we had to teach the child valuable lessons. But in an atmosphere of acceptance and love, discipline becomes a nurturing act.

We are under control, doing what we know is right, not reacting unpredictably in the heat of the moment. Our children know *they* are loved and accepted even when their behavior is not. They know we are acting for their benefit, not our own, and they grow to respect us more.

Healthy discipline presupposes we are in relationship with our children and that we care deeply about them.

Shortly after being disciplined, a child is often most receptive to nurturing. This is actually the best time to go back to the child, talk through his behavior with words of blessing and gestures of affection, and soothe the wounds his ego has suffered. When he can experience such affirming love, he will be much more positive about the guidelines you set for him, the entire discipline process (realizing it is correction, not punishment), and your devotion to him as his father.

Going Too Far

As with each of the "I CANs," nurturance can go out of balance; it is possible to overdo it. Overnurturing fathers, more often than not, smother their children. These fathers tend to lavish their children with false praise, sometimes even going so far as to manipulate their children with affection. They become blind to their children's faults, giving them excessive comfort, even in situations where they don't really need it.

These fathers may, in fact, look like "model" fathers. For example, a father showers his daughter with affection, and she quickly becomes "daddy's little girl." He gives his daughter everything that is in his power to give, and she soaks it up. To him it seems like successful fathering. After all, she doesn't challenge his authority and she seems happy. However, subtly the father is failing to lead her into independence. Instead, she expects a good life given to her without any effort. She may become what Maureen Murdock termed a "hero's daughter"—"a woman who identifies with her father and imitates men in her pursuit of success." But in the end, says Murdock, "the more strongly she identifies with him, the more difficulty she has establishing a separate identity of her own."[14] She may have trouble with intimate relationships and at the same time, an overnurturing father may find it difficult to entrust his children to get married.

Children who grow up with overly nurturing fathers often lack structure in their lives. Their fathers seldom discipline them. Children who have been given rules of conduct will test the limits of those rules constantly as they grow up; many children will openly rebel against them. These are ways children figure out the basic values that lie behind the rules, and whether their father truly believes in them. When a well-meaning father raises a child without guidelines, the son or daughter often concludes that Dad doesn't really care what he or she does. The child is essentially left alone in a large and confusing world.

Learning to Nurture

Like most men, you may have a problem with expressing yourself emotionally to your children, which is at the core of nurturing. What do you do?

My first advice is to "practice" on your wife. The commitment of marriage allows us the freedom to enrich our nurturing skills in a natural emotional atmosphere. For many of us, marriage opens up a side of us that we never knew existed. We learn to relate to our wives and express love in a variety of ways and on a daily basis. Women are more naturally affectionate. They typically deal in the emotional realm easier and more often than we do, and we can learn a lot from watching their relationships. Even though our children do benefit from the unique masculine approach to parenting that a father brings, many of us could stand to adjust our masculinity to include more emotion and sensitivity, qualities that have long been thought of as "feminine."

You can also watch other men who model healthy emotional expression. Consider also meeting with a group of fathers who share each other's struggles and celebrate each other's progress. Fathering groups almost automatically produce mutual nurturance. Joe made it through an important talk with his daughter. "I knew you could do it," says Marcus, a member of Joe's group. Someone tells the men about the constant tension lately between his teenage son and him, and Bill gives a squeeze on the shoulder: "I know that can be rough. Feel free to give me a call at home or at the office any time." Men can teach each other the kind of encouragement that transfers directly to their kids.

As we learn to show affection to our children, it begins to spill over into the other areas of our lives. According to author Joseph Pleck, the more we nurture our own children, the more caring and giving we'll be as we approach middle age. We'll become more altruistic and more likely to give to those in need.[15]

Four Sturdy Walls

Now that all four walls have been raised and are solidly in place, I want you to step back for a minute. We need a larger perspective on our building project.

In a sense, I have done a disservice to the "I CANs" by separating them into their own individual chapters. There are very few fathering tasks that do not include most, if not all four, of the fathering functions. Active listening is nurturance but is also a key way in which we gain awareness of who our children are and how we can best meet their needs. If you're sitting down to a game of chess with your son, you're involving yourself in his life, but how you react when he creams you in the first game will have a bearing on your consistency as a father. You'll also increase your awareness about your son's competitive spirit. Pick any fathering activity, and several of the "I CANs" can be applied to it.

I wish I could tell you to work on just one of the "I CANs," and then pick up the rest when you have that one mastered, but they don't work that way. Only when your house has all four reliable walls will you be able to best protect your most prized possession, your children.

FATHER INVENTORY #8
Nurturance

INSTRUCTIONS:

Take your responses from the statements on pages 91 and 92 and place them next to the corresponding items below. Total the scores for the items under each of the I CANs and plot the appropriate score on the graph on page 156.

P S 4	It is easy for me to encourage my children.	Score	_____
P S 8	I praise my children for things they do well.	Score	_____
P S 12	I express affection to my children.	Score	_____
P S 16	I constantly tell my children that I love them.	Score	_____
P S 20	I show my children that I care when they share a problem with me.	Score	_____
P S 24	I tell my children that they are special to me.	Score	_____
P S 28	When my children are upset, I usually try to listen to them.	Score	_____
P S 32	I point out qualities in my children that I like about them.	Score	_____
		TOTAL	_____

Plot your score below and on page 156.

8	10	12	14	16	18	20	22	24	26	28	30	32	34	36	38	40

FATHER INVENTORY #9
The I CANs of Fathering Summary

INSTRUCTIONS:

Transfer the scores from each of the I CANs (pages 107, 122, 137, 155) to the corresponding scales on this page to identify your specific strengths and areas that "need work."

Involvement	8	16	24	31	36	40
Consistency	8	16	24	31	36	40
Awareness	8	16	24	31	36	40
Nurturance	8	16	24	31	36	40
	LOW		AVERAGE		HIGH	

INTERPRETING THE RESULTS:

The I CANs Profile has been designed to help fathers obtain feedback on their approach to fathering. Recognize that fathering is a creative, complex, and challenging occupation. It has many aspects and requires different approaches for different circumstances and conditions.

Be easy on yourself as you review your results. This profile is limited. It cannot assess your heart, your desire. It can only give you a reference point about your relationship with your children. The profile is a tool that can assist you in evaluating your fathering practices for the purpose of planning ways to modify and strengthen the areas you desire.

There are some things that you do better than others—your strengths. Don't shortchange yourself. Don't say, "I have no strengths." Review your profile and note your strengths in the space below. Rejoice and capitalize on your strengths. Don't forget them.

There are other areas where you have opportunity for improvement. Note them in the space below. You need to work on these. But don't try to apply yourself to all of these at once. Pick one—maybe two—areas that you want to strengthen, and focus your efforts there. Begin your improvement work with the help of other men.

Remember this is a snapshot of where you are today. With a firm commitment and a good plan, you can improve your fathering and become the dad you want to be.

My strengths are:

-
-
-
-
-
-

My opportunities are:

-
-
-
-
-
-

Personal Action Plan:

Part Three

THE DISCIPLINED HEART

THROUGH
THE YEARS

T he healed and strong heart of a father, even one capable of functioning on several different levels, does not guarantee success. A man can deal with past hurts and embrace the four crucial functions of successful fathering, yet he may not finish in the race called fatherhood.

I like to compare the job of a father to that of a long-distance runner. Fathering isn't a sprint—it's a marathon. It's a long and often trying journey. And, like the marathon runner, we must have disciplined hearts if we hope to successfully finish the course.

I'm amazed at how many fathers don't run the entire race. To them, fathering seems to be a series of isolated events rather than a continuous, and continuing, identity. The map of fatherhood for them is a point on the map ("here is home") instead of a line that stretches along a road to be traveled. These fathers feel the false freedom to just "pop in" on their children's lives. They may wait until after infancy to begin interacting with the kids. They may skip out on adolescence altogether and make up for it with an expensive graduation gift or final family vacation. They convince themselves that, because they have made some contact at specific points, they have fathered.

But such in-and-out fathering is bound to fail. Fathers who try to be involved only at fixed points are usually miles behind their children, who are always on the move, always developing, never at the same place twice. If you simply try to connect with them here and there, you always find yourself playing catch-up. We need to accompany our children on their journey, walking with them each step of the way, carrying them when necessary, pointing out the dangers just over this hill, encouraging them with the opportunity that lies just around that bend.

We need to be prepared.

That's why I love the metaphor of the marathon. A race of 26 miles, 385 yards, the marathon isn't so much a race competing against other people as a race against yourself—a race testing commitment, endurance, training, and mental toughness. Some try to cheat by starting the race somewhere down the course. They think, *Babies are just too fragile and messy. I'll get involved when she's two.* Others start during the first months, helping with bottle feeding and bathing; years later, though, they are contemplating dropping out. Maybe it's at "the wall," when all their energy reserves seem depleted and their muscles are starting to self-destruct. *Teenagers!* Some skimp on training. *Who needs to learn how to be a father?* Or, once having run most of the good race, there are others who will simply never finish, missing out on the celebration. *My kids are grown up; they don't need me anymore.* They do, however. As a friend and supporter, you can give advice and a clasp on the shoulder to your adult children that provide valuable support.

Indeed, the marathon course presents challenges from nearly every conceivable angle. A father who is unprepared is committing himself to mistakes, many of which might have been avoided.

But a father who is committed to his children will diligently prepare and train his heart for the long run. This, of course, involves difficult work. Much careful planning goes into the training and then into the race itself. The marathon runner examines the terrain, plans his pace, determines when he'll get drinks along the way, and makes adjustments based on his time splits and body condition. He is a man committed and prepared to stay in the race.

Fortunately, the marathon a father must traverse—the stages of his children's growth—has been well-mapped. But the map that's missing has been one that combines stages of the child's growth with the father's own growth. The pioneering work of researchers like Erik Erikson, Daniel Levinson, and Gail Sheehy described developmental stages that adults go through. Yet those researchers rarely mentioned men as fathers or described the challenges and needs men have in that role. So we took our investigations beyond their work and looked at specific challenges and changes that dads go through as their children grow. We've begun a fruitful field of research, and the National Center for Fathering plans to contribute more in the years ahead.

Some of those who talk about development will use the term "life cycle." This implies all humans go through similar stages (e.g., birth, puberty, mating, death). But I will talk about the "life course" of a father because "cycle" can imply you'll be doing something again, going through the same stage again. Of course, if you have more than one child, you'll encounter similar challenges as they grow. But as dads, we won't be going through exactly the same stages as before because we're developing at the same time. We'll have gone through our own transitions, whether it's what Gail Sheehy calls "the passage to first adulthood" at age thirty, or a midlife transition, or even the so-called "male menopause" later on.[1]

Our research at the National Center for Fathering identified six stages in the life course, with distinct differences. The stages, based on the age of a father's oldest child, are: attachment (birth through age one), idealism (ages two through five), understanding (ages six through twelve), enlightenment (teenage), reflection (young adults), and generativity (adults with children). In this final section we will explore the stages in detail.

Like a marathon runner understanding the terrain of his course, an understanding of the stages we'll go through will help us fathers meet our children's changing needs.

If you don't devote yourself to scouting out the life-course terrain ahead of your children, you usually spend the journey looking over your shoulder, surveying where you've traveled and muttering to yourself, "If I had to do it over again, I'd do it differently," or "If I only knew then what I know now," or "Boy, I really missed out." It doesn't have to be that way.

By understanding the terrain and map of our course, we can learn to discipline and pace ourselves. We understand that no one stage will last forever; we will be trained to endure; we will push toward the vision and celebration of the finish line. We will also understand that there will be peaks and valleys in terms of our own fathering satisfaction and pain.

As any good marathon runner knows, much of the real struggle is not against the course, but an internal battle of motivation and will. It's a matter of mental toughness. A father, like a good runner, needs to know what is going on inside his own heart.

His children are not the only ones who are changing. A man as he matures through the years is also moving through a life stage of his own. In *The Seasons of a Man's Life,* Daniel Levinson proposes three main periods of an adult male's life: early, middle, and late adulthood. He then subdivides the first two "eras" into four periods each.[2] The fathering life course must recognize that both children and men are going through stages of development, but that neither fathers nor their children are developing in a vacuum. Your children are developing within the context of your habits and preferences, and so you need to make allowances for the ways in which you are changing as a man. Similarly, as a male adult who is also a dad, you need to realize that your child's growth through his or her life course will affect you as you go through your life course.

In the following chapters, we will examine how the two developmental paths interact. Often, the fathering life course is an integration of the childhood life course and the male adult life course. By devoting ourselves to guiding our children through their childhood course, we are actually being assisted in moving through our own life course.

Marathoning may seem like a very individualistic sport. And in one way it is—just like fathering. But, in another way, team support is critical. Many marathoners would have given up the training necessary to compete—except for someone else encouraging them along. When they ultimately run the race, there's a strong sense of camaraderie rather than competition. Along the race route, signs are posted and arrows are spray painted on the pavement so runners can gauge their progress and pace, as well as stay on the right course. Beverage tables are carefully spaced along the way so runners can grab a paper cupful of water or Gatorade as they go by.

For fathers running the life course, there is also assistance. And it's wise to seek it out. Seek out the advice of those who have run different parts of the course so that you will know what to expect. Find those who will be willing to ride alongside of you on a bicycle, encouraging you to the next water station.

Use the fathering life course of these next six chapters as the map for the marathon. The six stages of the fathering life course will serve as mile markers, laying out the course before you, giving you direction. You can assess yourself at each stage along the way, in the same manner that a runner looks at his time splits or checks his heart rate. In this long journey, there are fathering resources that can help you win the race.

The work of disciplining your heart for the long run is difficult work. But the rewards, which often take you by surprise, are worth the effort.

FOR FATHERS OF INFANTS: ATTACHMENT

I pulled into the gravel driveway in front of our house, turned off the ignition, and listened to the engine sputter to a stop. A yawn quickly escaped from me; I could hide it no longer. Another yawn came over me and then another. Each yawn seemed to come from deeper in my hollow chest than the one before. It was three o'clock in the afternoon, and I was exhausted.

Twenty-four hours earlier Dee had started contractions, and I knew our first child was coming. The contractions soon became more intense and regular; Dee entered the hospital, and we began a long, sleepless night together. The chair next to Dee's bed was cruelly uncomfortable, unwilling to let me doze, yet it was no more discomforting than listening to Dee groan as the baby pressed against her cervix. It was one of those marathon labor/endurance tests, unlike anything our wonderfully optimistic instructor had mentioned in the Lamaze classes.

At 7:10 the next morning, more than fourteen hours later, the doctor ordered Pitocin added to the IV drip to help stimulate the labor. Two hours after that Dr. Barba broke the water bag around the baby. At 10:00 heavy labor began, and Hannah was born at 10:45 a.m.

We were parents. Our first child. I was a father.

I stayed at the hospital with Dee and Hannah through most of the afternoon. I was absolutely amazed: Hannah cried for just a moment. The nurse wrapped a blanket around her and she quieted. Her eyes were open and she looked around. Best of all, she took her mother's breast and began sucking immediately. What a wonderful little human being!

After a sleepless night and the emotional drama of Hannah's delivery, I was badly in need of a shower and drove home. Now, with our '79 Datsun resting in the driveway and my mind dazed by the exciting yet draining events, I stared out through the windshield at the wooden steps leading up into our house. My vision seemed to have a heightened focus: I noticed the steps were rickety. One board was a little rotten on one end, and the rusty nails had gouged their way to the surface. Another board had warped up off the supports.

My mind snapped to attention. In less than forty-eight hours, a new mother carrying a new baby would be climbing those rickety stairs.

So, exhausted as I was, with bloodshot eyes and the aroma of my sleepless hospital visit about me, I got out the power saw, some wood, a handful of nails, a square, and a hammer. For the next three hours, I built steps.

When I was done, I went in, took a shower, and then headed right back to the hospital.

I was a father ready to protect his family. I was a father in the stage of attachment.

The Birth of a Child

As your first child is delivered into this world, your wife is giving birth to more than just a baby. A father is also born. And in the meeting of father and child, an entirely new perspective is birthed, and the world never looks the same. Don't ask me how it happens, but it is a drama (and often comedy) of magnificent proportions.

The characters in this drama are clear enough. First, there is the baby. A purple, often bald lump of humanity, who mostly drools, poops, and cries. And then there is this other new creature, the father. Previously a straight-thinking, steady, mostly unflappable male, he is reborn into this world as a bug-eyed, cigar-toting, back-slapping fanatic. With his baby tucked into his arm like a football, he is often seen wandering aimlessly down hospital corridors, saying, "Isn't she the most beautiful child in the whole world?" Several of his nose prints can be seen, at virtually any hour of the day, on the nursery room window. At the mention of his baby's name, he might light up like a firefly, or begin to cry. He may weigh in at 180 pounds of muscle, but now he's completely overcome by a few pounds of baby fat. He is obsessed.

The experts even have a name for his new condition: *engrossment*. The characteristics are absorption, preoccupation, and overwhelming interest. As physician Martin Greenberg writes, "He has an intense desire to look at his baby, to touch and hold him. It is as if he is hooked, drawn to his newborn child by some involuntary force over which he has no control."[1] It's not something that he has willed to happen; it just does. Certainly it defies explanation; it's reserved for the realm of mystery.

Now this may not be your experience. Having a baby can lead to feelings of fear and helplessness. Some fathers take their time to attach to their baby. But for all fathers, events have now become larger than life. They seek to understand—and often idealize—what this new child means. Over the years, the father matures, but he never grows completely immune to the child's pull on his heart. Who can explain what happens when a little child grabs your finger in her tiny hand, looks up into your face, and says, "I love you, Daddy"?

Maybe it's their innocence, maybe it's their helplessness, but there is a power that young children exert over men.

The Birth of a New Perspective

Engrossment

When a child is born, so is a father. Nothing is the same. Suddenly, life seems larger than life. The word *engross*, in fact, means to "make large." Even fathers themselves feel as if they have suddenly grown. They feel bigger, stronger, older, and more powerful. Although this feeling is sometimes overwhelming, causing periods of doubt and insecurity, it is mostly exhilarating. Such men are charged with enthusiasm.

Just like a marathon runner, the enthusiasm is easy to maintain at the beginning. You're fresh; the crowd is concentrated near the starting line. For the first number of months, the novelty itself is invigorating. Although the sleepless nights and constant demands begin to take their toll, you get new shots of adrenaline along the way—people who haven't yet seen your newborn, your child's first step or first word.

In the mix of engrossment and enthusiasm, something stirs deep within a father's heart. It is called love. But it is a love like none other, this bond between father and child. It causes him to look at the world from a new perspective. In his desire to protect and care for his child, he sees things that he never saw before. It's great to be a dad!

Responsibility

For me, driving home from the hospital, I saw rusty nails and a warped board on our front steps. My perception and imagination had been totally recircuited when Dee gave birth: "Oh no, Dee will be walking up and down these steps. She'll be carrying Hannah. She might slip. Hannah is so fragile . . ." But I had a power saw and fresh lumber and new sense of responsibility: "I will protect my family!" Afterward, when I would tell people, "We have a new baby," Dee would add with a proud smile, "and new steps."

Fathers care for and protect their families. Perhaps at no time do we feel responsibility more profoundly than during the stage of attachment, which continues through the first two years of the child's life. We realize that, for really the first time in our lives, another person is depending on us for his basic, daily needs. And though it's often gradual, we also begin to grasp that our priorities have to change; the needs of this child (and his mother) will require us to give up some activities or habits that we have grown to enjoy.

It's amazing where this sense of responsibility surfaces. One man tells of driving more safely, even when alone, and of wearing his seat belt for the first time in his life. "I became aware, when my wife was pregnant, that I no longer had any right to die. . . . I was now important to this little thing, and I couldn't die because he needed me."[2]

And of course, when it comes to responsibility, new fathers quickly think of finances. I've talked with men whose voices actually dipped from the enthusiasm of "We're going to have a baby!" to the softness of their next words: "I hope we can afford it." These men may be accused of being cold and unfeeling, but it's really just the opposite. They want to be able to give their children what they need.

Many new fathers dream dreams. They long to give their children the desires of their heart, to protect, care, and provide for them in the best way that they can. If a father's childhood was one of contentment and security, he vows that his children will have the same. If he was fathered at a distance, he promises to break the cycle—to give his children what he's never had. He wants life to be wonderful for his children.

Know Your Emotions

Being a good father is primarily a heart activity, not a head activity. And relationships require a set of tools that men do not often employ. Our emotions are close to the surface during the stage of Attachment. In fact, that is one of the purposes of this stage in the original design: We men, wrapped up in our world of logic and action, get a chance to experience and identify the emotional side of life. We can lay the groundwork for an emotional intimacy with our children that will last throughout the life course.

I have described some of the positive desires and emotions that surface during the first two years of a child's life—the engrossment and enthusiasm that are a natural part of being a dad. But as I'm sure you know, it's much more complex than that. You'll also find some emotions welling up that will challenge your ability to respond in a positive way. Here are a couple:

Jealousy

In the midst of all the changes your wife has gone through with the pregnancy, delivery, and now adjusting to motherhood, it's easy for a dad to wonder where he fits in. She's getting most of the attention, she has a natural bond with the child after carrying him for nine months and now possibly breast-feeding him, and she probably handles most of the child-care duties. She has a deep connection with the child that you can never quite understand or participate in, and it's likely that you'll feel jealous from time to time.

You may feel jealous of the baby, who's getting all of your wife's best attention and energy. You may feel jealous of your wife, who has bonded easily with the child and is, in a sense, a "gatekeeper" for your fathering activities—she probably knows more about what the child needs and how to satisfy him.

Some fathers get discouraged and decide to sit out the first few years of their baby's life, hoping to build a relationship later on, when the child can talk, and play ball, and go on outings. That may seem like the easiest approach, but it isn't the best for you or your child. Being involved with your child during these early stages will greatly enhance your fathering satisfaction throughout the life course, and your marriage will benefit as well.

If you feel discouraged, the best approach is not withdrawal. You need to talk about it, preferably with your wife. Ask her what she's going through, and communicate your concerns. If that sounds impossible at the moment, try talking to another father who's been through this life stage. He can share insights about how he got through it, and show you that it's really a common experience for new dads. Eventually, you should discuss your feelings with your wife if you want any real resolution and improvement in this area. Work through these issues together, and start healthy habits that will help you deal with potential conflicts down the road.

Anger

This is another emotion that may sneak up on you before you expect it. Let's say you have committed to being highly involved in caring for your child, and one evening you take over so your wife can run some errands and get out of the house. Your child wakes up from her nap and begins to cry for no apparent reason, and you can't get her to stop. Every logical remedy fails; she keeps right on crying. Or, when your child reaches eighteen months, you might begin to wonder if she came from Tasmania. She whirls and swirls and twists and jumps and leaps and breaks things at a greater speed than a cartoon devil. Turmoil is in her very wake.

Frustration is inevitable. And, depending on the specific circumstances—such as your tolerance level, the tasks you had hoped to accomplish, other issues that are on your mind, and how much fatigue you feel after a long day—that frustration could drive you over the edge. You may feel like yelling at your baby or even hitting her.

Clearly, those are things you should never do, but unfortunately, clear thinking most likely isn't your strong suit at the moment. As Martin Greenberg points out, there is a difference between feeling out of control and being out of control, but rising emotions like frustration and anger tend to make that distinction much more blurry.[3] If those thoughts start coming into your mind, find a way to express the emotion in a harmless way, directed away from the child. Set her in the crib for a minute and do push-ups or jumping jacks to let off steam. Turn on some soothing music. Open the window shades. Pray.

Do whatever it takes to protect your child from the possible dangers that can result from intense emotions. Identify chains of events or certain situations that could make you susceptible to outbursts. Learn to expect your baby's fussiness, and plan ways to handle it calmly. Ask a friend if you can call and talk—at any hour—when you feel yourself nearing the edge. Consider counseling if you just can't shake it. It's vital that you learn to control your emotions. Right now, your baby's physical safety is at stake, and that's serious. But if you don't conquer anger now, you could easily settle into negative habits of relating to your children that, through the years, will do lifelong damage to their emotional and spiritual well-being.

At the heart of this struggle is the question of competing priorities. As a father, you know your child's needs are much more important than your own sleep, watching your favorite team on TV, or whatever else you could be doing instead of dealing with a fussy baby. Being a responsible father requires significant investments of your time, energy, and emotions. It takes sacrifice! The problem is that it often takes time to fully embrace that shift in priorities. For some dads, it may take many years. But when you do make that mental shift and place your children's needs above your own desires, there's no more competition for your attention and energy. You'll feel less frustrated and angry because the matter has been decided; you have already determined that you'll be available to rock your baby, mix up a bottle of formula or oatmeal, or whatever she needs. I don't mean to imply that this is an easy process. It isn't! But it can be helpful for young fathers to recognize and begin making adjustments early in their fathering careers.

These emotions also highlight the importance of the parenting teamwork in a marriage. When strong emotions arise, you can check each other, draw strength from one another, or step in and provide relief. If your wife stays home with the baby during the day, knowing you'll be walking in the door soon may be her greatest hope. You can take over for a while and give her a chance to get away and regain her composure. And new dads caring for their babies alone for the first time know what a welcome sight it can be when Mom comes back home.

The Virtue of Patience

When mothers leave the hospital after a delivery, it's common for the hospital to send them home with a few articles of parenting paraphernalia—perhaps a diaper bag, a thermometer, and other necessary items. If I could send new fathers home with anything, I'd send them home with a good dose of patience.

I could state this negatively: "Let me tell you, Dad, you'll really pay if you're not patient in these first few years." But I prefer to state it positively: "Dads, patience is the virtue that will allow you to bond with your child and mesh together your schedules, ideals, and personalities. It will become the basis for building your relationship together. Patience allows you to make the sacrifices you need for the sake of your children."

Patience is crucial because your child moves at a different pace and operates at a different size than you, Mr. 180-pound Bulk of Busy Purpose. Kids are going to slow you down. I tell you, if General Patton had taken a platoon of one-year-olds on his march to Berlin, he would have had to order up a whole new supply convoy. The accessories needed for a diaper change make packing for a trip across town a prolonged procedure.

The list of things that require patience is a long one. There will be numerous 2:00 a.m. feedings. There will be occasions when your child is ill, but she can't tell you or the pediatrician where she hurts.

As I described, fathering a young child involves sacrifice. You'll be asked to change or put on hold some of the things you have enjoyed in the past—eight hours of sleep, speedy arrivals, intimacy with your wife, spending money on yourself, fulfilling certain dreams. Patience builds relationship. It is a vital component in any situation where two people must learn to mesh together their personalities, paces, and priorities. Patience will help you maintain your sanity, and even better, it will help you build a close bond with your child.

Create a Job Description

What is our official job description? At no time do we feel the need for a fathering job description more than when we first become fathers. We hold our little son in our arms and ask, "Now what do I do?" Conceiving the little tyke was probably the easy part, but where do we go from here?

Despite what may seem to be a backdrop of turmoil, a child's demands on his father are relatively few during these first two stages. Mothers, particularly if they are breast-feeding, are as busy as they'll ever be, but fathers are not quite so taxed in their roles. These early stages provide a man with a window of opportunity to think through the issues of fathering, plan his fathering strategy, and begin to put it into place. You can develop a "Father Job Description" that goes well beyond the traditional role of financial provider for your children. There are several factors to consider as you put together a fathering strategy that is unique to your own personality and gifts.

How You Define "Father"

I hope the first two sections of this book provided a good starting point for you. As you explored your relationship with your own father, I encouraged you to reflect on his strengths and weaknesses as a dad. There are probably ways you want to follow his example, and ways you want to do the opposite of what he did. Maybe there were other father figures in your life—or other dads you know right now—who have modeled healthy fathering for you. Put those insights to use with your own kids. Then, hang on to the "I CANs" of fathering as big-picture guidelines for your fathering. Strive to be involved, consistent, aware, and nurturing.

Remember, the position of father is an honorable one in and of itself. We can take pride and gain motivation simply because we are fathers, and that office carries great power. But sitting in an office of honor doesn't always mean we're acting honorably. In other words, biology doesn't always provide the best fathers. And, in the same way, the most devoted fathers are not necessarily biological ones.

In some cases, courts have recognized a child's "psychological father" as more legitimate than the biological father. Many men are claiming ownership of their kids not on a biological basis, but on a practical one—a day-to-day living out of their commitment to the children they love. That's the kind of resolve I would urge you to add to your job description.

Expectations

During these early years, it may seem like everyone has an idea of what you should be doing and how you should be doing it. The culture places both high and low expectations on how you should father. Most likely, your colleagues at work also communicate expectations. Your parents and your in-laws, whether they communicate them or not, also have expectations for you as a father. After all, you are raising their grandchildren!

Your wife's expectations also play a large role in your fathering. The most important man in her life, before she met you, was her father. When she thinks of the job title "father," her mind naturally returns to him. The expectations she has for you as the father of her children will probably be based on the responsibilities that were fulfilled by her dad, or the ways in which she feels that her father failed her, or, more likely, some combination of the two.

Maureen had a lousy relationship with her dad. He was away from home often and not too pleasant when he was there. Maureen determined that things would be different between her daughter, Jessie, and her husband, Ted. So she wrote her husband a job description. But she never considered her own expectations, and whether they were realistic, which they were not. Ted reacted to the pressure of having to march to the beat of someone else's drum. He often bailed out by going hunting or fishing, or else he "punished" Maureen by withholding emotion or communication. It has hurt their marriage, and it's affecting Jessie, who senses the tension even at her young age.

Some of Maureen's faulty expectations may be the results of male-female gender differences. Consumed as she is with the task of mothering, Maureen may assume that parenting equals mothering. In other words, she may not know that there are distinctive ways in which men interact with children. Mothers, for example, are trained for immediate reaction. When a child cries, they respond. A child's hungry cry will even make a mother's milk move toward her breast. Maureen expected Ted to have her same, immediate reaction. But like Ted, most men are able to keep a more objective distance. They assess the situation and come to their own conclusions about what is an appropriate response.

How to raise children can be a major source of conflict for parents. If you are to be effective, you must discuss your expectations with your wife. You need to be able to ask her, "Honey, what is it that you expect me to do as a father?" Get specific. Talk about the schedule of diaper changes, or the amount of time spent with the kids, or what part you play when it comes to discipline.

Talking about expectations includes listening to our wives' expectations for us and giving them strong consideration. Primarily, we need to listen for our own good. I know Dee has taught me more about good parenting than I can thank her for. We men need to learn from our wives.

Some of the expectations your wife voices may appear to you to be unrealistic, or you may simply disagree about the contents of your fathering job description. You do have the right (as the one expected to do the job) to reject bad or improper expectations. The only stipulation is that you have to be able to defend your choice. Talk with your wife, and tell her why you don't think you can do what she has asked. Dealing with expectations has to be a conscious, verbalized procedure. Then we are in the position to be instructed by good expectations, not driven by bad ones.

Bonding with Your Baby

The first few years of a child's life can be relatively "low maintenance" for a father. Involvement at this stage means things like: changing a dirty diaper, feeding, reading simple books, and lots of talking, cooing, holding, and playing. Your most important task is found in the word that defines this stage: attachment.

One of the many positive effects of bonding is your child's strengthened self-concept. Young children experience security and protection when they have a healthy bond with their fathers, and those seemingly small positives now will translate into much more tangible benefits later in life.

Bonding is really something that happens more than something you do. It is, however, a wonderful by-product of the things you do. Not surprisingly, simply spending time with a child is one of the greatest contributors to bonding. For many fathers, being involved with their infant is a natural next step based on the overwhelming emotions—the "engrossment"—that they feel.

Some dads don't feel an immediate closeness to their babies. After all, this is a brand-new relationship—a brand-new person—and it may take time to get used to each other. If you don't feel that bond right away, don't pressure yourself. Give it time. You can still become just as caring and loving and close to your child as any other father.

I want to give you permission to defend your unique, "manly" approach to parenting. You don't have to be a mother, or even some kind of generic parent. Be a father. Take some initiative, dive in, learn about what your child needs, and gain the experience and confidence you need.

But I also want to caution you. In many cases, the mother may have a better feel for what's best for the baby from her months of reading and her keen intuition. If she fears that you're not being careful enough in playing with your baby, she may have a good point. And you may get frustrated when it seems your wife keeps correcting you in how you're handling your child. Much of her advice may be justified, and some of it may not. If you do find it necessary to defend your way of doing things, stay committed to what's best for the child, whether you "win" or not. And even if you have to swallow your pride every now and then, consider it a small sacrifice for the benefit of a harmonious household atmosphere at a time of great adjustment.

Playtime!

Playing seems to come naturally to most dads. Whenever I see a father and child playing and laughing together, I wonder who's having more fun. Usually, it's a toss-up. But more than just being fun, playtime is good for children. Even at this young age, play encourages their imagination, physical and mental prowess, and a healthy spirit of competition. They are exposed to risk taking and problem solving in a safe environment.

In the book *The New Father,* Armin Brott and Jennifer Ash list some helpful reminders for fathers playing with infants:

- Use moderation. Especially with very young babies, restrict play sessions to around five minutes. Too much play can make them fussy or irritable.
- Take cues from the baby. Adjust what you're doing based on the baby's crying, boredom, or discomfort.

- Schedule your fun. Choose a time when the baby is alert and when you can give him your full attention. Be careful about playing immediately after a feeding.
- Be patient. Don't expect too much too soon.
- Be encouraging. Use lots of facial and verbal encouragement, smiles and laughter. The baby can't yet understand the words, but she can definitely understand the feelings. At just a few days old, she will want to please you, and your encouragement will build her self-confidence.
- Be gentle—especially with the baby's head. His neck muscles will take time to develop, so be sure to support his head from behind. Avoid sudden or jerky motions, and never shake your child. Also, be very careful about throwing him up in the air.[4]

Dads and Child Care

Many of us dads will readily admit that we feel out of our element when it comes to child care. We get in an unfamiliar situation with our child, freeze up, and give the child back to her mother A.S.A.P. We can stand up to an angry boss or muster the courage to land an important client, but we cower in fear at the sight of a one-year-old in need.

New fathers must become comfortable with the everyday care of children. Committed fathers are willing to brave screams and tears, messy faces, and, yes, even "atomic bomb" diapers. The best way to master child care is to dive right in, make mistakes, learn from experience, and gain confidence for the next time. We can't afford to skip out during this stage, because these everyday forms of involvement play a large role in our ability to bond with our babies.

Whether you're dealing with a messy diaper, a crying baby, or the challenges of bath time, do your best to keep a few important principles in mind:

When your baby is unhappy, focus on the cause of the behavior. Babies generally cry to let us know they are uncomfortable, in pain, hungry, wet, needing to burp, sick, too hot, too cold, overstimulated, or missing their caretakers. They have a limited number of ways to express themselves, so we must be sensitive to facial expressions, subtle differences between cries, and other conditions that might clue us in to the problem.

View child care as bonding time. You're doing more than just changing a diaper or giving a bottle or a bath. You're relating to your son or daughter. Try to make these positive experiences for both of you, not just daily (or hourly) chores. If you're frustrated and tense, your infant will sense that, and it will only make things harder.

The more you hold, massage, sing to, laugh with, cradle, play with, and talk lovingly to your child as part of meeting his everyday needs, the better. Looking at the larger picture, this approach can create patterns of behavior that develop trust in your baby. He will know that, no matter what is happening, you can be counted on to restore a sense of security, support, and love.

Building a Support Team

No matter how well you develop and implement your fathering job description, there is one thing you need to remember: Fathering is not a one-man job. This great drama/comedy does not take place without a supporting cast. Your wife, a father role model, and other couples typically comprise the supporting players, and they can be rich resources during the final five stages of the fathering life course, offering advice and assistance when you need it most.

Your wife should be your primary colleague on your fathering team. She will be your most valuable asset throughout your fathering life course, whether in her parenting knowledge, her complementary perspective, or her womanly comfort. But during the stages of attachment and idealism, it is likely that you will need to be more supportive of her than she is of you. Young kids make for exhausted mothers. Do all you can to make her pregnancy as comfortable as possible. When the child arrives, do your share of the child-care chores. Volunteer your help; anticipate her needs. In fact, offer her some refreshing time away from the kids. And, yes, work at keeping romance alive in your marriage.

You need to also look for good fathering examples, including men who may be strong in areas where you are weak. You need to be bold in taking the initiative. Approach a trusted friend and ask, "I'm having a little trouble figuring something out about my daughter. Could you give me some advice?"

And finally, spend time interacting with other families. You may be tempted to work on your fathering just by meeting with other fathers or sticking your nose in a good parenting book. But young families also need interaction with other families to see how they solve problems and interact.

When Rachel was still a toddler, my friend Danny and his son, Ryan, came visiting. Sitting on the couch, Danny and I witnessed Ryan take a swipe at Rachel. Danny launched into a profuse apology, which I accepted. I encouraged Danny to stay on top of Ryan's aggressive behavior. I also told him, "If Ryan hadn't taken a swipe at Rachel first, it wouldn't have been long before Rachel would have tried to work him over."

Ryan is Danny's only child, so he's had no one else to compare the boy to as he tries to determine what's "normal." But by visiting our home and comparing notes with me, Danny managed to avoid the isolation that makes a father feel hung out to dry.

Strong from the Start

It's fairly easy to make the case that the beginning of something is always the most important part. But the message of the fathering life course is that of the whole: Each leg is important. We need to run the race with endurance.

If you've already missed out on the stages of attachment, you can still work on developing your fathering style. You may feel like you are playing catch-up—and you are—but a marathon is a long race. It's never too late to pick up the pace and finish strongly.

But if you are still a father in the stages of attachment, I would encourage you to come out strong off the blocks. Use the natural enthusiasm and sense of responsibility of this period to propel yourself miles down the course to fathering success.

FOR FATHERS OF PRESCHOOLERS: IDEALISM

I remember the afternoon years ago when my wife, Dee, called me at the office. "We've got a problem," she blurted out. "Rachel's gone." "She's what? How can she be gone?" I ran to the van and raced home. There, in the passenger seat of a police car parked not far from our house, sat little, sweet, three-year-old Rachel. While everyone else was in the basement working on school projects, this little descendent of Houdini had escaped out the front door, crossed the street, traversed the park, and navigated a busy intersection. Authorities speculated that she was headed for the ice-cream store, but we'll never know for sure. Fortunately, a friendly passerby coaxed her into his pickup and called the police.

Some ten days later, Dee received a visit from a state child services official. Obviously, we weren't keeping very good track of our three-year-old. Dee was a bit angry and embarrassed until she realized the woman was just doing her job, and probably had a right to be concerned. Eventually we were able to convince her that we are responsible parents, and that this was one of those unusual situations when we simply lost track of a curious child.

Dad, you may not have realized it since you've been so busy chasing your youngster around, doing your best to clear his path of everything that's dangerous, breakable, or both—but when your oldest child turned two, you entered the stage of idealism, which will continue through your child's preschool years.

Now your baby is developing new capacities to reason, and move about more quickly, and manipulate objects with some precision and dexterity, and communicate more clearly. Your child will keep you on the verge of wonder. He's learning something new every day.

You have probably looked forward to this time when you're able to relate to your child on more concrete terms. Now your child can understand and use words rather than forcing you to interpret various types of sounds and gestures. You can ask questions and get answers; you can say, "I love you," and be confident that your daughter has a good idea what you mean; you can ask your son, "What do you want to do this afternoon?" and know that his answer will guide you toward something that will make him happy.

In the marathon of fathering, having a preschooler would be like miles four to ten. It probably took you about three miles to loosen up your joints and persuade yourself that, yes, you're actually running a 26-plus-mile race. It took a few miles for your system to adjust, for your heart rate to level off, and for your hamstrings to work out the stiffness. But now you've adjusted to being a father. You've set a comfortable pace. Sure, there will be hills that challenge you, but your energy is still pretty high. You can navigate those and have something left for later stages of the race. Your arms swing effortlessly at your sides; you're just hitting your stride.

Establish Ideals

The adult male life course adds its own distinctives to the fathering stage of idealism. Most men in this stage are somewhere between ages 25 and 35, though as a nation we are marrying later and delaying the start of our families. Often fathers of preschoolers are not too distantly removed from college or technical training and are working their first "jobs," if not already started in their "careers."

Daniel J. Levinson, author of *The Seasons of a Man's Life*, claims that during this time a man is consumed with "two primary yet antithetical tasks:

(a) He needs to explore the possibilities for adult living: to keep his options open, avoid strong commitments and maximize the alternatives, and (b) The contrasting task is to create a stable life structure: become more responsible and 'make something of my life.'"[1] Now such a man has a little son or a little daughter to factor into the equation.

It is during this season that the young father is establishing his priorities and deepening his commitment to the fathering role. You probably identified your aspirations during your first few years as a father, factoring in your relationship with your own dad and other father figures in your life. Now you have begun to grasp the many demands fathering puts on your time and energy, and you have a better idea of what it's going to take for you to be a good father. Idealism is where you take all those desires as a father and come up with specific goals and actions you want to put into motion. Now is the time to decide: "It will be a challenge, but I'm going to place fathering among the very highest priorities in my life."

It's time to translate your sense of enthusiasm and responsibility into a set of ideals, a method of operation, your own personal fathering policy. Get some understanding of the personal costs of putting those ideals into place. You are going for your personal best as a father. Now admittedly, things rarely work out as they are planned. But that's no reason not to plan.

Involvement During Idealism

I'm going to try to inspire you to fathering greatness by instilling in you a sense of wonder about your child and his world. A few years ago your child was born into the world, but now he is further "born" into the world of speaking and toilet training and learning and relating. Growth is so rapid in our children's early years that development can be tracked in weeks and months. Your child can now run and climb with confidence, and seems to have boundless energy and a hunger for more and more physical activity. He can't get enough running, racing, wrestling, playing games, swinging, sliding, and on and on. Be prepared, because your child will really test your stamina.

He is active socially and needs lots of interaction with you, other adults, and playmates his age. He will start imitating you in many ways, learning and singing songs, and asking all kinds of curious questions. His imagination is now running wild with stories, pretend games, and even imaginary friends. By the time the stage of idealism has run its course, this toddler will grow to become a school-age playground sophisticate with a vocabulary of 2,000-3,000 words.

A child is an incredible being! Don't let yours grow up without you. I suspect I won't have to give you too many ideas in this area. Your involvement with your young child probably comes pretty easily. Your child is very active and willing to learn a variety of games, stunts, sports, and other activities. I would encourage you to be creative, but you really don't need to dream up anything brilliant here. Just be resourceful; there are plenty of great dad/kid activities all around you, and your child will probably love them all. Best of all is your own natural sense of playfulness: a romp on the living room carpet, or a bucking bronco ride on your back as you cart your son off to bed. An impromptu snowball fight. A tickle-fest. Dads are the perfect playmates, and these can be great times of involvement with your child.

Reading Together

A 1644 Massachusetts Colony law stated that heads of households should be responsible for teaching their children to read. Not a bad law! I would love to see the fathers of today make that law their own. You can start with reading to and with your children. Here are four of the many important benefits:

1. *Reading fosters intellectual development.* Reading together gives your child plenty of opportunities to learn new things. He'll be exposed to basic plot development from beginning, to middle, to end; he'll absorb many new words into his vocabulary; he'll learn the basics of rhythm and rhyme. He'll enjoy pictures and stories about the world around him, and tales of adventure and repetition. One of the best ways to positively influence your child's future education is to foster a deep appreciation for books and reading, and the time to start is now.

2. *Reading together gives you a chance to observe and enjoy your children.* When my son Micah was younger, I used to love to watch him out of the corner of my eye as I read him a story. He'd think. He'd wonder. He'd worry. He'd smile.

Reading a story to your child can teach you how he thinks and reacts and responds. Welcome interruptions—your child's questions allow him to participate more fully. You can ask questions like, "What does that mean?" "Why do you think he did that?" or "What do you think you would have done?" These are great opportunities to learn more about your child, teach him your values, and monitor his level of understanding and mental maturity. These kinds of insights will help you later, when you want to communicate about more important issues.

3. *Reading helps you be creative and interesting.* Children long for the fun-loving excitement and creativity that their dads provide so well. With something like Dr. Seuss or the Berenstain Bears, it's nearly impossible to read without changing your voice for different characters, acting scared or surprised, and involving yourself in the story line. Exploring different emotions with your child helps him to be honest about his feelings with you.

4. *Reading brings you into close proximity to your child.* One of the best things about reading with your children is that it encourages physical closeness. You can watch TV from opposite sides of the room. Not so with reading. You share the same book. You look at the pictures together. It brings a little child into the lap of her father.

Learn Healthy Discipline

Helping your children learn about responsibility and the consequences of their choices is a lifelong pursuit for fathers. Fathers of adult children are still trying to help their children make wise decisions and avoid the trials that come with mistakes. Healthy discipline is an important aspect of fathering in every stage of the life course. But during idealism, your children have grown to the point where they are making thoughtful choices, balancing right and wrong, and testing your resolve. The patterns that you establish now with your child will pay long-term dividends in your relationship.

I'd much rather discuss the importance of establishing proper habits of discipline with dads at this stage than try to help dads of teenagers who feel like they've lost control, who may be trying to undo years of harmful patterns in relating to their children. Dads of preschoolers are usually open— and sometimes eager—to learn positive fathering practices. Fathers of rebellious teenagers tend to be more desperate; they'd give anything to be able to go back and change the past. Sometimes they can repair, to some degree, the hurts from past mistakes, but they never have another chance to start out at ground zero, decide what's best when it comes to disciplining their children, and then proceed with confidence. You have that opportunity, and I hope you'll make the most of it.

What Is Healthy Discipline?

Let me affirm that discipline—in a healthy balance with love—is good for children. We all need to think about and discuss with our children's mother the specifics of the way we'll express and carry out discipline. For example, what does the word "discipline" make you think of? Punishment? A struggle for control? Time-out?

I'd like to expand the idea of discipline and talk about it in terms of relationship. We need to banish the idea that discipline is an event—a one-shot act of punishment—and view it instead as a process. It's part of the way we relate to our children every day, whenever we're together. We need to consistently model a virtuous life, communicate that actions have consequences, and impart a healthy respect for authority and justice.

We're seeking to create an environment in which our children become self-disciplined—confident, self-controlled, making wise choices, taking responsibility for their actions, and proactively working to fix their problems. Most schoolteachers will tell you discipline is lacking in today's kids. As committed fathers, we can train our children in a way that they'll become positive models among their undisciplined peers.

An Overview

There are many different approaches out there for training and correcting children, and I'm convinced that more than one of them can work well with your children. Perhaps the most important part is finding a method that you and your child's mother believe in and that you're willing to carry out together. It's vital that you exercise discipline with consistency and a common purpose. Also, the method you choose will be impacted by how you (and your wife) were disciplined when you were young, your unique personalities and how you handle emotions, and the values that you seek to maintain in your family.

More specifically, I believe healthy discipline includes some key principles:

- balancing high expectations with encouragement and affirmation
- setting clearly defined boundaries
- administering unpleasant (and often natural) consequences when your child does wrong
- knowing what is appropriate and effective for each individual child
- maintaining your self-control
- having your child's best interests in mind, instead of your own emotions or a need to be "right"
- using mistakes and conflicts as opportunities for your child to learn and grow
- reassuring your child often that he is deeply loved, regardless of mistakes and misbehavior

Discipline and teaching responsibility are such vital concepts for fathers, and it's important that you get a good handle on them now, when your children are still young. You'll create a healthy pattern for relating to one another, and you'll probably save yourself and your child a good deal of heartache later on. I encourage you and your child's mother to work out the details of how you'll handle discipline. In the back of the book, I have included some recommendations for books you might like to read on this and other topics.

Your Child's Safety

A concern for your child's safety is something that lasts throughout the fathering life course. During your baby's first few years, you and your wife were able to keep pretty close tabs on him—you had to, because he needed someone there to care for him. Now, he's more able to move around and investigate things on his own, though he's still pretty naive about many of the potential dangers all around him. He's learning to communicate well enough to understand your warnings about what he shouldn't do, and to whom he shouldn't talk. This is a time when you need to be especially attentive to protecting your child.

Some Specific Concerns

The incident with Rachel escaping from our house was a close call, and those kinds of things do tend to happen with young children. If we're smart, these can be wake-up calls for us dads. Here's a checklist for starters:

- Teach your children proper fire escape routes.
- Teach them how and when to call 9-1-1, and how to make a long-distance call, dial direct, and get operator assistance.
- Be sure your children know what things in the house are off-limits: matches, medicines, power tools, etc.
- Teach your children how to respond in a tornado or earthquake, or if they are caught outside in a lightning storm.
- As soon as they can speak, have each of your children memorize their phone number and street address in case they get lost.
- Be sure your children learn how to swim.
- Make it a priority that your child knows what to do if someone else has a medical emergency: whom to call and, for older children, how to administer CPR.
- Teach your children how you want them to handle encounters with strangers, including how much distance to keep, not talking with them, not taking anything from them, and not going anywhere with them.
- Make sure your children understand proper and improper touches, and that they have a right to say who touches them and how. If anyone touches them in a way that feels funny or uncomfortable or in a way that you would think is wrong, they should say, "No, stop it." They should tell another adult or create a scene in public, if necessary.
- Teach your children how to verify that a person is, in fact, an employee of a particular store.
- Make sure your child knows that, when he's home alone, he shouldn't answer the door or tell someone on the phone that he's alone.
- Have your child come and tell you if any adult asks her to keep a secret from you.

I urge you to read up and get more specifics about how to protect your child in these areas. Your local fire and police stations and your library should have more information.

Crisis situations are part of parenting. Accepting that role as protector of your children will help you prepare for the challenges and will help your kids feel more secure in a world that can be scary.

Thoughtless Mistakes

I'm embarrassed to admit it, but sometimes our children need to be protected from us! I have always been very enthusiastic about being a dad. When I was younger, sometimes my enthusiasm overwhelmed my common sense, leading to some pretty ignorant actions on my part, and I overlooked my own children's safety.

Earlier, I told you about the time I left our two young daughters, Hannah and Sarah, alone in our apartment so I could run two blocks to buy chocolate chips. There was another day when my two young daughters and I hopped in our red wagon. I grabbed the black steel handle, and with several powerful kicks sent us careening down a long hill. It was exhilarating . . . until my pregnant wife caught up to us and pointed out that I had put the girls in a situation that was potentially very dangerous.

These stories are a bit embarrassing today, and I hope you're guided more by common sense than enthusiasm—unlike I was. I'm fortunate that I can tell these stories today with a self-effacing smirk rather than with deep pain and regret. I was fortunate, but don't assume things will always turn out for the best. Learn from my mistakes: slow down, exercise some caring common sense, and protect your children even from the dangers of your own parenting decisions.

The Virtue of Gentleness

The patience that carried you through the first two years of being a father is still a great virtue to practice and develop. In fact, patience is a big part of the gentleness that is required during these preschool years: patience for toilet training; patience for his seemingly boundless energy; patience for her endless curiosity; patience when you're trying to teach manners; patience when it seems like you're failing as a parent.

You exercise gentleness during temper tantrums; gentleness when he is trying to deal with new emotions; gentleness when she becomes selfish and possessive; gentleness as your youngster pushes against your boundaries; gentleness as he learns appropriate ways to use his developing vocabulary; gentleness as you praise good behavior; and gentleness when you exercise discipline.

You'll need patience and gentleness when it comes to the questions your preschooler will ask. Do you know that more than 10 percent of your four- to five-year-old's speech will consist of questions? "Daddy, why do birds fly? . . . Daddy, what's in your briefcase? . . . Daddy, where do babies come from?" And then, when you feel like you've given a solid answer: *"Why?"*

Your gentleness will allow you to treat these questions with respect, giving them brief, confident answers and assuring your child that you consider her important enough to take time and listen (without letting her ask questions on and on just to keep you going).

You'll also need gentleness for what I call the "training twos" (more commonly known as the "terrible twos"). This is the time when your child is trying to get a firm hold on her own self-identity while learning to conform to your guidelines and expectations. I remember thinking, *Where does this little two-year-old get off defying me? Doesn't she know I'm bigger than she is?* Your child's acts of defiance could rattle you. But be gentle—even through whatever action you take to discipline the child. For your kids, rattling you is part of their job description.

Calm Fathers

In our stressful lifestyles, it can be easy for a dad to begin reacting to the urgent issues pressing on him—which aren't always the most important ones—rather than being proactive and choosing a course of action based on the principles he believes in. A dad who's reactive is prone to fly off the handle when one of his children messes up, defies him, or makes one more request of his time. But a dad who's *proactive* looks at his priorities and chooses how to act. He sees that his child is more important than other demands, and he treats the request with gentleness and love. He's the kind of dad who makes his children feel comfortable and secure. He listens and accepts. He's slow to anger and seldom overreacts. He keeps his cool.

Gentle dads can still correct their children. It's just that the punishment probably won't be as loud, and it's much more likely that the consequences will fit the crime. Every child wants a gentle father: a dad who's approachable and accepting, who listens to his child's concerns and remains open to her ideas. Keeping our cool will allow us that opportunity, and it's an opportunity that leads to the real joys and rewards of fathering.

So, chill out, dad. Realize that your young children are going to occasionally put you on some emotional roller coasters. You're going to be tested. Your child may even say things that are designed to hurt you personally. That's okay; stay calm. Don't go ballistic when you talk to your kid. And don't wait until the heat of the moment—decide now to react with calmness at your next opportunity.

Demonstrate a life of self-control and character. Be a gentle father.

FOR FATHERS OF SCHOOL-AGE CHILDREN: UNDERSTANDING

The first formal talk I had with my son Joel about sex was when he was seven years old. Actually, it was his mother who suggested the talk. Dee had seen Joel's curiosity about his older sisters, so I agreed to take this quiet gentleman out for lunch and discuss the differences between "them" and "us."

We found a booth at Pizza Hut, then ordered a pan pizza and a couple man-size sodas. Now this wasn't the full-blown "birds and bees" talk; it was simply a discussion of human anatomy—male and female differences—something certainly appropriate for a boy Joel's age to know. But I was taking the talk seriously. I knew I was doing "father stuff."

I started out asking questions to see what he knew already, but his brief answers—"yes, no, maybe, I don't know"—led me to think that pepperoni and sausage still held more interest to him at this age than the fact that girls exist in the world. But I plodded on with my explanations. Finally, I wanted to know whether he had listened and understood.

"Joel," I asked, "do you understand the differences between a girl's body and a boy's?"

"Yes."

"OK, then. Tell me, what is the difference between your mother's body and my body?"

Joel thought for a moment. I was convinced he was reviewing my lecture carefully. But then he looked out the window and replied, "Mom has a different color of eyes."

I smiled. He smiled back.

What happened? One minute I was engrossed in the stage of idealism, happily dangling toys above my baby's pudgy outstretched arms, but in just a few short years, my oldest children had propelled me into the third stage of the fathering life course: the stage of understanding. Like Joel, children in the stage of understanding cross over from the four walls of home into a vast world, one that seems to be without boundaries. It is a time of great transition, which produces even greater questions. Our children need our help as they wrestle with such critical issues as social status, spirituality, and sex.

As I gave Joel my Anatomy 101 talk, I remember thinking that he seemed so young, sitting across from me in his Chicago Cubs baseball cap. Yet I am aware that a child's innocence is being tested at younger and younger ages by streetwise friends, television, and magazines. Increasingly, the pressure builds on our young children. That is why active parental involvement in the stage of understanding takes on higher stakes. If we are to err, it should be on the side of communication.

I don't know, for example, if my lecture on sexuality did my son any good, at least at the moment. When we came home from Pizza Hut and walked in the back door, Dee was waiting in the kitchen. On an impulse, I grabbed Dee, swung her around, and gave her a big kiss. Then I said, "I sure do like those eyes!" Dee looked surprised, but I glanced at Joel and his normally solemn face had broken into a huge smile. I nodded to him and he nodded back, then ran out the door to the park where his friends were playing.

I realized then that fathers teach their children in a million different ways, and I had just successfully communicated the point I most desired my son to know.

A Brave New World

As a father, you enter the stage of understanding when your children enter their school-age years. The stage will continue until they reach adolescence.

Our children, who have been residents in our homes, are now becoming citizens of a larger world. Their primary loyalty is still to the family, but their energies are shifting increasingly to their friends. Meanwhile, your fathering is being augmented by other adults: teachers, coaches, music instructors, and so on. These are not mere babysitters; they are influencers.

Certainly, the most obvious change in the routine of your child's life is that she is now going off to school. But formal education is not the only type of learning going on. Your son is seeking to understand his entire world: how to develop a good move on the basketball court, what type of sneaker is hot, why Susie isn't cool, or what lies around the corner.

During this stage, the father's great task is to facilitate understanding. It's your privilege to introduce your children to the world. This involves a critical balance between allowing your children the freedom to explore their worlds and, at the same time, providing them with a safe and secure environment (as much as that is possible). This may sound like a contradiction, but it is not.

At first glance, rock climbing may appear to be a dangerous sport: a handful of people going up hard, unforgiving crags, held to each other by ropes. However, under the leadership of a trained professional climber the sport is relatively safe. A leader anticipates every potential disaster and takes precautions against them. Ideally two support ropes are anchored into rocks from different angles, taking into account different possible stresses. And while the climber is ascending, he is supported by the belay man, who is responsible for letting out rope, as well as holding the climber in case he should fall. In addition, the belay man is often viewing the climb from an overall perspective—either below or above the climber—and can offer encouragement and suggestions to help the climber complete his climb.

This is a great analogy for fathering during the stage of understanding. We can create the support, encouragement, and perspective necessary for the child to feel safe to explore. As fathers, we must give our children the sense of security and confidence to explore. In rock climbing, a good belayer is one who is both focused and calm, alert and patient. A good father, in a like manner, must cultivate the virtue of peace in his life. He needs this peace in his internal life, in his relationship with his wife, and finally with his children.

A Father's Stage of Discovery

The stage of understanding is a period of transition and tension. Not only is the child in a stage of discovery, but so is the father. Typically, the father is in his late twenties to early forties, settling into life and a career. In essence, just as your children are trying to understand their world, you are trying to come to grips with the adult world. Daniel Levinson, a social researcher who has taught at the Yale School of Medicine, says a man in this period of life is trying "to establish a niche in society: to anchor his life more firmly, develop competence in a chosen craft, become a valued member of a valued world."[1]

The Good and the Bad

This overlapping between adult and child stages—your trying to understand the adult world, your child his new world—can be both good and bad. On the positive side, it provides possible connection points between you and your children. At this time in your lives, you and your children have a lot in common. You're both settling into a routine. Much of a child's attention at this time is occupied with formal education, regular activities, and the development of new skills as he tries to increase his understanding. In a parallel fashion, a father is settling into a career, acquiring occupational skills, or starting a new business as he tries to further his position. Consequently, a father may be more in tune with his children than he realizes. Both are actually working on similar conceptual tasks, even though they may be different issues. The challenge for a father is to look for "intersection" points with his children to assure that he and they are growing together, not apart.

On the negative side, your stage of understanding may disrupt your sense of peace, throwing priorities out of their proper order. When the National Center for Fathering surveyed fathers with children in stage three, we found that the greatest obstacle in fathering was not having enough time. The biggest question of fathers was, "How do I balance my career and my family?"

Levinson mentions this tension. At the same time a man is trying "to establish a niche in society," he is also working at "making it: striving to advance, to progress on a timetable." In "making it" Levinson includes "all efforts to build a better life for oneself and to be affirmed by the tribe."[2]

Finding Peace Within

We will deal with this tension in depth in the next chapter on adolescence (when a man is most likely to "escape" into his work). But let's note here that the conflict, although very real, can be dealt with during the stage of understanding. It's my hope that during the stage of idealism, every man was able to sit down and ask himself, "What is really most important in my life?"

FATHER FACT #5
The Work-Family Challenge

The tension between work and family will continue to be a major issue for both employers and employees. Success and productivity in both the workplace and family relationship will require companies to develop strategies and programs to alleviate the tension.

Two items in the NCF/Gallup Poll measured the degree to which employers understood the tension between work and family demands. The results show most employers recognize the challenge but need to do much more to make the workplace family-friendly:

Your employer recognizes the strain you face between the demands of your family and the demands of work. (Results for men)

Mostly true	36.4%
Somewhat true	18.7%
Uncertain	9.8%
Somewhat false	12.8%
Mostly false	14.9%

If your employer implemented more family-friendly policies, you would be more productive at work.

	Dads	Moms About Dads
Mostly true	40.2%	33.8%
Somewhat true	20.9%	17.3%
Somewhat false	10.4%	6.2%
Mostly false	8.1%	9.9%

Employees link family satisfaction with productivity at work, and many companies are starting to recognize this. At DuPont Corp, a study concluded that "the most striking finding . . . is the positive impact that DuPont's work-life programs have had on business results." In their study of 18,000 employees, the company found that the top three reasons employees rejected changes in their duties or promotions were family related. Thirty-four percent refused relocation, 24 percent refused increased travel, and 21 percent refused overtime.

Knowing what is really important and having a plan to live out those priorities will bring peace. Without a clear answer, we may look for ultimate fulfillment and identity in our own work. Sometimes we feel stranded in the wasteland, abandoned by our own fathers, unsure of our own masculinity. In a sense, we are thirsty: "Give me respect and worth." We look out over a parched landscape and see the shimmer of water in the distance. So we set out to find it. Some of us break into a run. But when we get there, it's gone. Or more accurately, there it is, a little farther in the distance, holding out the same false promise of quenching our thirst. You can die chasing mirages of career.

We need to put things in perspective. Tonight, when your children are asleep, sneak into their bedrooms and sit down on the corner of the bed. Pull the covers back slightly and watch the moonlight fall quietly on their tousled hair. There should be no doubt of what is ultimately important in our lives.

Reconciling the "Daddy Track"
and the "Career Track"

The key to resolving this tension is integration. Don't perceive of your career and your family as separate rails—the "daddy track" or the "career track"—but think of them as a set. Effective fathers undergo a key change in thinking during the stage of understanding: They begin to think of their work in the context of their family, and they begin to think of their family in work-related terms.

Men normally begin their careers with little reference to anyone else but themselves. This is understandable. Most of us were still unmarried when we left high school. We chose our college majors and career directions based on what we thought would best fulfill us—supply our particular dreams, best use our particular strengths and talents. But now *I* has become *we*—I have been joined by a wife and children. An effective father makes a transition; he begins to reconceive his career as a means to an end: supplying for the physical and emotional well-being of his family. Consequently, he makes decisions about promotions, transfers, and work schedules based on how he thinks they will affect his family.

Interestingly, researchers are finding that in the tension between the increasing demands of our children and those of our jobs, involved fathers not only endure the tension, they appear to do better through it. An Emory University study found that, overall, involved fathers "may have delayed writing a paper, or put off some other project, but in the long run [such] fathers went just as far in their work as comparable men did who were less involved with their kids."[3] This longitudinal study conducted by psychologist John Snarey spanned four decades with the same group of men and their children (many of whom now had children as well). His research also showed that fathers who were involved in their children's mental development and their adolescents' social development went further on average in their careers than dads who were not.

Similarly, a study by a Wellesley College researcher found that being actively involved fathers "buffered men from the negative mental-health effects associated with a poor experience on the job."[4]

Rediscovering Your Wife

During the stage of understanding, a peculiar thing is likely to happen: You will have time to take a look around and discover a woman in your house. That would be your wife. During the stage of idealism, with its turmoil of diapers and sick children and spilled drinks, it's easy for spouses to lose track of each other. The needs of the children simply overwhelm the family. But during the understanding stage, when children go to school, there may exist the strong possibility of rediscovering each other.

It is critical that you do so, not only to strengthen your marriage, but also your fathering. In an NCF study, we analyzed the fathering scores of a group of effective fathers (identified as such by their peers and professionals who knew them, and by their wives and children) and compared them with the scores of all other fathers in our data bank. Seven significant differences emerged, showing what made these fathers a cut above the rest.[5] One of the differences was that effective fathers cultivated a healthy marital relationship. This strong bond with their wives, in turn, profoundly benefited their relationship with their kids.

A healthy marriage helps create an atmosphere of security and love for the children. In one NCF Father of the Year essay contest, a fourth-grade girl refers to her dad's relationship with her mom. Of her father, Tasha wrote, "He treats my mom very nicely, which makes me feel wanted." It's an interesting comment. Shouldn't Tasha write, "He treats my mom very nicely, which makes her (my mom) feel wanted"? Instead, Tasha has identified that her father's love for her mother indirectly supplies that love to her too. She is wanted. Her family and all that she cares about is not going to suddenly fall apart.

Tim, now in his late thirties, remembers as a child coming down the stairs one night for a cup of water and stopping as he heard his parents' raised voices. They were in the kitchen arguing with one another. For the next six months, Tim had nightmares. His mother and father, he was convinced, were going to get a divorce. Now Tim's world was overrun with fear. He remembered that his cousins, whom he often played with, were sad and confused after their parents had gone through a bitter divorce.

In terms of the consistency function of fathering, children need to see their father in a loving, steady, and faithful relationship with their mother, especially during the understanding stage. It is, perhaps, the greatest gift a father can give to his children. During this stage of fathering, look for those opportunities (they will come) to renew the relationship with your wife. Your children don't need their parents' constant attention, and they're old enough to spend more time with grandparents and friends. It's important that you and your wife get to know each other again. Put a date night back into your weekly calendar. Take an occasional weekend for a romantic excursion. The renewed relationship will pay dividends in ways you couldn't even imagine.

One of those benefits will be in terms of partnering with one another to rear your children. Fathers need support, and the greatest member of that team can be your wife. She has a different perspective on the kids. She can help round out your awareness of them. In addition, your wife is likely to be more knowledgeable about parenting and child development than you. Most women are. I continually turn to Dee for insight and advice. We are a parenting team. Especially when we are a united front, we work much better together than we do alone.

Peace with Fathering

In his book *Fatherhood,* comedian Bill Cosby writes, "I must admit I did ask God to give me a son because I wanted someone to carry the family name. Well, God did just that and I now confess that there have been times when I've told my son not to reveal who he is. 'You make up a name,' I've said. 'Just don't tell anybody who you are.'"[6]

Cosby reminds us of one profound truth: When your child goes out into the world, so does your reputation. The stage of understanding marks a clear and often awkward transition, as your fathering goes public.

The stage of understanding is the time of performances (baseball and soccer games, track meets, school musicals) and recitals (piano, dance, violin, etc.). I remember the feeling I experienced while finding my seat in a small auditorium for my daughter's violin recital. I knew that in a few moments my daughter Sarah would walk up onstage, place her chin firmly on the chin piece, position her feet, and extend her bow to the "up" position. I would see her eyes focus on her instructor. When she received an affirming nod, Sarah would begin to play "Ode to Joy," by Ludwig van Beethoven. I had heard the piece at least fifty times at home.

I think we fathers hate to admit it, but it's true: Every time our children step up to bat, or walk out onstage, or sit down to take an exam, we are acutely aware that these kids bear our last names. I remember the first recital of our young violinist, Sarah. "Sarah Canfield is the third performer," the emcee announced. No doubt some listening parents thought, *Hmmm. Canfield. Now where have I heard that name before? Oh yeah, her father's the one who . . .* As Sarah played, people listened to see if she hit all the notes and if her bow strokes were confident and in rhythm.

Why was I so invested in this little concert? Because my daughter was becoming known to the world. She had changed from the little infant of years past. She had acquired new skills. She was expressing those talents and would receive the recognition of applause. I felt that my fathering was on trial. As she played, the questions haunted me: Did I get Sarah to lessons? Did I help her set up a practice schedule at home? Did I listen to her practice the piece behind closed doors and give her the encouragement she needed? In a sense, I had the feeling that I was giving a "shadow" performance along with my daughter.

Dealing with Pride and Embarrassment

When fathering goes public, we wrestle with our own egos. Pride and embarrassment are common fathering emotions—they are perfectly natural feelings. We have no control over them. What we do have is control over how we express them. For example, pride should be expressed at every legitimate moment. "Sarah, you played that piece beautifully. Beethoven would be proud." But personal pride should not be our goal. I put Sarah in violin lessons because she had a desire to explore music. I took her to practice because I want to facilitate connections between her and the outside world. I didn't force Sarah into lessons to compensate for my lack of musical ability. Pride becomes a destructive emotion when it causes us to push our children.

Pride may actually be a cloak for a fear of embarrassment. And *embarrassment, when it is expressed to your children, is almost always a powerfully destructive force.* You may feel it—it's a natural part of being a father—but don't express it. Above all else you do as a father, let unconditional love govern how you relate to your children. It doesn't make any difference if they fail; they are still your children, and you claim them as your own. For that matter, failure is part of the job description of being a child, to the extent that trial and error are part of every child's exploring process in determining his own strengths and weaknesses.

One man told me how, when he was a kid, his piano teacher drove out to see his parents. "I think I should advise you," she said to them, "that there are probably better ways to spend your money than on piano lessons for Larry." The parents took the hint and decided to discontinue the lessons, but they praised Larry for what he did. He had no recital, but that was OK with his parents. Larry later lettered as a football player and became senior class president. He gave the speech at commencement. Some other child with different talents played the piano processional.

Dealing with Confusion and Feelings of Inadequacy

As children mature, and their questions get more probing, a father will also wrestle with the increasing complexity of fathering. At times he will feel inadequate, unable to act, or having done something, wondering if it was the right course of action. During this time, it is critical that he develop a support team to help: his wife, another fathering model, and another set of parents. In addition, a support team can include other fathers.

Remember, a support team helps you as a father to realize that you are not alone. For instance, Dan had a conversation with a couple of other men about their fathering, and he realized that what he's experiencing is something that men have experienced since the beginning of time: feeling awkward during their daughters' first menstrual period. Now he knows that his confusion about how to respond is normal.

A father's support network should begin to fall into place during the stage of idealism. During the stage of understanding, the father can begin to utilize his support team. The team can make it a point to get together— to work on problems, get feedback, and hold each other accountable. Together, they help each other become better fathers.

The Great Adventure Begins

Letting Them Explore

As you create an environment of peace where children feel safe to explore their world, you must now let them do so. This might sound simplistic, but it is often a difficult job. There will be a natural tendency to want to keep them at home, isolated and protected. Part of this is based on fear—the big world provides a lot more ways for our children to be hurt, both physically and emotionally. Part may be a matter of convenience—you will now have to spend a good deal of your time driving them to tee-ball practice and soccer games and computer classes.

Yet, even if you tried, you could not stop your child from exploring. The quest for understanding requires it. You could lock them in their rooms for six years, but their imaginations would carry them to distant lands, or they would find a way to pry the window open, slide down the drainpipe, and take off down the street. Every child, in his or her own way, is a Huck Finn, accompanied now by other mentors, floating down the Mississippi, meeting riverboat captains and Shakespearean charlatans. The four walls of your home can no longer contain them.

For them, a great adventure begins in the stage of understanding. I suppose we all keep learning throughout our lives, but I would contend that our attitudes toward what we discover—and toward discovery itself—are formed early on. One of the unique roles of fathers is in being a child's connection between the home and the outside world. I love what Nancy Swihart—a wife, mother, college professor, and coauthor of *Beside Every Great Dad*—writes about her husband:

> When our boys were small, Judd loved to take them out on "manly" adventures such as climbing and hiking. . . . [I'd pack] a lunch for my mighty warriors and watch them swagger out to the car, full of three- and four-year-old confidence in this idol who would lead them out to conquer whatever challenges lay before them. Several hours later they would return, dirty, sweaty, and tired, but with wonderful tales to tell (horrific tales to a mother's ears) of falling, almost drowning, or of coming "close to the edge of certain death." From their jubilance it was evident that they had taken one more step closer to manhood, closer to becoming like the Hero—dad, and the bond of father-son was drawn a little closer.[7]

Their father served his children well. I know Judd's two sons, Derrick and Dan, and believe me, they both have confidence when it comes to discovery.

Establishing Links

You need to help your children establish links with the outside world by establishing your own links with that world. In other words, when your kids go out exploring, you accompany them. In the stage of understanding, the father must be actively involved in the lives of his children. One place it begins is at school. Hopefully, you and your wife were the ones who "introduced" your child to this new, significant adult—Mrs. Jones, the kindergarten teacher at Roosevelt Elementary. You visited Roosevelt before your child started attending and asked around the neighborhood: "How good a school is this? Are your kids functioning well there?" On the first day of school (and perhaps even one day during the semester before) you walked with your child, hand in hand, through those big doors. "Jackie, I want you to meet Mrs. Jones. She's going to be your teacher this year."

But then you stay with your child and monitor her progress as the link is established. You attend the parent-teacher conferences. You look—really look—at your child's cut-and-paste work. You observe her progress and grades, asking questions along the way. But monitoring your child's progress means more than looking at her grades in math, spelling, or geography. You're ultimately monitoring your child's integration out of your home and into the outside world.

Involvement, however, must be accompanied by awareness. That means you will be keenly interested in hearing how your child interacts with her teacher and with her friends. As the facilitator, you will also want to know if your child is receiving the essential things she needs. If not, it is your responsibility to make the changes necessary so that she does.

A genuine awareness means being open to criticism, especially at this stage of your child's life. You will need to keep an ear open as to your child's strengths and weaknesses, as well as a finger on the pulse of your own pride. Establishing a link with the outside world means receiving feedback. That first parent-teacher conference is a time of great pride and concern. *Is my child normal? Can she excel in this important environment?* Teachers, coaches, day-camp counselors, and music or arts instructors are all other adults who provide another perspective on your child. The reports will come back officially ("Here's your child's second-quarter report card") or unofficially ("Let me tell you what I saw David do yesterday. It astounded me"). Be willing to carefully consider the reports, even when they include several "Needs to improve." Admittedly, these adults will not fully understand your children —they only see them in one context and have known them only for a short while. But nothing is served by denying it if your child needs help. Avoid defensive reactions.

I know of one man, whose child was diagnosed with an attention deficit disorder, who refused to consider getting help for his child, or at least having him tested further. "It's all just psychobabble," he said. The man deeply desired, like we all do, for his child to be "normal." But for his child's sake, he needed to not automatically reject what he heard.

Awareness also involves not only a willingness to establish links with the world for your children, but also to limit them. Watch out here. Busy adults tend to have busy children. Psychologist and *Parents* magazine columnist David Elkind coined the term "hurried child" to refer to a child who was not so much *introduced* to the world as flung out into it.[8] Suddenly this child has schedules to keep and projects to complete and media-driven fads to follow. I think it's good that children experience a variety of different activities and come under the tutelage of den mothers, soccer coaches, piano teachers, and Sunday school instructors, but there's nothing that says your child has to do everything.

The Great Questions

As your child explores the world, the great questions of life will surface during the age of understanding. Think of the new things your child will experience during this period—developing and maintaining relationships, the need for acceptance, integration of values, the overwhelming intake of information. The questions they have will seem nonstop: Where do I fit? Why does Billy do wrong? Why doesn't Jane like me? Why can't I have a $150 pair of shoes? Why doesn't my body look more like other girls' bodies?

As you practice active listening and consistency in your own life, you will have the opportunities to nurture your child in almost every conceivable way developmentally—physically, emotionally, intellectually, and socially. Most fathers with a healthy and functioning heart for their children do admirably well instructing and guiding their children in most of these areas. However, one area is often neglected—spirituality.

Just as they are developing in their physical and intellectual lives, so they are developing in their spiritual lives. The question is not whether your children will develop spiritually; the question is how well or how poorly this aspect of their lives will be developed. Fathers in the stage of understanding seem to sense this. Young children begin to ask some pretty probing metaphysical questions. "Where do we come from?" "Who made the earth?" "Why isn't it right for me to take that toy?"

Our scientific answers might make sense to adults, but our kids aren't asking scientific questions. They've got a whiff of "mystery" in their nostrils and they want to know more about what's behind the smell.

Many parents return to churches as adults because of the concern for their children (see Father Fact #6). Most often, I believe this is by a parent's desire for his children. "I want my children in Sunday school. I want them to learn some values."

As a father, you don't need to be a theologian. But you do need to be a facilitator. That means knowing what you believe, living by a standard of truth, and assisting your child to do the same.

FATHER FACT #6
Great Questions

In the stage of understanding, the child will ask questions in almost every area of his life, including the metaphysical and the spiritual. Though most fathers are aware of their child's interest in the spiritual, they don't spend time dealing with this area. In a National Center for Fathering survey, we found men ranked "spiritual development" as the fathering area they were most dissatisfied with.[9] Nearly all of the men ranked themselves as either "very low" or "low" when asked to fill in the blank: "Compared with other fathers, my evaluation of my time spent with children in this area is _____"

I firmly believe that your child has a spirit. We all do. It's part of being human. That spirit is not like an ear for music or a mechanical aptitude your child may or may not possess and that you may or may not wish to encourage. Your child can no more decide whether to have a spiritual life than he can decide whether to be a human being.

Anecdotal evidence suggests that it is during the stage of

understanding that most men begin attending church again (if they have left in the first place). Among ministers in most Protestant denominations, it is common knowledge that this stage becomes the catalyst for many men to return to church with their families.

When she was just six, my daughter Sarah really caught me on this issue. During a family vacation, Sarah got a little ornery and pushed Hannah.

"Did you push your sister?" I asked later.

"No," she denied. Since this was becoming a growing pattern for Sarah, I decided to take a walk with her to get to the bottom of things.

"Sarah," I told her, "you know that I'm going to give you a spanking." I gave her the evidence of her lying. "I'm really disappointed with your behavior." I then asked her, "What do you need to do about it?"

I expected Sarah to tell me she needed to stop lying or apologize to her sister, but that wasn't what she said. She had tears in her eyes and she said, "I need to ask Jesus to come into my heart."

What? There I was, zeroing in on behavior modification, and my six-year-old daughter was dealing with bigger issues, the issues of needing forgiveness, cleansing, and internal spiritual change. I was focused on morality. She was focused on the spirituality that makes morality possible and sincere.

As a father, you don't need to be a theologian. But you do need to be a facilitator. That means knowing what you believe, living by a standard of truth, and assisting your child to do the same.

Preparing for the Teenage Years

As your children mature, they move closer to their teenage years—that period we have referred to as "the wall"—where great emotional, physical, and relational stresses occur in the father-child relationship. That is one of the reasons, I believe, it is so critical to build your relationship with your children now.

Let's compare our relationship with our children to a strand of twine. In its natural state, a single strand is very weak and vulnerable to breaking under stress. But what if you weave two strands together, or three or four? Then, the rope becomes strong and will hold up under a great number of stresses.

Consider your time spent with your children, during the time of understanding, as weaving together relational strands. You learn how to communicate, to listen, to respect one another. Then, when the stresses come during adolescence, which they surely will, you will have a relational rope, woven together with many strands of connections, that will be better able to deal with those inevitable tensions.

At this point, halfway through our tour of the six stages, you may want to pause and see where we've been and where we're headed. Take a look at the "Map to the Fathering Life Course" in appendix 2. It shows the changes during the stages for both father and child; it also outlines the differing goals the parent and child have. The needs of your child and yourself, so varied in stages one through three, will move in new directions during adolescence and beyond. Study the map, but don't let it overwhelm you. As you reach each stage, the previous stage should prepare you if you have been an active father. Now, let's move to the stage with the most change and challenge of all, the teen years.

Chapter Eleven

FOR FATHERS
OF TEENS:
ENLIGHTENMENT

Youth specialist Walt Mueller described a trip with junior high teens he once supervised. As the bus tooled down the road toward the campground, Walt observed an interesting phenomenon. The girls were all grouped in the front of the bus and the boys were in the back. Both groups were buzzing among themselves, occasionally stealing glances, occasionally sending messengers.

One young girl came and sat next to Walt. "Walt, you won't believe this, but . . . I'm going with Eddie," she said, referring to one of the boys in the back of the bus. Walt was surprised. From what he had seen, these two hadn't even been as close as four seats from one another, let alone talking to each other. Now, they were "going together." Ten minutes later, this same girl, with tears in her eyes, climbed back into the seat next to Walt. She told him the devastating news: She and Eddie had just broken up. Her world went from an ecstatic high and a deep connection with a boy to a devastating low and a broken relationship. In just ten minutes!

Such is life in the teenage world.

Fathering Ups and Downs

Fathers need to make a transition, even as they prepare their children for the transition to adolescence. But in a sense, the entire period is one long transition. That's why I've termed this stage of the father's life course *enlightenment*. This stage continues until his children leave home (typically at age eighteen). Enlightenment is the crucial stage when they learn about their identity, seek for necessary independence, and all the while, as not-yet-adults, need the support and guidance of their parents.

Though children experience major ups and downs during this period of change, so does the father. Some of the things that go up for dad: food bills, auto insurance premiums, the stereo volume, and anxiety and frustration levels. Some of the things that go down: free access to the bathroom and the mirror and the telephone, the number of victories in one-on-one basketball, and the gas gauge on the car. Of course, it is not just surface issues that change. Typically relationships between father and child become strained. Statistics show that a father during the stage of enlightenment will typically experience his lowest levels of satisfaction.[1]

During the stage of enlightenment, like the man well into a marathon run, a father often hits "the wall." Gone is the adrenaline and enthusiasm of the attachment/idealism stages, exhausted is the steady pace of the understanding period, and what overtakes a father is often pain. During the enlightenment stage, the heart of a father often gives out. The work just seems too grueling, too frustrating, too unrewarding. He faces rebellion, misunderstanding, and even apathy from his teenage child. Some fathers, while they may still be in the home, just quit. Others will persevere, most of whom will find their "second wind" and a new joy in fathering.

Radical Changes

As in the attachment/idealism stages, the period of enlightenment is filled with rapid change. In each of these stages, there are dramatic and often overwhelming transitions. But, there is one overriding difference in the stage of enlightenment: This time the child is not simply moving into another stage of childhood, but becoming an entirely different creature, an adult.

"[Adolescence] is a time of transition for both the child and the parent. The child has to learn to handle changing roles, moods, and body. You as parents have to learn to handle the changing child," according to education professor Cliff Schimmels.[2]

Relational Changes

From a father's perspective, the changes seem to often work in reverse from those in the attachment/idealism stages. In those early years, the child is moving *toward* relationship; in the enlightenment stage, the child seems to be moving *away* from relationship, at least with his parents.

Remember the feeling that you had when you bought your boy a baseball glove and ball, even before he could walk? You longed for the time when you could relate, when you could meaningfully enter into your child's world. Then, during the stage of understanding, you were finally able to engage this boy—body, soul, intellect, emotions, and will. Now, as a teenager, your son often barely acknowledges your presence, and certainly not when his friends are around.

At one point, I had children in both the idealism and enlightenment stages. To say the least, they related to me differently. When I'd come home after a day at work, the first sound I heard was the squeal of delight from my three-year-old daughter, Rachel. "Daddy! Daddy!" she'd scream. Boy, did I feel like a king! She'd race over and bury her face between my kneecaps. I'd reach down and lift her up and plant a wet kiss on her cheek.

Hannah, an adolescent at the time, would usually be out. Or, if she was home, she might be sitting on the couch, her face lowered into a Nancy Drew novel. I'd peel Rachel off my face long enough to say hi to Hannah. She'd lift her head from the novel for a second: "Oh hi, Dad," she'd say, then turn back to her reading. I learned not to expect her to come bouncing into my arms.

Physical Changes

As your child makes the transformation into an adult, hardly anything will remain the same. Puberty, which usually starts between the ages of eleven and fourteen, releases an onslaught of hormones that induce, among other things, mood swings and acne.

These physical changes are often bewildering, even frightening: "When will it end? . . . What will I look like? . . . Am I normal?" Media images of beauty, plus the wide variation in puberty's pace, leave most kids doubting their development. "My breasts are too small," bemoans Jenny. "My body isn't developing right," laments Elizabeth. Pete is obsessed with every pimple and goes into long complaints as each one appears. During P.E. class Dan doesn't say anything, but inside he's deeply affected by teasing in the locker room.

FATHER FACT #7
Changes, Changes

During stage four, enlightenment, major changes are occurring for both adolescents and their fathers. At the same time, though, adolescents and their dads are asking similar questions, and this provides a common ground where the two generations can meet and discuss disagreements.

According to Daniel Levinson, most men at midlife are asking these questions: (1) "What have I done with my life?" (2) "What do I really get from and give to my wife, children, friends, work, community, and self?" and (3) "What is it I truly want for myself and others?"

According to Walt Mueller, most teens are asking these questions: (1) "Who am I?" (What makes me different from all others?) (2) "Who are my friends?" (Where do I fit in?) and (3) "Where am I going?" (What does my future look like?).

Intellectual and Social Changes

Intellectually, your teenager is developing the capacity to think abstractly and logically (though you may wonder whether logic has anything to do with how your adolescent thinks). He can now hold his own in an argument. Earlier you may have been able to get away with saying, "Because I told you so," but no longer. Your teenager wants to know "why?" and will be able to tell you "why not." Not all arguments are conflicts, just like not all running races are competitions; sometimes it's just exercise. Teenagers are exercising their intellectual muscles.

Socially, adolescents typically switch their focus from family to peers. The talks he used to have with you he now has with his buddies. The things she used to do with you she now wants to do with her friends. They become busy and preoccupied. There are places to go: the mall, practice, homecoming committee. People to see: friends, friends, friends. Home, in one sense, becomes a way station, a place to load up on food and crash at night.

Although their lives may appear, in the rush of constant movement, to be superficial, they are not. Life is more than the mall or the baseball diamond. Spiritually, adolescence can involve a period of deep searching. Walt Mueller, author of *Understanding Today's Youth Culture,* claims that there are three great questions that a teenager is trying to answer: (1) "Who am I?" (What makes me different from all others?) (2) "Who are my friends?" (Where do I fit in?) and (3) "Where am I going?" (What does my future look like?).[3]

A Changing Father

A father, too, is often rapidly changing during this stage of his life. He may, in fact, be asking (or re-asking) many of the same questions as his teenager. A man during the stage of enlightenment is typically between the ages of thirty-three and forty-eight. According to Levinson, he is still engaged in the task of establishing a niche in life (stability) while still working for advancement (instability). During some portion of enlightenment, he will face what Levinson calls "Midlife Transition," but what most of us know as a midlife crisis; when a man searches out his identity and purpose. While some men make midlife corrections seemingly without effort, Levinson says, "For the great majority of men this is a period of great struggle within the self and with the external world. . . . They question nearly every aspect of their lives and feel that they cannot go on as before."[4]

Men need to recognize these transition times as opportunities during their fathering. Amazingly, this midlife transition can bring together a dad and his child on similar issues they're facing in their life course. The three questions fathers most frequently ask are nearly identical in nature to those that teenagers ask: (1) "What have I done with my life?" (2) "What do I really get from and give to my wife, children, friends, work, community, and to myself?" and (3) "What is it I truly want for myself and others?"

Such questions provide the possibility of connection between a father and his teenagers. Adolescence does not have to be a period that fathers simply "survive." It can be a process of mutual learning. As our children ask their three great questions of adolescence, they long for a father's input, and, as fathers, we are equipped to empathize because we're asking some very similar questions. Adolescence can be a journey that a father and his son or daughter walk together, even through some very rough terrain.

There can also be disconnection. The stage of enlightenment is fraught with seeds of conflict. The serious nature of the questions that both adolescents and adults ask during this period can lead to self-absorption. The energy to deal with such overwhelming change—both within yourself and your child—often does not seem to be there. The tendency is to withdraw.

A Different Relationship

The changes occurring in father and adolescent will result in a new relationship. During the stage of enlightenment, the familiar patterns of relating to one another, which were established (and often taken for granted) during the understanding stage, will undergo transformation.

Less Talk

One of the chief laments of both adolescent and father during this period is, "We never talk anymore." There are several factors that contribute to fewer and shorter conversations with your teenage son or daughter. First, adult and child are likely to be busy. During this stage, a father is likely to spend more time at work. As a father, your earning power is beginning to peak, and you are now in a position to accomplish more. And, if you aren't careful, you may also use your career as an escape from the difficulty of fathering during the enlightenment stage. The adolescent, as we have seen, is also busy. He has his own schedule, his own activities, his own friends, and, often, his own car.

FATHER FACT #8
Awareness of a Child's Needs

A potential blind spot for dads is awareness—understanding your children's needs as they change and mature. This blind spot surfaces in the data from the NCF/Gallup Poll "The Role of Fathers in America." Dads and moms have different perceptions of a father's awareness of his children. Dads were asked the questions as they are printed here, while moms were asked to respond based on their knowledge of the father of their children.

You have a good handle on how your child's needs change as he or she grows up.

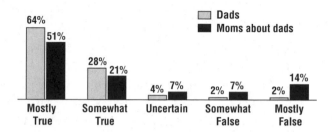

You know what your child needs to grow into a mature, responsible person.

	Dads	Moms about Dads
Mostly true	71%	59%
Somewhat true	21%	16%
Uncertain	7%	6%
Somewhat false	1%	7%
Mostly false	—	12%

Consistently, wives see their husbands as understanding less about the children's needs than their husbands believe. This contrast can be shown in other areas too. For instance, when dads with children over 18 read the statement "Your child and you often do things together," 71 percent answered "mostly true"; when the moms answer the same question about their husbands, the percentage drops to 55 percent.

Less Intimacy

As Hannah demonstrated, the teenage daughter (or son) is less intimate physically than when she was a little child. She will not naturally come for hugs or kisses. Some adolescent sons and daughters may entirely reject a clasp on the shoulder or a tousle of their hair (and some will secretly *want* it). They will be around less frequently and may seem more emotionally withdrawn.

More Independence

There will also be a distancing in the relationship in other ways. Enlightenment is a stage where teenagers naturally "test" everything they have been taught. Fathers who have dedicated themselves to instilling good moral and spiritual values may find, to their dismay, that their children have begun to question what they believe. It's easy for a parent to overreact: "Oh no, my rebellious kid is abandoning his upbringing. He's rejecting my values." He may. Giving them some space is a risk; but it's a risk that parents of even the healthiest teenagers must take. No matter what your child chooses to do, the most important thing is your relationship to him or her. So ask yourself, what is more important, my relationship to my children, or my reputation?

Teenagers are asserting their independence in thought and belief. They are also asserting their independence socially. When your children were little, they thought you were God. You knew everything. You were always right. And they always wanted to be with you. Have you ever had to peel a bawling kid off your leg to leave him at the day-care center? In adolescence, however, you've been dethroned. Many fathers go from "knowing everything" to "not having a clue." You've been displaced. Your child's peer group exerts much more influence.

A distancing occurs, which to a degree is natural and inevitable. But even the most healthy distancing removes one of the primary satisfactions that a man experiences as a dad: intimacy. Perhaps you enjoyed doing things with your son, but now he sits up in his room behind a closed door for a couple of weeks at a time. Perhaps you liked hanging out with your daughter, but now she gets embarrassed if you show up at the mall together.

Of course, such changes are unsettling. But realizing that they are normal can help your reaction to be more understanding.

Alienation and Control

I have a friend who is the pastor of a large church in the South. Martin has three children, and we have conducted fathering conferences together. I consider him quite knowledgeable on what makes an effective father. In fact,

I've watched him go through the stages of attachment, idealism, and under-standing with good success. The stage of enlightenment, however, threw him.

Martin's firstborn, Daniel, had always been a fairly compliant boy, but when he got into high school, he decided that he wanted to experiment with drugs and sex. Daniel wasn't afraid to be open about his exploits, especially among the peers whose acceptance he was courting. It wasn't long before many of the people in Martin's church began to express concern.

Martin's fathering world was turned upside down. Consider the new issues that he is facing. His beloved son is:

- Succumbing to new temptation and practicing very dangerous behavior;
- apparently rejecting his family's values;
- publicly embarrassing his father;
- calling into question the integrity of his father's occupation. How can a minister preach against what his own son is practicing?

At first, Martin reacted to his son's behavior by attempting to change it. He used many of the fathering principles from the understanding stage to try to "fix" his son. In a way he believed to be constructive, he began pointing out Daniel's problems to his son. He would then give his advice on why and how his son's behavior should be changed. Martin, in fact, was doing what he knew worked on the job: Each Sunday as a pastor, he could step into the pulpit and sway the moral decisions of hundreds with his words.

But Martin's push for control was counterproductive. Daniel com-plained that his father was always criticizing him and trying to force him into a mold. He reacted by involving himself in more destructive and rebel-lious behavior. In a last-ditch effort to maintain control over his son, Martin threatened to send him to military school. That threat, too, backfired.

Issues of Control

Martin is now attempting to come to grips with what he can do that will best help his son. Painfully, after many well-intentioned errors, he has become "enlightened" about a fundamental paradox: A father holds close, but he also lets go. Even the best of parents are forced to realize that a child's transformation into an adult is risky business.

Given the danger that a child faces as she changes into an adult, it is only natural that a father would want to control circumstances. However, it is during enlightenment that we will see, often painfully, the reality of the truth that we cannot "run" our children; they run themselves. What we as fathers do is build a safe, secure, and affirming home around our children in which they make the transition into adults in good health. If our kids want to bang their heads against the walls, that is their choice, but we fathers will build soft, resilient walls. If our kids want to take a pickax to the basement floor, that's their choice, but we will build a solid, reinforced foundation for them.

In other words, we must always focus on those things that are under our control as fathers, not on things that are beyond our control. This is especially true during enlightenment, which paradoxically is often when our children seem to be most out of control. We can try to exert control over them, or we can choose to do what works—namely, focus on controlling ourselves.

Our Reaction: Self-Control

Self-control is rooted in a sense of recognition. During the stage of enlightenment, a father must come to grips with this startling fact: Things will never be the same. His child is turning into an adult. Armed with a knowledge that change is inevitable and necessary, a father will be less likely to view changes in his teenager as personal attacks. The emotional swings will be part of the overall picture, not a personal affront.

It will not come as a surprise that one day your son will talk to you for two hours straight and then, for no apparent reason, disappear into his room for six straight days. Or, when your daughter tells you about her junior high school trip where she started dating Eddie one minute and, ten minutes later, broke up with him. When she starts to cry on your shoulder and you want to say, "Don't be so silly," you don't. Instead you realize that change, even highly irrational change, is to be expected.

You cannot control the changes taking place in your adolescent, but you can control your reactions and actions. You have a choice in how you relate to your child/adult. You could choose to stick to the "tried-and-true" parenting strategies that served you well during earlier stages but that are destined to fail during enlightenment—or you can relate to your children in new and appropriate ways.

Ask yourself how you treat your adolescent son or daughter. Do you seek to squelch all signs of independence, damaging your child's transition into adulthood, or do you encourage and facilitate the change by relating in new ways?

This is obviously an awkward and difficult transition. It involves treating your adolescent progressively like an equal.

Same Functions, New Approaches

In order to facilitate a child's transformation into an adult, a father must rethink and redevelop his fathering strategies. Your child's need for the "I CANs" will not change, but they will assume new faces. Consistency, for example, takes on a critical role during the enlightenment stage. Your children need you to model—not so much lecture on—ethics, morality, and faith. Although your children may seem to be outwardly rejecting your value system, you can be sure they are actively and inwardly processing your behavior. Consistent actions—those that square with your declared beliefs—will count greatly in their eyes.

Involvement

Such modeling means staying involved. And unfortunately, time for a father and adolescent relationship seems to be in short supply. Fathers need to develop new strategies for spending time with their teenagers. In one research study, adolescents were asked the following question: "What would you like to do with your dad?" For sons, the top three answers were joint recreation, working together, and going places. The daughters listed going places, talking together, and performing an activity (like going to a movie or hunting down an item at a store).[5] The top three were almost identical for both sexes.

Fathers need to take the initiative: "Hey, let's make plans to go to the races, or work together on your car, or go golfing." The opportunities for involvement might be more limited than before, so it becomes especially important to schedule in significant events—and your child is the one who should determine which activities are indeed significant, whether they're specific school functions, birthdays, or whatever.

Listening

Spending time together provides an opportunity for communicating—but it doesn't mean real communication will happen just because you're together. In the study mentioned above, researchers also asked teens, "When you talk with your dads, what do you talk about?" Sons listed school performance, politics, and sports. Daughters most often mentioned school performance and politics. These are hardly the meaty issues that teens have on their minds. Only 4 percent of sons and 1 percent of the daughters surveyed could agree with the statement "My father and I always talk openly with each other."[6]

Why don't dads talk openly? Has "the wall" made them take leave from the fathering marathon?

Part of the reluctance is that talking is hard work. Teens can ask deep questions. And in answering we may have to think through some of the struggles of our own adolescent years. Sometimes our reluctance to talk about real issues may come from fear of looking foolish or being humiliated in our child's eyes. But humble pie brings real intimacy, and that's what a marathoner needs to keep going.

Of course, communication is two-way. Often teens don't talk openly with dads. Why? I firmly believe that most adolescents don't talk to their fathers during the enlightenment stage because they don't believe their fathers really listen. Gwen was sixteen when she stopped talking to her father. Even though he made it a point to regularly and systematically talk to his daughter, Gwen sensed he wasn't really there. "My father always asked me questions," Gwen once told me, "because he knows he is supposed to ask questions. But when I looked him in the eye, I could tell that he wasn't listening to what I was telling him; he was thinking about his response."

We must listen for the sake of listening. This will be difficult. Teenagers often have wild ideas and questions. But you, as a loving father, must respect them. However crazy your son's or daughter's ideas may seem, behind almost every one of them is a search for identity, love, and purpose. Awareness must take the form of active listening. Maintain your self-control and listen to what your child is really saying. Nothing says you have to agree. Nothing says you aren't allowed to state your own opinion. And nothing says you shouldn't exercise your authority to set limits where limits need to be set. Doing so means you're fulfilling your role as a father. But don't throw off your adolescent's ideas with a "Don't be silly" or a "Because I said so." Seeking first to understand takes time and effort, but it is a sign of respect that our teenagers will respond to, even while they complain, "You treat me like a little kid."

Never forget the great question of adolescence: "Who am I?" Your teenager will have to answer that question for himself. What he wants to hear from you is, "Whoever you end up being, I'll still love you." Never forget the great fear of adolescence: "Am I normal?" The likely answer to that question is "Yes," but what the teenager wants to hear from his dad is, "Even if you were abnormal, I'd still love you."

Perhaps no period of a person's life is marked by more self-doubt and self-consciousness than adolescence. Our children need to ask their questions in an atmosphere of security.

Active listening is not just an awareness activity; it also is a form of nurturance. Child psychiatrist Ross Campbell draws the link between nurturance and active listening, which he calls focused attention:

> Focused attention is giving a child our full, undivided attention in such a way that he feels without doubt that he is completely loved. That he is valuable enough *in his own right* to warrant parents' undistracted watchfulness, appreciation, and uncompromising regard.[7]

Remember, the father who is an active listener fights off the urge to lecture. Ludicrous, false, and blatantly selfish statements—it is likely you will hear them all at one time or another from your teen, and it will be tempting to jump in with a pontificating lecture. But if your child has lived in your home for sixteen-odd years, it is likely she already knows what you will say. If you simply provide an empathetic sounding board, you may be surprised how easily she reaches your conclusions too. A father's wise lecture fulfills an important fathering role, but the dad who listens first will find that his words bear more fruit. Listening conveys—and earns—respect.

Devoting yourself to the task of active listening can help you both survive and thrive during enlightenment. Our research showed that the trait most associated with fathering satisfaction during this stage is verbal inter-action.[8] My friend Martin is learning it, and that gives me additional confidence he will see his son, Daniel, through a turbulent adolescence and continue into a loving future relationship.

Sex, Vocation, and Rearing Children

Don't control your children. Learn how to relate in new ways. Model —not just lecture about—your morality. Listen actively. You may concur that all those recommendations are noble and good, yet wonder how they can work in the real world. Does *anything* work with adolescents?

To answer that legitimate question, I want to examine two critical areas of particular importance to the adolescent—sex and vocation. It is not an accident that these two issues are vital during this stage. Sexual behavior— an ultimate expression of human relationship—deals with the questions "Who am I?" and "Who loves me?" Vocation becomes the search for an answer to the question "What am I going to do?" These questions cause our adolescents great struggle because the questions represent new, and often overpowering, concerns.

About Sex

When it comes to sex, your teenager searches for sexual mentors to answer his questions. What is good? What is right? What is normal? They'll pick up clues from friends. They may watch MTV and take subconscious notes. The latest teen diva or hot music performer may have some influence too. And, we hope, they will turn to you, because you are still the most influential man in their lives. The viewpoint your children adopt is outside your control. Having a view, however, and living consistently according to it is within your control. What do you want your teenager's sexual life to look like?

One of parents' biggest concerns about their teens' sexuality is their health. Many daughters find themselves pregnant and unsure what to do or whom to turn to. The Centers for Disease Control and Prevention estimates that over 9 million new STD infections occur each year among young people ages 15 to 24.[9] We do not want our children to have to face difficult consequences from the wrong decisions about sex. Discussion of these issues is certainly appropriate; in fact, it's imperative. But many fathers never get as far as talking about sex with their children.

But most fathers agree safe sex and pregnancy prevention are not the only issues they care about when it comes to their teens' sex lives. Fathers want them to have a healthy view of sexuality.

You may remember the episode of *The Cosby Show* where Denise, the college-age daughter, had just returned from Africa. To everyone's surprise, she had come back as the wife of a naval officer, Martin. At one point Bill Cosby, as her father Heathcliff Huxtable, escorts his new son-in-law into the kitchen for a chat. "I just want to know," he asks the young man, "before you got married, did you and Denise . . . you know . . ."

Martin laughs nervously. He admits that he did try, but that Denise would "have none of that." Huxtable smiles his broad smile, drawing his son-in-law out. "Yeah yeah. Go on."

"Let me put it this way," Martin says. "On our wedding night, only one of us had experience, and as you know, I'm the one with the daughter" (referring to Olivia, his little girl from a previous marriage).

"Yes!" Huxtable exclaims and then jumps up to do his little shuffle of delight.

The writers of one of the most popular sitcoms in television history gave honest expression to something men really feel. In this age of sexual freedom, most men I know, if they could have their heart-of-heart's desire, would still prefer that their children wait until marriage before becoming sexually active.

The great sexual-development need for teens is not to have sex but to learn about sex—to understand their budding sexuality and to incorporate it into their life experience. We fathers can and should lead our children into an understanding of sexuality in healthy, creative ways. Discussion, role modeling, and even an occasional lecture that outlines our morality can help our teens channel sexual desire into the proper paths of expression.

We must also listen to our children. Often, a child who allows herself to be in a sexual relationship is not looking for sex at all, but to fulfill deep, unmet needs for love, touch, and connection. As fathers, we should listen to our children, and then dive below their words to find out what is in their hearts. Our children may reveal to us if they are vulnerable sexually. We must be involved and aware.

But our goal should not be just to prevent our children from having sex, but to educate them as to its real purpose—the ultimate and exclusive expression of love in a marital relationship. This cannot be taught by our words alone. For children to develop a healthy view of the wonderful and powerful nature of sex, they must see their father and mother in a loving, affirming relationship, which allows them to place sex in its proper context. This is a function of consistency.

A father must also prioritize intimacy with his children. He must nurture them. For it is intimacy—the tender and loving heart-to-heart connection —that is the foundation of our longings for sex. Recently I talked with a nineteen-year-old woman who had become involved in a tangled, unhealthy relationship with her boyfriend. As I questioned her, she told me about her relationships with her father and stepfather. Her dad was faithful in paying child support and visiting her according to the custody arrangements. He fulfilled his "responsibilities" like clockwork, but he was deaf and mute when it came to communicating his feelings about her. As a consequence, Wendy has always questioned her inner beauty and sense of worth.

Her stepfather, on the other hand, had no trouble expressing his feelings. He constantly berated Wendy. Ever since he married Wendy's mom, her new weekday dad ripped into her about her weight, her attitudes, and her feelings with words that are not suitable to print. She described her feelings about him in outbursts of sadness and anger. Her relationship with her boyfriend, it was clear, was a misguided attempt to meet her needs for intimacy and acceptance.

In educating our children on any moral issue, we must always be careful to respect them. We need to be honest. Transparency, in itself, teaches our teens. They want to know, "Is it normal to have struggles?" By admitting your own struggles, you can assure them, "Yes, it is."

About Vocation

In the turmoil of emotions, hormones, and ideas, a child/adult longs to find a direction in life. She wants to find a career. Here, too, a father can play a valuable role. Not so much in dictating to his teen his own desires, but in helping her discover and develop her own unique gifts and passions.

Traditionally, financial provision has been one of the ways a father helps his young adult into college or the job market. He will help with tuition or put a down payment on a house. But the issues are more than financial. A father who is interested in facilitating his children's transition into the real world will help them find the answers to the following questions: "What am I good at? . . . What do I like doing? . . . What comes most naturally to me?"

Perhaps they have sales savvy, or design skills, or even political abilities. Your primary task is to identify skills and aptitudes at this point; matching them up to colleges and careers is secondary. This means you're aware and involved in your teenager's life. You need to talk with him about what classes he likes and doesn't like, and why or why not. You can also discuss his skills and interests with teachers, guidance counselors, and coaches. Your student may want to take advantage of some of the school's assessment tools—aptitude, personality, and career assessment tests. After the tests, make it a point to discuss the results: "Do you think this is accurate? . . . Have you ever thought you might possess this skill?"

Again, you will need to listen actively, especially in day-to-day conversations. You might begin a discussion by simply asking, "Why do you like to do this?" If he says, "I don't know, I just like it," you can explore it further with him by listing some possibilities. You can brainstorm together.

Volunteering and community service can provide youth with opportunities to identify interests and to see beyond their immediate day-to-day worlds. Helping others often gives teens better "big picture" perspectives. A long-term study of teens involved in community service found that they had a 32 percent lower rate of receiving Fs, a 37 percent lower rate of school suspension, a 43 percent lower rate of pregnancy, and a 75 percent lower rate of school dropout, compared to the control group.[10]

Whether your teen is volunteering or beginning her first job, monitor her experience and help to make it a positive experience. Before an interview, you can coach her and relieve some of the fear. You can make sure she knows you're supporting her on the first day on the job, and thus nurture her confidence. Keep the focus on a character quality or the skill, not on the job (which might be selling shoes or grilling burgers): "Honey, you really seem to have good people skills. You know how to make your customers' feet comfortable"; or "Son, I appreciate how hard you work. Your boss told me you keep going strong right up to quitting time."

After beginning a first job, teens often begin thinking more about a specific career. You can help here too. Arrange an interview with someone who is doing what your teen has shown an interest in. If she has a gift and passion for helping others, for example, arrange to have her spend time with a nurse. If your son is mechanically gifted and likes to draw, ask him if he would like to spend some time with a draftsman or engineer.

But there is one thing you should never do—force your own choice of career on your son or daughter. Do not try to use your son or daughter to fulfill your own plans or dreams, or to derive personal satisfaction. As fathers, we must assist our children in finding their own career niche—one that fits their unique gifts and interests—so they can feel fulfilled in *whatever* they choose to do.

Running Through the Wall

No one is trying to kid you. Fathering in the stage of enlightenment is difficult, often painful work. But, perhaps in ways like no other, your teenager needs you during this period. The transition from child to adult is traumatic. Even if teens won't admit it, they desperately could use your help.

Like a man hitting "the wall" in a marathon, it is easy to give up. The pain is just too much. Many simply stop fathering and pull away from their children. In the study quoted earlier in this chapter, adolescents were also asked, "How do you feel when you are with your father?" The daughters said distant, uncomfortable, or withdrawn. Only 1 percent said they are most likely to feel playful, open, or accepted. The sons in the survey said they are most likely to feel withdrawn, insensitive, careful, serious, uncomfortable, criticized, unwanted, or distant.[11]

As fathers, we must run through "the wall." We must remind ourselves of the motivation for our fathering—unconditional love. You express that love by being willing to keep running, to simply do your duty. It is only then, as the heart of a father pounds against the overwhelming stresses, that we will continue. And, in our second wind, we will once again catch the cooling breeze of loving, connected relationships.

Chapter Twelve

FOR FATHERS OF YOUNG ADULTS: REFLECTION

You have two suitcases under your arm, and you're struggling up
the final flight of stairs in your daughter's new dormitory. She's
already negotiated with her roommate for the bottom bunk. You hear
"music" blaring from an open door down the hallway. As you walk onto the
lawn to leave, an errant Frisbee almost beans you. This will be home until
Thanksgiving break—a long three months away—for the girl who used to
sleep under your roof.

Or maybe you're under the sink in your son's new apartment. He's got
a new job and a new apartment. It's an old place, but the rent is cheap; and
besides, too modern a pad would clash with his menagerie of ragtag garage-
sale couches, chairs, and end tables. Now, after two months at the place, he
reports that the sink has been backing up. The landlord's out of town, but
your son figures you'll know how to replace a trap. He gives you a call and,
of course, you stop by.

Letting Go

Welcome to the postadolescent years, the stage of Reflection. You walk these young adult kids out to their cars. They climb in and roll down the window, and you say a few more good-byes. Then you see them back the car out of the driveway then toss you a wave, and you stand there and watch for a second as they take a corner and are lost to view. Oh, they'll be back. But for now, you turn and wrap one arm around your wife's waist and walk back into a house that is suddenly quieter than you ever wanted it to be.

When your adult children leave home, you, too, in a sense are launched into a new stage of life. Although this stage is filled with critical fathering tasks, this initial phase of our children leaving home often feels like death. Letting go is painful.

An Emotional Change

When our children move out, it strikes a deadening note of finality. Even the language we use to describe this event—"let our children go" and "cut the umbilical cord"—whispers of deep, irretrievable separation. In actuality, it is just another transition in the fathering life course. But it is, at first, a very emotional change.

The fifth stage of reflection, which lasts from the time our children leave home to the birth of the first grandchild, is true to its name: It is marked (especially at first) by inward reflection. A father reflects on the past, his eighteen or so years with his child. His memory is keen. He'll be putting on a tie in the mirror and remember the Father's Day when his young son "borrowed" money to buy him that very tie. He'll be fishing at the lake, and in the moment of casting, he'll be flooded with a memory of how he used to take his daughter out in this boat and put the worms on the hook for her.

Too, he may be thinking about past mistakes, whether perceived or real. He may regret never having taken that big family vacation or having told his son he loved him. He may also be anxious: "Will my child choose to live according to the standards I've tried to instill?" These are powerful emotions.

Your Child's Emotions

Your young adult will also be processing these emotions, some of them about how he thinks you are as a father. In college, he lives with others who are also sons—but not his brothers. He will hear a lot about other fathers. This may be good or bad news for you.

Some young adults will come back and say, "You know, Dad, my room-mate tells some horrible stories about what it was like growing up in her home, and it really makes me realize how grateful I am for our relation-ship." Others will express less positive emotions.

Your son or daughter may come to feel that, in one aspect or another, you have failed as a father. You need to let them express those feelings, even if it results in some pain or regret for you. In fact, your sympathetic listen-ing ear at such moments can serve to redeem those memories for your child. Hold off the temptation to say, "Why don't we just leave that in the past?" or "Why don't you grow up and leave that behind you?"

Steve had an important lunch appointment. He had traveled several hundred miles to be at this landmark event. He was exhausted and more than a little nervous. But his meeting wasn't scheduled so he could cut a new deal with some corporate exec. It was to start a new relationship. His luncheon partner was his daughter.

Michelle had left home for college two years earlier. She came home for Christmas and spring break, and also during the summer, but Steve never really felt like he got to sit down and talk with her. Michelle was nervous too. Her friends kidded her about being in the "major of the month" club. She just couldn't seem to find the educational track appropri-ate for her. Each false start seemed to indicate one additional semester tacked on to the end of her college career. And college costs money. But Michelle had a dad who, in some sense, awakened as a father during the stage of reflection. He chose to be proactive. He arranged to visit with Michelle and to take her to lunch.

There Steve spoke these words: "Michelle, I've been thinking about you a lot lately, and I want you to know that though you've been having a tough time finding your niche the past two years, your mother and I are still 100 percent behind you."

"Thanks, Dad." She stared out the window. Finally, Steve said it. It took him three repetitions of her name to finally get it out: "Michelle, I . . . want you to know that I love you."

In the stage of reflection, we come face-to-face with the realization that our children need to reconcile with us about some issues. Steve had an immediate occasion to put action behind his words of love. Michelle needed to talk. He found out from her just how highly controlling he had been as a father. He was a strict disciplinarian who made his daughter's heart "just cold, just really cold" toward him.

Michelle began to find healing. Steve's willingness to discuss his influence on her life—and admit his shortcomings—allowed her the freedom to confront her emotions. She continues to work through feelings of resentment toward men, cynicism toward authority, and a compulsion to try to impress her dad. Steve did not allow his emotions to dictate the moment when his daughter described to him her "cold heart." By refusing to act defensively, he opened up the possibility of a new relationship with his daughter.

A Time for Dialogue

Emotions will flare up during this stage—both the child's and the parents' (or parent's). How, for example, do you react when your adult child disagrees openly with your morals or opinions? If you're like many fathers, you'll feel the need—no, make that *duty*—to set your son or daughter straight. Don't.

Remember that the young adult has to question at least some of the premises on which you've built your life—it's part of the independence he or she is establishing. You may have taught him to be a loyal Republican, but after the most recent election, he went out of his way to tell you why he voted mostly for Democrats. Or maybe your daughter comes home wearing a ragged T-shirt and a pair of torn blue jeans. She announces she's joining the Peace Corps. You applaud her altruism, but inside you wonder why she has to look so sloppy.

This is a time when your adult children are making decisions that will affect the rest of their lives, and it's difficult to stand back and watch them go down a path that you don't think is best for them. If handled correctly, disagreements don't have to be disagreeable. The stage of reflection is a time for dialogue, not monologue. Remember, two adults—not an adult and child—are having a discussion. Jim Conway, who wrote one of the earliest books about men in midlife crisis, claims, "If a man is going to resolve the tension with his young-adult offspring, he must learn what they face, how they think, and come to love and respect them."[1] When we engage our adult children, we need to engage them as independent thinkers. Such dialogue begins with respect.

But, I can hear you object, "What if my daughter is engaging in destructive thinking or behavior? Don't I have a duty to protect her?" My answer is simple, and not meant to be glib: "No." You need to let her go. You cannot rescue her and, if you try, you will likely push her further into the behavior that you are trying to prevent. She is an adult, able and even required to make decisions. She may come to you for advice; be there, ready to listen. She may not come to you.

What I always suggest is to look five or ten years down the road. Your child may be facing any number of challenges—huge or small. In any case, you want to have a strong relationship, and you could be jeopardizing that by laying guilt trips or trying to impose your viewpoint. Sure, the stakes are high. All young adults make mistakes—sometimes big ones. It's a given, and we can't insulate our children from pain. While the consequences could be difficult, the future of your relationship is on the line. It's the dad's job to build the kind of relationship where his son or daughter will want to come back for more discussions about important decisions. If irreconcilable differences develop, proceed with your own life based on your own values. Repeated conflicts aren't healthy for anyone. All you can do is try to keep up the relationship.

A Return

Children's departures from the home inevitably cause certain emotions to arise. We need to process those emotions in a healthy manner, not only so we connect in new ways with our children, but also because our fathering skills still need to be in peak condition. Paradoxically, when a child leaves home, in more sense than one, he returns to his father. Need is often the driving force.

In the move from child to adult, the rules also change. But the problem is that adult society doesn't come with a rule book. Young adults often feel abandoned in a strange new world, as they move from an "age-graded" society in which school and age gave certain privileges and duties, to a social-status society that assigns prestige and power "not so much on age as on skill and strength and wisdom and family connections."[2]

As the young adult comes to realize that his peers (an age-graded concept) can help much less in such a world, he may want to turn to you, his father. Robert Havinghurst of the University of Chicago lists eight developmental tasks that your early adult child faces: selecting a mate, learning to live with a marriage partner, starting a family, rearing children, managing a home, getting started in an occupation, taking on civic responsibilities, and finding a congenial social group.[3]

Before we begin to discuss how a father can assist in some of these critical areas, we need to first discuss a great obstacle that most fathers face during the last two stages of fatherhood: distance.

How to Shorten the Distance

The "I CANs" at the heart of a father all rest, in one way or another, on involvement. It is the environment, the oxygen, of all the other functions—consistency, awareness, and nurturance. And it doesn't take an Einstein to realize that, during the stages of reflection and generativity, our children no longer live with us. Patterns of involvement are suddenly broken: gathering around the supper table, hanging out on the back porch, watching a television program together. In fact, seeing one of your adult children now may mean buying a plane ticket and flying across the country. Obvious opportunities to do what we've normally done as fathers seem few and far between.

Involvement during the stage of reflection will require two great characteristics: initiative and creativity. Involvement rarely just happens; you have to make it happen. But there are some ways to remain involved, to cross the great barrier of distance. We'll start with this: write and call. That seems so obvious that it's hardly worth listing, but let me tell you: Fathers need to realize how powerful their letters and phone calls are. My friend Judd Swihart was telling me about a young woman he had been counseling as part of his practice. One day she came in for her session and Judd noticed immediately that something had changed about her. Her face radiated, her arms swung freely. This was a happy woman.

"Yesterday was my birthday, and guess what happened?" she asked.

Judd thought maybe her friends had thrown a party for her, or she had received a really luxurious gift.

"My dad called me!" she said, not even giving Judd a chance to answer. "He called to wish me a happy birthday. It absolutely made my week!" Our adult children not only need, but desire, to hear from their father.

Creativity is as important as initiative when it comes to bridging physical distance. I recently heard of one father whose work took him and his family overseas. His son spent most of his childhood growing up in a foreign culture, but when it came time to go to college, he applied and was accepted at an American university. The father knew this transition back into American culture—let alone into responsible adulthood—was going to be a difficult one, so he and his wife talked and made a decision. The father took a one-year sabbatical. The whole family moved back to the States and, in fact, rented an apartment in the very city where the son was going to college. The father took a menial job for the year. The son lived in the dorms, but he could always go out to the "folks' place" for an evening meal, to do his laundry, to spend the night, or just to talk.

This is an extreme example, but it does point out the rewards of being creative when trying to become more involved. Another father assisted during the purchase of his adult son's first car. The son asked for help in choosing a good, used vehicle, so the two of them combed the papers together for a couple weeks and visited used-car lots. Finally, the son decided on a Jeep CJ7 with 70,000 miles on it. In more ways than one, that Jeep has served to bring together father and son—drives in the country, mechanical repairs, and discussions about leaky hoses.

There are dozens of ways to get together with your older children. Invite your son on a weekend fishing trip. Call your daughter's dorm and ask her out for lunch, even if it occasionally requires a 2,000-mile flight. If you live far away, consider taking a vacation together. The distance can be subdued, if not conquered.

Distance will often give you a more objective perspective. When you are a father involved in the rearing of your children, it may be possible to lose sight of the "big picture." You see the kids day-in-and-day-out and may not have a sense of how they are changing over the weeks, months, and years. You also have your own ego invested in your children becoming responsible, productive, socially acceptable adults, so you may not be able to grant them the grace of failure. In addition, your schedule can leave little time to reflect on your family. Distance and time change all of this. They can help you see things in your adult child's relationships that you could not recognize before.

Track Your Adult Child's Development

The combination of involvement and perspective will lead a father into a healthy awareness of his children and grandchildren. By your thoughts and actions, you say, "You are still important to me. I've known you as a child. Now, I want to know you as an adult. I want to know how you are doing. I want to be ready without a second's delay to assist you when a crisis arises."

You will find yourself tracking your child's progress. Is she moving forward successfully into adulthood? Does she seem happy in her career? Is her job allowing her to use her special skills and interests? Does she have a clear and realistic picture of what she wants in a husband? Is this young married couple developing good patterns of communication? As you learn the answers, you will be able to give them advice, when asked, and may even become a mentor.

During the stage of reflection, a father's attention should be focused in three main areas: vocational establishment, marriage concerns, and financial assistance.

Vocational Establishment

Times are complicated. In 1890, the number of possible "Occupational Titles" was listed at 400. More than a century later, there are over 40,000 listed. Choosing—and getting established in—a career can be overwhelming. College has become not only a training ground but, with summer jobs and internships, a preliminary proving ground. "Is this what I really want to do with my life?" You need to be talking with your son or daughter about the desires of his or her heart, as well as his or her progress through school.

If you have business connections, you can also assist your adult children by providing contacts to help them get established in a job. Keeping a job will be their responsibility, but the process of getting one is certainly an area in which a father can legitimately offer his help.

Marriage Concerns

During the reflection stage your adult child probably will marry. Regarding marriage, the most obvious assistance is picking up the bill for the wedding. If your child is under thirty, he or she will probably need your financial help with wedding costs. In our part of the country, the bride's family pays for the ceremony and reception; the groom's family covers the rehearsal dinner.

But your assistance should start well before the wedding day. You need to be in active conversation with your son or daughter about the suitability of a marriage partner. In particular, you want to help him or her distinguish the difference between infatuation (based on immediate circumstances) and love (the commitment to remain together a lifetime). Your best work will be done long before your son or daughter brings home the potential spouse, sits on the couch across from you, and says, "We're getting married! Isn't that exciting! What do you think?"

Help your adult child think through what he or she wants in a marriage partner. "What qualities are you looking for in a potential spouse?" If your child has thought through these things ahead of time, then he will likely bring those criteria with him into marriage. Love is a choice, and choice means commitment. You encourage wise decisions to be made.

Financial Obligations

The most complicated area of assistance involves finances. A college student needs to pay her tuition. Do you help out? If so, how much? Your son needs to get his car fixed so he can get to work. Do you help out? If so, how much? There are other financial areas where you might be able to help: down payment on a car or home, last month's electric bill, a chance to go to graduate school in Rome, an engagement ring.

When we help our children financially, we should ask ourselves this question: Will this help them to more fully establish their independence? We should not always help simply because they ask, or because we assume it is our *duty*. For example, Dee and I are helping with our children's college tuition, but we aren't paying for all of it. First, we couldn't afford all of it, but second, it's important that our kids take ownership of their education. They need to have their wages invested in their schooling, so they'll also get a sense they have their future invested in it too.

When helping your adult child financially, you need to ask yourself other questions, as well: "Is my financial support shielding my child from the consequences of bad decisions he has made?" "Am I creating a dependence that would not allow her to make it on her own?"

It is possible, of course, to help too much. We can create children who are overly dependent upon us, who may even reappear in our homes and refuse to move out. When it comes to providing help to our adult children during the stage of reflection, a well-thought-through balance is critical.

The Virtue of Kindness

Simply defined, kindness is "love in action." We may also be familiar with its synonym "benevolence." Three characteristics of kindness reveal why it is such an essential virtue for the father of an adult child to cultivate:

First, kindness implies *generosity*. As I've mentioned, fathering an adult child involves a commitment of resources as you coparticipate in helping your child establish his or her own independence. In a tangible sense, this is a period where you might choose to use some of your savings to help pay for college, or vocational training, or a wedding. But there are other ways for a kind father to be generous—generous in praise, encouragement, affirmation, patience, advice, time, energy, etc.

Second, kindness implies *humility*. Humility reveals itself during this stage when you encounter the different life that your child is carving out for herself. You tell yourself, "She's an adult now. She's entitled to her own opinions."

There's another aspect of humility that we might call "condescension" —a term in disrepute, I'm afraid, in our time. In times past, a king was said to *condescend* when he would get down off his throne and walk out among the people. The king was admired for treating the peasants like equals; everyone considered it a demonstration of great kindness. In terms of fathering, this stage gives you the great privilege of stepping off your "throne" and treating your children like equals, like adults. You have embraced the fact that your fathering role is now one of *influence* instead of *authority*. It's an act of kindness.

Finally, kindness implies *service*. This is the love-in-action part. Sometimes this service comes in the form of rescue or help. Once or twice (or more) you will get *the call*. The phone rings and it's your son: "Dad, can you loan me fifty bucks? I'm overdrawn at the bank." Or maybe it's your daughter on the phone: "Dad, I ran out of gas. Could you come pick me up?" Of course, sometimes love in action means that you say "no" to your child's immediate request in favor of the greater kindness of helping to foster his or her independence.

Looking Forward

The fun is just about to begin. Your grandchildren are on the way. For many men, grandfathering is one of the most joy-filled roles they have ever had. Tossing a ball with a grandchild, going for a walk, reading a book, putting a puzzle together—these simple things put the bounce back in a man's step. What's behind that joy? Well, being a granddad is clearly different from being a father in many ways. But there's another dynamic, a switch that gets flipped when a man becomes a grandfather, and I think this can be an encouragement for dads who have adult children but no grandchildren yet.

Let's contrast these two stages of a dad's life. As I have described, Reflection is a time when dads look back on their kids' first eighteen or twenty years and evaluate what has happened. They ask: *What opportunities did I miss? What should I have done differently? Is it too late to make things better?* Simply the fact that the kids have moved out of the house can bring a sense of emptiness. And if a dad was too busy during his kids' early years, reflection can be a melancholy or even painful time. Even dads who were committed to their children will rethink their fathering careers—processing the good times and the not so good.

That's a big reason why being a grandfather is a magical time. Where a reflecting dad is focused largely on the past, grandchildren practically force him to look toward the future. Instead of focusing on what is ending, seeing the grandkids helps restore hope in what's ahead. Instead of dwelling on mistakes he may have made, now a granddad can start planning to leave a positive legacy for future generations.

So no matter how you did as a dad, I encourage you to think ahead: look forward to your new title someday, a wonderful new beginning— being a granddad.

FOR GRANDFATHERS: GENERATIVITY

The final stage of the fathering life course is Generativity. Your children now have children of their own. And no matter what your age or degree of preparation, those grandchildren are ready to hire you on for one more stint in one of the most important jobs in the world.

In the same way that my children benefit from father power over and above what I can supply, your grandkids will profit from the distinct advantages that you bring to their lives, which complement what your son or son-in-law can give them. Your work isn't done, granddad. It's just become more enjoyable.

Uniquely a Grandfather

Arthur Kornhaber, a child psychiatrist and researcher on grandparenting, comments, "There are three times when our lives are totally transformed by natural events without our having much to say about it: when we are born, when we die, and when we become grandparents."[1]

It is a role that a man swears he was made for. The dynamic of the relationship between the grandfather and grandchild is different from that between father and child, and it gives the older man some freedom he may never have experienced before. Kornhaber writes, "Since grandparents are not usually directly responsible for grandchildren, their egos are not as mixed up with them. Thus their affectionate bonds lack the conditionality of the parent-child love bond. Grandparents love grandchildren because they breathe."[2]

A Magical Bond

According to the Proverbs, "Children's children are the crown of old men."[3] Most grandfathers have reached the stage in life where they've done a lot of reflecting on their lives and what's most important. They may have regrets with their own children; they may look back on missed opportunities and misplaced priorities, and resolve to invest themselves fully in the lives of their grandchildren. They may have a strong desire to pass on the values and memories that make the family what it is. That sense of generativity is very motivating and energizing for a man, and it shows when he interacts with his grandkids.

I was the oldest grandchild on my father's side, and I always had an intuitive awareness that I brought a great sense of pride to my granddad. Here's how another grandfather, Leland Griffin, described an evening with his granddaughter:

> I returned home after another long day, anticipating a good meal and then a few hours of R&R. But when I opened the door, I noticed a pink coat, a small, glittery shoe, and then heard a shriek of delight as my granddaughter raced to greet me. Suddenly I was rejuvenated. After dinner, we set off on one of our adventures. We watched ants, talked to cats, played in the park and watched the sunset. I thought, "What better way to spend the end of this day—or any day?"

Who can explain what happens between a grandparent and grandchild? The grandfather sits down with his grandchild and tells stories no one has heard before. And it turns out he has an uncanny ability to draw faces with huge noses and bulging eyes that make the kids laugh whenever they look at them. The child starts asking to see that trick where Grandpa somehow pulls his thumb apart into two pieces, then puts it back together again. Others can try, but no one can do it quite like Grandpa.

Earlier, Grandpa complained that his back was acting up after he dragged thirty pounds of garbage out to the curbside. But now, when his six-year-old granddaughter arrives, he hoists her up for a hug without a second thought, without the slightest pain, almost effortlessly. Blake wants to go try to hook that big catfish in the creek, but he wants to wait until Grandpa can come, because only he knows where the "old monster" lives. How do you explain it? You don't. You just enjoy it.

Mystery. Amazement. Wonder. Grandfathers are magic. Their grand-children make them that way. As Kornhaber states, "This is what long life is for."[4]

Relating to Grandchildren

As a grandfather, you bring a wealth of wonderful resources for your children to enjoy. If you aren't there, they miss out. Studies reveal that adults who have had good relationships with their grandparents show a heightened self-esteem, a greater chance of success in later life, and a strong sense of family values.[5] What are the nuts and bolts of a relationship between a grandfather and his grandchild? At the risk of taking something magical, breaking it down, and robbing it of its charm, let's look at some practical ideas:

Make Time. Time is one of your secret weapons as a grandfather; it sets you apart from most of the other influences in your grandchild's life. My good friend Judd Swihart writes, "What a great experience it is for a grand-child to feast on time with someone who says, in essence, 'I have all the time you want. Help yourself to all you can use.'"[6] You can be a reminder that there are worthwhile pursuits that don't necessarily happen in a hurry: chess, reading, just sitting and talking, and much more of what happens in your day. Start regular activities together that will build memories through the years, like evening walks, breakfast out on Saturday mornings, or sit-ting on the porch swing and watching the sunset.

Little Things. Some of the best grandfathering comes in the cards and let-ters; a newspaper clipping that made you think of your grandchild; a poem; a small gift; little verbal affirmations along the way that communicate,

"You're special to me." Consistently recognize your grandchild for his good grades, or the ways she is showing her personal character. Reward her just for being the great kid that she is. Bring to life those features that make you the granddad that you are. Find the magic and mystery of a pocketknife or a pocket watch. Your hobby may be the key that unlocks a point of connection with your grandchild. My granddad was a car salesman who used his knowledge and his connections to help me fix up my first car—a 1964 Corvair.

Inspire and Motivate. One of the privileges that comes with the role of grandfather is being a wise and trusted counselor. You can be a consistent, long-term source of encouragement through all the changes that come with growing up. Your grandchild will have many teachers, coaches, and friends. There will be new challenges and risks around every corner. He will succeed in many ways, but he will also fail. He'll need comfort, and sometimes advice, and always someone to be positive and believe in him, no matter what.

Grandfather as a Living Library

There's a saying: "When an elderly person dies, a library burns down." Your grandchildren need a sense of family history. They need to hear your stories about what it was like growing up, about your grandparents, about what your sons and daughters (their parents) were like, about that old Chevy you used to drive, about the flood of '65, about canoeing the Boundary Waters, about "the good ol' days." Recall that prank that you pulled off with your brothers and sisters. Describe your house, your school, the baseball field where you hit your first home run, or the church you attended. What's the history of your last name? Share your ethnic or cultural heritage.

Pull out the photographs, yearbooks, awards, or other mementos. There are stories that go with all of them, and kids love to hear this kind of stuff. Here's how J. Allan Petersen, a pioneer in working with families, described it:

> I asked my 14-year-old grandson the other day, "What are grandparents supposed to do?" "Tell stories," he quickly replied. "What kind of stories?" I asked. "Old ones," he answered and began to recount a few I had told him earlier. He saw me as a bridge to another era, a more simple life before TV, computers and satellites.

Kids have a need to belong, to feel connected. When you tell stories about aunts and uncles, cousins and grandmas, you convey to them, "You are part of this family." Help them learn a skill that they can associate with you: whittling with a pocketknife, playing harmonica, driving a tractor, or calling cows. Introduce them to classical music; teach them dance steps from your youth, how to tie a bow tie, or magic tricks that always baffle family members.

A Transmitter of Values

The world in which your grandchild is growing up probably has different—or at least changing—definitions for concepts like commitment, sacrifice, faithfulness, self-discipline, respect, honesty, responsibility, work, faith, even love. Passing on values can be one of your grandest roles as a granddad.

Teaching Values. Often, when you are with your grandchild, she can relax a little more since there are no expectations from parents. She may listen better and ask you more thoughtful questions, like, "Grandpa, when Daddy was seven, was he like me?" "Did he have to clean up his plate?" Or maybe, "Why did Aunt Julie get a divorce?" She's trying to learn about her world, including school, her family, and relationships in general. With you, she may be more open to learn, and your simple yet wise perspective can help shape her young mind. Often, these opportunities can't be planned—they just happen. That's why it's good to spend lots of unstructured time with your grandchildren. Sometimes you're able to teach something without really even realizing it. Something happens, you take an action, answer a question, or explain something, and the child learns something new.

Modeling Values. Are your actions backing up the qualities you'd like to see in your grandchildren? If you want your grandchildren to appreciate a life of simplicity—and not the materialism you see in our culture—how does your life show it? Do you miss the days when a man's word really was his bond? What agreements or promises have you made to your grandchild, and how can you show her that it's important to keep them? If you believe in a strong sense of family, make that clear by your words and actions. Children are natural observers, and they can learn powerful, lasting lessons from watching a grandfather go through life with dignity, selflessness, and a childlike sense of wonder.

Support Your Adult Children as Parents

You can have a great impact on the lives of your adult children related to their parenting. Support them by backing up what they're doing as parents. Reinforce their limits, their routines, their desires for their children. And don't forget to brag on your adult children to their children. "Wow! You're lucky to have such a great dad!" "Wasn't that neat of him to miss his golf game so he could take you to the zoo?" Notice the good that your children are doing and praise them to their children.

Provide Feedback

The increasing fragmentation of the extended family in America means that a grandfather may learn about his grandchildren during brief, intermittent interaction. But distance has advantages when it's applied to your perspective. Your adult child sees the kids every day and may not have a sense of how they are changing over the weeks, months, and years.

It's different for a grandpa. Changes in the grandkids are obvious. "My how you've grown." "She's much better on the clarinet now than last time we visited." This removed perspective also enables grandparents to notice potential developmental issues.

Micah, my youngest son, had some difficulty learning how to speak. Dee and I would find him talking out the side of his mouth and being generally "slushy" in his speech. We assumed he'd grow out of it. "You ought to have his mouth checked," my dad told me during one visit. Sure enough, the doctor who checked Micah told us that his upper palate wasn't spreading adequately. He built a retainer that enabled Micah to enunciate his words. My dad was able to see things that neither Dee nor I had caught.

Involvement Versus Interference

You may have lots of wisdom and experience that would be a great benefit to your adult children in their parenting; you may see them walking down the same wrong path you took as a young parent; they may be trying a new approach that really causes you some concern. But if they don't know they need your advice, your efforts may be seen as a judgment on their parenting or an unwelcome intrusion into what they're trying to accomplish with their kids.

How do you know when you have passed from helpful to intrusive? The conventional wisdom is that, when it comes to giving your adult children advice on parenting, *don't*. Allow them to make mistakes and learn some things on their own—many people need to learn that way. Try taking a back-seat and enjoy being a grandfather. Be your adult child's cheerleader even when he fails or disagrees with you on some issue. Psychiatrist Paul Warren writes, "No grandparent has the right to interfere with or undermine the parents' authority. You don't raise kids by committee. The parents have the final word, regardless of what you think."[7] Any advice you give should be prefaced by a request for permission to do so: "If you'd be interested in hearing some ideas on that sometime, let me know." Of course, if they refuse your advice, accept that gracefully and continue to be a positive influence where you can.[8]

In his book *The Gift of Grandparenting*, Eric Wiggin suggests that grand-parents can address concerns for their grandchildren in an indirect way, and accompanied by an offer of generosity. For example: "Hey, you've taught Erica to count! Would you like us to get her a phonetic reader?" Or, "I'm afraid for little Justin with all those trucks rumbling past your house. Could you folks use a fenced backyard? I've been looking for an excuse to use some of my new tools, and I think we have enough in our rainy day account for the materials. I'll build it however you want it."[9]

In finding this balance—where a grandfather gives all he can give but no more than he should give—you'll protect your son's or daughter's dig-nity, build their confidence as a parent, affirm their authority with their kids, and preserve the peace of their relationship with you. And if you become a source of encouragement and help for your adult child and his or her spouse rather than bringing pressure and guilt, they'll be much more likely to come to you when they do have questions.

The Fine Art of Spoiling

You will have special connection points with your grandchildren that make up part of the joy and magic that is a grandfather: Letting them stay up later than usual . . . Making trips to the local ice-cream parlor . . . Giving them a five-dollar bill for something they want . . . Letting your eleven-year-old grandson sit on your lap and steer the old truck on a deserted country road.

Most of it is good fun, but you need to know about the potential dangers. Some grandparents, whether they mean to or not, spoil their grandchildren to the point of angering the child's parents. The grandparents insist that it's harmless, but the parents are genuinely offended. Their lives will be much more difficult the next few days because of the liberties allowed at Grandpa's house. The grandparents, convinced they are right, may push back again or indulge the kids even more just to make a point.

Harmless spoiling is the great duty and privilege of grandparents, as long as it remains in the realm of healthy companionship and good cheer. Examine your motives and be sure your overall goal is to support what your children are trying to do in their home. When they succeed, you succeed.

The Virtue of Faithfulness

Faithfulness implies a steadfast perseverance. You have hung in there over the years. Now you have a relationship with those who will be the leaders of the next generation, your children and grandchildren. They now represent your contribution to the world. Perhaps your greatest legacy—the best honor your children can give you—is to become the best fathers and mothers and grandparents that they can be. That's a legacy that will be a blessing to children who come along several generations from now.

During a National Center for Fathering essay contest, a nine-year-old named Jordan wrote this about his faithful grandpa:

> Four months before I was born, my real father left my mommy. My Grandpa drove 400 miles to come get my mommy and me and brought us back to Minnesota. He took care of my mommy until I was born. When I came home from the hospital, there was a cradle that Grandpa made just for me. Someday, my kids will sleep in the same cradle.
>
> When I was a baby I cried a lot at night. Grandpa would walk me around and around the kitchen table. He rocked me to sleep and he was my first baby-sitter. Now I'm nine years old and Grandpa is my best buddy. We do lots of things together. We go to zoos, museums, and parks. We watch baseball games on TV and we have Chex Mix together, just the two of us.

When I was four my Grandpa spent a whole summer building me a playhouse with a big sandbox underneath. He made me a tire swing and pushes me lots of times in it. He pushes me real high, way up over his head. Now he spends all his extra time building new rooms on our house so that Mommy and I will have our own apartment.

He likes to tell me about things that happened when he was a little boy and when my mommy and uncle were little. My Grandpa is really patient. When he is busy building things he always takes time to start a nail so that I can pound it in. After he's spent all day mowing our big lawn he is really tired but he will still hook my wagon up to the lawn mower and drive me all over the place.

Sometimes people on TV talk about kids from single parent families. I'm not one of them because I have three parents in my family. My Grandpa isn't my Father, but I wouldn't trade him for all the Dads in the world.

The Heart of a Grandfather

Faithfulness as a grandfather means stepping in to help out when you see a child in need. With the number of broken homes in our society, chances are good that you'll find that child right in your own family. But if you don't, I encourage you to look outside your family, to single-parent families or abandoned children. They're in your neighborhood and church. Or, maybe it's a family whose grandparents live far away. All of your grandfatherly assets that I've listed—a link to the past, a transmitter of values, a wise teacher, a role model, an enthusiastic companion—can apply to children outside your family as well. They may need these things from you even more than your own grandchildren. Invite them over for a meal. Include them in some outing or activity. Do special favors for them. Invest yourself in their lives.

Generativity is about extending your legacy into future generations, and being a grandfather to all the children who need you is faithfulness at its best. If you really do believe you have something valuable to give to those coming after you, then it's worth it to find a way to carry it out.

A FATHER'S LEGACY

Blake Ashdown is a good friend of mine who, like many of us, works hard to make a living while staying connected to his wife and children. Several years ago he started an exercise that helps him keep his priorities in focus. Every once in a while, he imagines what it would be like to attend his own funeral as a spectator.

I know it sounds morbid, but try it. Put down the book if you want. Take a minute and imagine your own funeral. Where will it take place? Who will be there? What inscription will be on your grave marker? Perhaps most important, who will give your eulogy, and what will that person say? At many funerals, a close friend or family member gives a verbal testimony of honor and remembrance.

Who would give yours, and what specifically would he or she say about you? Would your daughter talk about your attentive listening ear? Would your son describe many simple yet meaningful times just hanging out together? What kind of experiences are so ingrained in your daughter that they will naturally flow out during her time of grieving? Or will she make vague, general comments about your dedication to your work?

Then, someone will read your obituary, which will describe your life's information, with memberships and achievements. The obituary saves the best for last, when it lists who will "survive" you—your descendants. It's a powerful and sobering thought: Your children (biological, step, or adopted) will effectively represent you for decades to come.

The point of this whole exercise is simple. As fathers, our actions today are writing the future—not with ink and paper, but with flesh and blood, through our practice of involvement, consistency, awareness, and nurturance. When we die, we will all leave an inheritance of some kind. Some of that inheritance may be in *stuff*: heirlooms, land, furniture, stocks and bonds, etc. But those things are temporary. The more meaningful inheritance will be memories, relational skills, and values that will be steady guides for our children as they mature.

Frederick Buechner didn't inherit much, yet he was able to overcome the pain of a fatherless youth to become a successful novelist. His father committed suicide when he was ten—a very difficult and embarrassing time for his entire family.

Yet when Frederick grew older, he somehow knew that "although death ended my father, it has never ended my relationship with my father—a secret that I had never so clearly understood before."[1] Forty-four years after his father's death, Buechner dedicated his prize-winning novel *Godric* to his father. He wrote the dedication in Latin because he wanted to be "obedient to the ancient family law that the secret of my father must be at all costs kept secret."[2]

After years of contemplation, Buechner wrote this about his father's death:

> Who knows how I might have turned out if my father had lived, but through the loss of him all those long years ago I think that I learned something about how even tragedy can be a means of grace that I might never have come to any other way.[3]

No one would wish for the opportunity to learn from tragedy, but if fatherlessness can be a means of grace, how much more can purposeful fathering be a blessing to children and grandchildren?

The brilliant allegorical writer C. S. Lewis reached a conclusion about fatherhood that demonstrates a yearning for which this book is written. His Welsh father displayed a fierce temper to the entire family, and Lewis was shipped off to boarding school at age ten (then a common practice in the British Empire). For years he was separated from his father by the Irish Sea.

Though his parents, who normally would have established him in the world, were taken away from him, Lewis became a man of letters at Oxford, and one of a few men in the twentieth century who possessed a seemingly intuitive grasp of truth. Where did his balance and prudence come from? Interestingly, he did not remain orphaned for long. He soon found other father figures. The most immediate was his older brother, Warren. He found perhaps his most profound father substitute when he converted to Christianity, where he experienced a loving relationship with his heavenly Father.

Lewis also had a fascinating and unique relationship with fellow author George MacDonald. I call it a "relationship," even though MacDonald had lived in the previous century. "All I know about MacDonald," Lewis confessed, "is what I've read in his books or in his biography written by his son. Nor have I but once talked to anyone who knew him." And yet MacDonald, nonetheless, served as a kind of mentor to Lewis, so much so that Lewis would claim, "I fancy that I have never written a book in which I did not quote from him."[4]

At one point, looking back on all he learned from MacDonald, Lewis focused on the issue of father power. He wrote of MacDonald, "An almost perfect relationship with his father was the earthly root of all his wisdom. From his own father, he said, he first learned that fatherhood must be at the core of the universe."[5]

What a claim! MacDonald apparently benefited so greatly from a positive relationship with his father that it was natural for him to think of healthy fathering as a basic need of our existence.

I couldn't agree more. In fact, I'd like to take it one more step: Should fatherhood be at the core of *your* universe? When you think about all the tasks to which you are devoting your life's energies, do you ever get the sense that what you do as a father will have the greatest lasting impact and provide you the deepest personal satisfaction?

After a Tornado

Several years ago I drove ten miles out into the Kansas farmlands only hours after a tornado had swept through. I saw pieces of houses scattered all over the fields, and canceled checks miles away from anyone's home. I saw victims who were overwhelmed at the sight of their personal belongings, their homes, their very lives strewn across the countryside. I'm sure they were thankful to still be alive, but in that moment they had nothing left to deal with the process of putting their lives back together. Suddenly their lives were out of order, and they retreated to the basics to try to restore that order.

As I've reflected on that evening and the destruction I witnessed, I couldn't help thinking of fathers. I hesitate to draw too many comparisons between fathering and a tornado, but I believe there are at least two valuable lessons here.

First, we must recognize that *there are no guarantees* in fathering. We can sail along with barely a concern and then be devastated in a moment's notice. There are fantastic fathers who raise rebellious kids, and there are "distant" fathers whose kids do well. As fathers, we are investing in the future—and we have every reason to invest wisely and confidently—but we can't guarantee a payoff.

Second, *we must make our homes a priority.* After a storm comes the time to clean up, reflect, and rebuild what has been destroyed. Often, it takes a disaster before we'll take notice of what needs to be done. Maybe your relationship with your children has been damaged by selfish habits, uncontrolled emotions, or the busyness of life. Maybe something has happened to a child that, as a father, you consider to be a disaster: drug use, educational failure, unplanned pregnancy, or something else. In those cases, I'm sure you feel the urgency of picking up the pieces and repairing what has been broken.

It's much tougher to sense the urgency when you haven't gone through a disaster, even though your relationships with your kids may be in need of repairs. Perhaps you can't talk to your teenage daughter like you used to, and she has grown distant. Or maybe you've been extra hard on your son lately when he steps out of line. These aren't emergencies yet, but the buildings definitely need some stabilizing, some patching up here and there, and some preventive maintenance. Maybe things are piling up at work and you've been putting things off for a while.

Now is the time to proactively repair what has been damaged in those relationships. We fathers must be the ones who take the initiative. Seize the moment and don't let it seize you.

Finally, one of the most inspiring aspects of any disaster is the way people rally and unite to help the victims. Neighbors, acquaintances, and total strangers see people in need and show up to help put things back together. So when I see tornadoes rip into the Midwest, floods ravaging Louisiana and Mississippi, earthquakes in California, or even terrorist attacks, I grieve with those who are suffering, but I am also stirred by the sense of community that develops.

And I believe there is also a fellowship of fathers forming in this nation that can serve much the same purpose. When one man falls, other dads must be there to help him work through his pain and get him back on his feet. If you're feeling like a victim of tragedy, let me encourage you: If you are open enough to let your needs be known, there are other fathers who will extend their hands to you. Even if you have lost touch with your kids— or lost them completely—don't lose heart. There are others willing to help.

The Sound of Voices

Indeed, I hear a rumbling in the land. It's the sound of voices—deep basses and baritones—saying, "We're coming home." They're like an army of fathers, marching as one.

We "ordinary" fathers are connecting with thousands of other fathers who are simply committed to being the best dads we can be. No longer will our own pasts, nor our current pursuits and aspirations, keep us from developing a deep, abiding relationship with our children. Our children deserve so much more—not just the leftovers of our energies and emotions.

More than anything, I hope this book stimulates you to join this army of men. What it requires on your part is a commitment of the *heart*.

The Heart of a Hero

One of my favorite sayings comes from a prophetic piece of Hebrew literature: "See, I will send you the prophet Elijah before that great and dreadful day of the LORD comes. He will turn the hearts of the fathers to their children, and the hearts of the children to their fathers; or else I will come and strike the land with a curse."[6]

The problem is that most men work too much out of their heads—whether they are working, solving problems, or just relating to people. Sometimes that's necessary, but relating to children is more a matter of the heart. And I'm finding that when you can reach a man's heart, that's when he's most likely to experience a powerful and lasting change in the way he relates to his children.

Our research at NCF has shown that some of the most effective fathers have a heartfelt relationship with another Father[7]—a heavenly one—who strengthens and equips them in their fathering, and has their best interests at heart. He wants to change their hearts—to equip them not only in a relationship with Him, but also in responsible and loving relationship with their children. As men come to a better understanding of who their heavenly Father is, they also learn how to be the fathers their children truly need.

I believe men are at their best when their hearts are engaged. The coming generation needs fathers who relate to their children and wives with their *hearts*—hearts that overflow with love and compassion, and hearts that are very intentional and committed to doing what's best for those they love.

Maybe your heart is disengaged. Maybe the only emotions you express to those you love are anger or disappointment. Or maybe your heart is hardened by destructive habits, and you need to seek forgiveness and restoration.

As you become a more effective father, you learn what a powerful tool an engaged heart can be: You are more sensitive to your children's needs; you're more likely to act on their behalf, not your own; you show unconditional love and acceptance, and provide protection, comfort, and guidance.

Those may seem like pretty insignificant qualities, but to me, these are the qualities of a hero. America has a way of venerating its heroes. They are given a place of respect and honor. George Washington is pictured on our currency; Martin Luther King Jr. has a holiday; Michael Jordan and Joe Montana have their rightful places in their halls of fame. Other sports stars, clergymen, and civic, corporate, and military leaders are all important role models to the coming generation. Such heroes are esteemed due to their power or prestige.

But I see a new group of heroes emerging—fathers who have faithfully and quietly forgone power, prestige, position, and their own desires to become successful with their kids. These heroes know that the true litmus test of greatness is service. They rise early and labor diligently to provide for their families. They help with homework, become taxi drivers for their children, and write notes of encouragement. Even if they are in difficult circumstances, they are faithful in paying child support and in visitation. They respect women. They know that true manhood is based on commitment to children, giving their all for the next generation.

Such heroes come from every ethnic heritage, economic situation, and age group, but they are united by their shared purpose—becoming better dads. And their very lives become their message—they walk their talk, they keep their promises, and their hearts are turned toward their children.

What does one of these heroes look like? Dad, go look in the mirror. They are men like you, who may consider themselves ordinary and common, but who are extraordinary in the eyes of their children.

Do you want to be great? Turn your heart toward your children, because greatness is defined by service. Do you want to do something profound? Turn your heart toward your children, because the profound is often discovered in the simple. Do you want to change the world? Turn your heart toward your children; for just as the hand that rocks the cradle rules the world, men now have the opportunity to rock the cradle. Do you want to do something to honor God? Turn your heart toward your children, then reach out to a child who is fatherless.

I hear a rumbling. I see an army of fathers. And I smell a fresh wind of renewal blowing across our land. Stop for a minute and take a good, long, deep breath.

Preface: Father Power

1. Gordon Dalbey, *Father and Son: The Wound, the Healing, the Call to Manhood* (Nashville: Nelson, 1992), xii.

Introduction: The Heart of a Father

1. Henry Biller wrote *Father Power* in 1974 (Doubleday/Anchor). This significant book helped to turn the attention of research to the forgotten role of fathering. I am indebted to Biller and Dave Simmons for developing my understanding of father power. Simmons wrote *Dad, the Family Coach* in 1991 (Victor).

2. Wade Horn, *The ABC Evening News with Peter Jennings,* interview, December 1994.

3. Sam Keen, *Fire in the Belly* (New York: Bantam, 1991), 224.

4. Wade Horn, *Father Facts* (Lancaster, Pa.: National Fatherhood Initiative, 2004). www.fatherhood.org/fatherfacts_int.asp.

5. National Center for Fathering, *National Survey of Men,* 1994, 2001.

6. Gale H. Roid and Ken R. Canfield, "Measuring the Dimensions of Effective Fathering," *Educational and Psychological Measurement* 54 (Spring 1994): 212–17.

7. The National Center on Addiction and Substance Abuse at Columbia University (CASA). The Importance of Family Dinners. Survey conducted by QEV Analytics (New York: 2003).

8. Henri Nouwen, "Generation Without Fathers," *Commonweal,* 12 June 1970; as reprinted in Henri Nouwen, *The Wounded Healer* (New York: Doubleday, 1972), 27.

9. Phyllis Schlafly, "Federal Incentives Make Children Fatherless" (Alton, Ill.: Eagle Forum, May 11, 2005; www.eagleforum.org).

10. The Promise Keepers movement has filled stadiums and arenas across the country, with more than 5.3 million attending. The Million Man March attracted an estimated 800,000 in October 1995, mainly African-American men who applauded the call to be involved in raising their sons and daughters.

11. *Newsweek,* 24 January 1990.

12. Sam Osherson, *The Passions of Fatherhood* (New York: Fawcett Columbine, 1995), 10.

13. Andrew Merton, "Father Hunger," *New Age Journal* (September/October 1986): 24.

14. Lewis Yablonsky, *Fathers and Sons* (Berkeley: Berkeley, 1982); and Robert Meister, *Fathers* (New York: Richard Marek, 1981).

Part 1 Introduction: Examining Your Heart

1. Mike Downey, "Gathers Had It All—Everything Except Luck," *Sporting News,* 19 March 1990, 4. See also Shelley Smith, "Death on the Court," *Sports Illustrated,* 12 March 1990, 14.

2. Samuel Osherson, *Finding Our Fathers* (New York: Fawcett Columbine, 1987), 6.

3. Donald Joy, *Unfinished Business* (Wheaton: Victor, 1989), 34.

4. Robert Bly, *Iron John* (Reading, Mass.: Addison-Wesley, 1990), 94.

5. C. S. Lewis, *The Abolition of Man* (New York: Macmillan, 1947), 101.

6. Gordon Dalbey, *Fathers and Sons* (Nashville: Thomas Nelson, 1992), 179.

Chapter 1: Recognize Your Past

1. See http://www.publicdebt.treas.gov/opd/opdpenny.htm. As of January 2006.

2. Samuel Osherson, *Finding Our Fathers* (New York: Free Press, 1986), 198.

3. David Stoop, *Making Peace with Your Father* (Wheaton: Tyndale, 1993), 7.

4. Donald Joy, *Unfinished Business* (Wheaton: Victor, 1989), 34.

5. Elisabeth Kubler-Ross, *On Death and Dying* (New York: Macmillan, 1969).

6. Gordon Dalbey, *Healing the Masculine Soul* (Waco: Word, 1988), 138.

Chapter 2: Resolve Your Past

1. Lynn Smith, "Need Good Dads? Yes, Kids Do," Los Angeles Times News Service, appearing 26 March 1994. See also Jane Drew, *Where Were You When I Needed You, Dad?: A Guide for Healing Your Father Wound* (Newport Beach, Calif.: Tiger Lily, 1992).

2. Ralph Keyes, "If Only I Could Say 'I Love You, Dad,'" *Parade,* 7 February 1993, 4.

3. Ibid., 5.

4. Luis Zayas, "As Son Becomes Father: Reflections of Expectant Fathers on Their Fathers in Dreams," *Psychoanalytic Review* 74:4 (1987): 443.

5. Samuel Osherson, *Finding Our Fathers* (New York: Free Press, 1986), 194.

6. Keyes, "If Only I Could Say," 6.

7. Elva McAllaster, *When a Father Is Hard to Honor* (Elgin, Ill.: Brethren, 1984), 31.

8. 1 Timothy 5:1. The Greek words *epiplesso* and *prahaleo* in this verse have a range of meanings; thus this is the author's amplified translation of the verse.

9. Keyes, "If Only I Could Say," 5.

10. Judith S. Wallerstein, *Second Chances* (New York: Ticknor and Fields, 1990), 13–14, 290–91.

11. W. E. Vine, "Reconcile," *An Expository Dictionary of New Testament Words* (Old Tappan, N.J.: Revell, 1940).

12. David Stoop, *Making Peace with Your Father* (Wheaton: Tyndale, 1993), 238.

13. Gordon Dalbey, *Healing the Masculine Soul* (Waco: Word, 1988), 49–58.

Chapter 3: Relate to Your Father

1. Robert Bly, *Iron John* (Reading, Mass.: Addison-Wesley, 1990), 25.

2. Ray Oldenburg, *The Great Good Place,* as quoted in David Morris, "Rootlessness Undermines Our Economy As Well As the Quality of Our Lives," *Utne Reader*, May/June 1990, 88.

3. William J. Bennett, "Raising Cain on Values," *Newsweek,* 18 April 1994.

4. David Stoop, *Making Peace with Your Father* (Wheaton: Tyndale, 1992), 246.

5. Ralph Keyes, "If Only I Could Say, 'I Love You, Dad,'" *Parade Magazine,* 7 February 1993, 5.

Part 2 Introduction: The Four "I CANs"

1. As quoted in Louis Sullivan, "Absentee Fathers Tarnish Tradition of Father's Day," *Allen American,* (Tex.) 16 June 1991, 9A.

Chapter 4: Involvement

1. The National Center on Addiction and Substance Abuse at Columbia University (CASA). The Importance of Family Dinners. Survey conducted by QEV Analytics (New York: 2003).

2. Garret D. Evans, Psy.D. and Kate Fogarty, Ph.D., "The Hidden Benefits of Being an Involved Father" (Family, Youth, and Community Sciences Department, Florida Cooperative Extension Service, Institute of Food and Agricultural Sciences, University of Florida: 1999. Rev., July 2005). http://edis.ifas.ufl.edu.

3. Henry Biller, "The Father Factor and the Two-Parent Advantage: Reducing the Paternal Deficit," presented to the Father-to-Father working group meeting with White House advisor William Gaiston, 17 December 1993 and 15 April 1994.

4. Ronald P. Rohner and Robert A. Veneziano. "The Importance of Father Love: History and Contemporary Evidence," *Review of General Psychology* 5.4, (December 2001): 382–405, taken from www.fatherhood.org/fatherfacts_lb.asp.

5. Carla Cantor, "The Father Factor," *Working Mother,* June 1991, 40–42.

6. Ibid., 39.

7. Ibid., 39–40.

8. Ibid., 143. Studies cited: Kathleen Mullan Harris and S. Philip Morgan, "Fathers, Sons, and Daughters: Differential Paternal Involvement in Parenting," *Journal of Marriage and the Family* 53 (August 1991): 539; John Snarey, *How Fathers Care for the Next Generation* (Cambridge, Mass.: Harvard Univ. Press, 1993), 115.

9. The letter has been revised for grammar, and profanities have been removed.

10. Nick Stinnett, "Six Qualities That Make Families Strong," in *Family Building,* 40.

11. Michael Lamb, ed., *The Father's Role: Applied Perspectives* (New York: Wiley & Sons, 1986, 1996), 8.

12. Michael Lamb, ed., "A Biosocial Perspective on Paternal Behavior and Involvement," in Jane B. Lancaster et al., eds., *Parenting Across the Life Span: Biosocial Dimensions* (New York: Aldine De Gruyter, 1987), 131–34.

13. Ibid., 132–33.

14. Aaron Latham, "Fathering the Nest," May 1992, 68.

15. Julia Lawlor, "Men Seeking More Family Time Fear 'Wimp Factor,'" *USA Today,* 14 June 1991, B1.

Chapter 5: Consistency

1. Alan C. Acock and V. L. Bengston, "Socialization and attribution processes: Actual versus perceived similarity among parents and youth," *Journal of Marriage and Family* 43 (1980): 501–18.

Chapter 6: Awareness

1. LouAnne Johnson, "My Posse Don't Do Homework," *Reader's Digest,* September 1992, 207.

2. Rebecca Hagelin, "Men of Character, Boys of Fortune" (Washington, D.C.: Heritage Foundation, 2005). http://www.heritage.org/Press/Commentary/ed110105a.cfm.

3. J. Youniss and J. Smollar, *Adolescent Relations with Mothers, Fathers, and Friends* (Chicago: Univ. of Chicago Press, 1985); quoted in James Youniss and Robert D. Ketterlinus, "Communication and Connectedness in Mother- and Father-Adolescent Relationships," *Journal of Youth and Adolescence* 16 (1987): 266.

4. Many books contain charts that help you map out a typical child's development in key areas, such as physical, intellectual, social, sexual, and spiritual. I recommend John M. Drescher, *Seven Things Children Need,* 2nd ed. (Scottdale, Penn.: Herald Press, 1988). (See particularly appendix B.)

5. "Teen Tipplers: America's Underage Drinking Epidemic," press release (Washington, D.C.: The National Press Club, February 26, 2002.) www.casacolumbia.org.

6. "Generation Rx: National Study Reveals New Category of Substance Abuse Emerging" (Washington, D.C.: Partnership for a Drug-Free America, 2005.) www.drugfree.org.

7. "Teenagers in the United States: Sexual Activity, Contraceptive Use, and Childbearing, 2002" (Hyattsville, Md.: National Center for Health Statistics, 2004). http://www.cdc.gov/nchs/pressroom/04news/teens.htm.

Chapter 7: Nurturance

1. Wade Horn, *Father Facts* (Lancaster, Pa.: National Fatherhood Initiative, 2004). www.fatherhood.org/fatherfacts_t10.asp.

2. Garret D. Evans, Psy.D. and Kate Fogarty, Ph.D., "The Hidden Benefits of Being an Involved Father" (Family, Youth, and Community Sciences Department, Florida Cooperative Extension Service, Institute of Food and Agricultural Sciences, University of Florida: 1999. Rev., July 2005). http://edis.ifas.ufl.edu.

3. *UCLA Monthly,* Alumni Association News, March-April 1981; as quoted in Gary Smalley and John Trent, *The Blessing* (Nashville: Nelson, 1986), 42.

4. J. Allan Petersen, "Expressing Appreciation," in George Rekers, ed., *Family Building* (Ventura, Calif.: Regal, 1985), 89.

5. Carla Cantor, "The Father Factor," *Working Mother,* June 1992, 39–42.

6. Dolores Krieger, "Therapeutic Touch: The Imprimatur of Nursing," *American Journal of Nursing;* Helen Colton, *The Gift of Touch,* as quoted in Smalley and Trent, *The Blessing,* 40.

7. Cantor, "The Father Factor," 40.

8. Dave Simmons, *Dad, the Family Coach* (Wheaton: Victor, 1991), 45–46.

9. B. Rollins and D. Thomas, "Parental Support, Power, and Control Techniques in the Socialization of Children," in Wesley R. Burr, Rubin Hill, F. Ivan Nye, and I.L. Reiss, eds., *Contemporary Theories About the Family,* vol. 1 (New York: Free Press), 792.

10. Cantor, "The Father Factor," 41.

11. Michael Lamb, ed., *The Father's Role: Applied Perspectives* (New York: Wiley & Sons, 1986), 14.

12. Gary Smalley, video series, *Hidden Keys to Loving Relationships* (Branson, Mo.: Relationships Today, 1993).

13. Karen S. Peterson, "Dads and Daughters, Tricky Tango," *USA Today,* 5 April 1993, 6D.

14. Maureen Murdock, *Hero's Daughter* and *Ties That Bind* (New York: Ballantine, 1994), xiv, xv.

15. Joseph Pleck as quoted in Cantor, "The Father Factor," 43.

Part 3 Introduction: Through the Years

1. Gail Sheehy, *New Passages: Mapping Your Life Across Time* (New York: Random House, 1995).

2. Daniel J. Levinson, *The Seasons of a Man's Life* (New York: Ballantine, 1978), 57.

Chapter 8: For Fathers of Infants: Attachment

1. Martin Greenberg, *The Birth of a Father* (New York: Avon, 1985), 22.

2. Jerrold Lee Shapiro, "The Expectant Father," *Psychology Today,* January 1987, 36–39, 42.

3. Greenberg, *The Birth of a Father,* 201.

4. Armin A. Brott, *The New Father* (New York: Abbeville Press, 1997), 21–22.

Chapter 9: For Fathers of Preschoolers: Idealism

1. Daniel J. Levinson, *The Seasons of a Man's Life* (New York: Ballantine, 1978), 58.

Chapter 10: For Fathers of School-Age Children: Understanding

1. Daniel J. Levinson, *The Seasons of a Man's Life* (New York: Ballantine, 1978), 59. For an updated look beyond his book, see Daniel Levinson, "A Conception of Adult Development," *American Psychologist,* January 1986, 3–13.

2. Ibid., 59.

3. Marjory Roberts, "When Father Puts in Time with Kids, He and They Gain, Study Finds," *Kansas City Times,* 9 June 1989, C–2. See also John Snarey, *How Fathers Care for the Next Generation* (Cambridge, Mass.: Harvard Univ. Press, 1993), 115.

4. Aaron Latham, "Fathering the Nest," M, May 1992, 75.

5. Ken R. Canfield, *The 7 Secrets of Effective Fathers* (Wheaton: Tyndale, 1992).

6. Bill Cosby, *Fatherhood* (New York: Doubleday, 1986), 15.

7. Ken R. Canfield and Nancy L. Swihart, *Beside Every Great Dad* (Wheaton: Tyndale, 1993), 208–9.

8. David Elkind, *The Hurried Child: Growing Up Too Fast Too Soon* (Reading, Mass.: Addison-Wesley, 1984).

9. Ken R. Canfield, *The National Survey of Fathering Practices* (Julian, Calif.: Family Development Foundation, 1989). See details in appendix 1.

Chapter 11: For Fathers of Teens: Enlightenment

1. Ken R. Canfield, *Effective Fathering Practices and Fathering Satisfaction Related to a Father's Life Course,* doctoral dissertation, Kansas State University, 1995.

2. Cliff Schimmels, *What Parents Try to Forget About Adolescence* (Elgin, Ill.: David C. Cook, 1989), 179.

3. Walt Mueller, *Understanding Today's Youth Culture* (Wheaton: Tyndale, 1994), 28.

4. Daniel J. Levinson, *The Seasons of a Man's Life* (New York: Ballantine, 1978), 60.

5. James Youniss and Jacqueline Smollar, *Adolescent Relations with Mothers, Fathers, and Friends* (Chicago: Univ. of Chicago, 1985), 68.

6. Ibid., 49, 68.

7. Ross Campbell, *How to Really Love Your Child* (Wheaton: Victor, 1979), 56.

8. Ken R. Canfield, *The 7 Secrets of Effective Fathers* (Wheaton: Tyndale, 1992), 154.

9. H. Weinstock, S. Berman, W. Cates, "Sexually transmitted diseases among American youth: incidence and prevalence estimates, 2000," *Perspectives on Sexual and Reproductive Health* 2004, 36 (1):6–10; www.cdc.gov/std/stats/trends2004.htm.

10. Cynthia Moore and Joseph Allen, "The Effects of Volunteering on the Young Volunteer," *The Journal of Primary Prevention,* 1996. As quoted in "Teens and Their Parents in the 21st Century: An Examination of Trends in Teen Behavior and the Role of Parental Involvement," *Council of Economic Advisors.* Report presented at the White House Conference on Teenagers: Raising

Responsible and Resourceful Youth, 2 May, 2000; http://clinton3.nara.gov/WH/New/html/teenconf.html.

11. Youniss and Smollar, 49–51, 68–72, 87.

Chapter 12: For Fathers of Young Adults: Reflection

1. Jim Conway, *Men in Mid-life Crisis* (Elgin, Ill.: David C. Cook, 1978), 247.

2. Robert J. Havinghurst, *Developmental Tasks and Education* (New York: David McKay, 1948), 75.

3. Ibid.

Chapter 13: For Grandfathers: Generativity

1. Arthur Kornhaber, *Between Parents and Grandparents* (New York: St. Martin's Press, 1986), 13.

2. Ibid., 26.

3. Proverbs 17:6, *New King James Version*.

4. Arthur Kornhaber, *Grandparent Power!* (New York: Crown, 1994), 53.

5. Judson J. Swihart, "Older Grandparents' Perception of Generativity in the Grandparent/Grandchild Relationship," unpublished doctoral dissertation, Kansas State University, Manhattan, Kansas, 1985.

6. Ibid.

7. Dr. Frank Minirth, Dr. Brian Newman, and Dr. Paul Warren, *The Father Book* (Nashville: Thomas Nelson, 1992), 259.

8. Jim Fay and Foster Cline, M.D., *Grandparenting with Love & Logic* (Golden, Colo.: Love and Logic Press, 1994), 115.

9. Eric Wiggin, *The Gift of Grandparenting* (Wheaton: Tyndale, 2001), 175–79.

Epilogue

1. Frederick Buechner, *Telling Secrets* (San Francisco: HarperCollins, 1991), 22.

2. Ibid., 32.

3. Ibid., 20–21.

4. C. S. Lewis, *George MacDonald: An Anthology* (London, Geoffry Bles, 1946), 20.

5. Ibid.

6. Malachi 4:5–6, *New International Version*.

7. See Ken R. Canfield, *The 7 Secrets of Effective Fathers* (Wheaton: Tyndale, 1992), 18–19.

The following three books offer additional guidance in rearing your children through the six stages of fathering.

The New First Three Years of Life by Burton White, M.D. (Fireside)
This collection of ideas on how to raise infants and toddlers has been tested by hundreds of families and preschools. This new and revised edition, based on thirty-three years of research by the author, is the classic guide to the child's early mental, physical, social, and emotional development. A good supplement for understanding the attachment and idealism stages.

How to Really Love Your Child by Ross Campbell, M.D. (Life Journey)
Practical and inspiring, this book reminds us of the basics and makes clear how parents can build a confident foundation of acceptance and trust in their children. A good supplement for the understanding and enlightenment stages.

Parenting Your Adult Child by Ross Campbell, M.D. and Gary Chapman (Northfield)

This book provides help with key issues that are likely to surface: "nests" that don't empty, conflicts over lifestyle choices, questions related to financial support, and helping adult children succeed in careers, marriages, and families.

Here are several other books that are valuable resources in understanding fathering, marriage, and being a man.

General Men's Issues

Healing the Masculine Soul by Gordon Dalbey (Word)
Seasons of a Man's Life by Daniel Levinson (Ballantine)

Dealing with Your Fathering Past

Finding Our Fathers by Samuel Osherson (Fawcett Columbine)
FatherLoss by Neil Chethik (Hyperion)

Marriage

Men and Marriage by George Gilder (Pelican)
10 Great Dates to Energize Your Marriage by David and Claudia Arp (Zondervan)
Love & Respect by Dr. Emerson Eggerichs (Integrity)
The Five Love Languages by Gary Chapman (Northfield)

Single/Divorced Dads

Live-Away Dads by William Klatte (Penguin)

Stepdads

Keys to Successful Stepfathering by Carl E. Pickhardt, Ph.D. (Barron's)

Educating Your Child

School Starts at Home by Cheri Fuller (Piñon)
Talkers, Watchers, and Doers by Cheri Fuller (Piñon)

Parenting and Disciplining Your Child

Parenting with Love and Logic by Foster Cline, M.D. and Jim Fay (Piñon)
Boys! by William Beausay (Thomas Nelson)
Girls! by William & Kathryn Beausay (Baker)
King Me by Steve Farrar (Moody)

Parenting Teens

Parenting Teens with Love and Logic by Foster Cline, M.D. and Jim Fay
    (Piñon)
Suddenly They're 13 by David & Claudia Arp (Zondervan)
The Five Love Languages of Teenagers by Gary Chapman (Northfield)

Grandfathers

Grandparenting with Love and Logic by Jim Fay and Foster Cline, M.D. (Love
    & Logic)
The Gift of Grandparenting by Eric Wiggin (Tyndale)

NATIONAL SURVEY OF FATHERING PRACTICES

The following questions are excerpted from the National Survey of Fathering Practices. Section One contained 116 questions, followed by 8 open-ended questions, 17 questions on satisfaction, and extensive demographics (n=2006). Key findings follow these questions, and are based on answers of 2,066 fathers.

IMPORTANCE	HOW IMPORTANT ARE THE FOLLOWING FACTORS TO BEING A SUCCESSFUL FATHER?:	APPLICATION
How important do you think this item is?		How effective are you in performing this item?
Not at all = 1		Poor = 1
Slightly = 2		Fair = 2
Somewhat = 3		Good = 3
Very important = 4		Very good = 4
Critically = 5		Excellent = 5

1 2 3 4 5	Allowing my children to express fear, anger, joy, or pain.	1 2 3 4 5
1 2 3 4 5	Having a job that I enjoy.	1 2 3 4 5
1 2 3 4 5	Being acquainted with my child's friends.	1 2 3 4 5
1 2 3 4 5	Having someone, other than my wife, to talk to about problems in fathering.	1 2 3 4 5
1 2 3 4 5	Having a good relationship with my father.	1 2 3 4 5
1 2 3 4 5	Being able to respond calmly when my children say hurtful things to me.	1 2 3 4 5
1 2 3 4 5	Helping my children understand what they are learning at school.	1 2 3 4 5
1 2 3 4 5	Being able to share my inner feelings with my wife.	1 2 3 4 5
1 2 3 4 5	Pointing out spiritual insights when I talk to my children.	1 2 3 4 5
1 2 3 4 5	Telling stories and/or reading to my children.	1 2 3 4 5
1 2 3 4 5	Limiting the outside activities of the family.	1 2 3 4 5
1 2 3 4 5	Being involved in helping my children better understand their sexuality.	1 2 3 4 5

Open-Ended Questions

What are the three most important goals you have for your relationship with your children?

Who was the best role model you had in fathering?

What makes a father successful?

What would help you to be a better father?

What was the most significant thing your father did with you?

Given your experience, what advice would you give a new father?

Satisfaction Questions

The following items concern your opinion of marriage, parenting, and family life. Rank on a seven-point scale: 1=Extremely Dissatisfied, 2=Very Dissatisfied, 3=Somewhat Dissatisfied, 4=Mixed, 5=Somewhat Satisfied, 6=Very Satisfied, 7=Extremely Satisfied.

How satisfied are you with your marriage? _____

How satisfied are you with your relationship with your wife? _____

How satisfied are you with yourself as a father? _____

How satisfied are you with your children's behavior? _____

How satisfied are you with your family life? _____

Selected Findings

The above sample includes 12 of the 116 statements that reflect factors in fathering. The findings for the top 27 statements are ranked below. From these the four primary fathering functions were derived: involvement, consistency, awareness, and nurturance. Again, the respondents ranked the statements on a scale of 1 to 5, with 5 being "critically" important.

FATHERING SCALES: ORDER OF IMPORTANCE

Scale	Scale Mean	Adjusted Mean	Rank Order
Showing affection/affirmation	21.82	4.36	1
Parental discussion	12.76	4.25	2
Role modeling	16.86	4.22	3
Dealing with a family crisis	16.76	4.19	4
Involvement in discipline	12.57	4.19	5
Moral and spiritual development	32.88	4.11	6
Knowing my child	24.55	4.09	7
Involvement in education	16.27	4.07	8
Wife's role	8.13	4.06	9
Parental confidence	16.24	4.06	10
Male identity	15.68	4.06	11
Marital interaction	31.37	3.92	12
Involvement in child's development	11.71	3.90	13
Time committed to child	19.41	3.88	14
Freedom of expression	23.17	3.86	15
Verbal interaction with child	15.22	3.80	16
Relationship with parents	7.60	3.80	17
Planning child's future	14.89	3.72	18
Child care	14.43	3.61	19

Scale	Scale Mean	Adjusted Mean	Rank Order
Financial provider	21.35	3.56	20
Role in planning family activities	17.48	3.50	21
Extended family activities	10.38	3.46	22
Job satisfaction/stress	13.66	3.41	23
Personal goals/hobbies	9.91	3.30	24
Expectations for child	9.89	3.29	25
Seeking outside advice/help	18.43	3.07	26
Involvement in household chores	9.00	3.00	27

The study went further and asked fathers to rate themselves on "How effective are you in performing this item?" The fathers rated themselves using the same 116 items that they had rated for importance.

A comparison revealed areas where fathers were experiencing large gaps between what they considered to be important for being a good father and their actual performance in the family. These gaps indicate that the father is experiencing dissonance, a tension between what he believes is important and what he treats as important in rearing his children. This dissonance may lead to guilt, as the father is not living up to what he considers to be important. To determine the level of discrepancy between a father's belief and action, the father's mean rating of his performance (or "application") for each item was subtracted from his mean rating for the item's "important" rating.

Areas with higher mean difference are likely to be areas of highest dissonance and guilt. Thus, the top four areas of guilt for a father are likely to be moral and spiritual development, freedom of expression, role modeling, and involvement in education.

DISCREPANCIES BETWEEN
IMPORTANCE AND APPLICATION

Scale	Scale Mean	Adjusted Mean*	Rank Order
Moral and spiritual development	6.94	.87	1
Freedom of expression	4.71	.79	2
Role modeling	3.03	.76	3
Involvement in education	2.88	.72	4
Dealing with family crisis	2.79	.70	5
Role in family planning	3.32	.66	6
Parental confidence	2.57	.64	7
Marital interaction	5.12	.64	8
Verbal interaction with child	2.46	.62	9
Parental discussion	1.83	.61	10
Knowing my child	3.62	.60	11
Planning child's future	2.40	.60	12
Time committed to children	2.76	.55	13
Showing affection/affirmation	2.66	.53	14
Seeking outside advice/help	2.94	.49	15
Involvement in discipline	1.38	.46	16
Personal goals/hobbies	1.21	.40	17
Involvement in child's development	1.13	.38	18
Relationships with parents	.62	.31	19
Male identity	1.22	.30	20
Extended family activities	.80	.27	21
Job satisfaction/stress	.76	.19	22
Child care	.65	.16	23
Financial provider	.84	.14	24
Expectations for child	.10	-.03	25
Wife's role	.16	-.08	26
Involvement in household chores	.40	-.13	27

*Calculated by dividing the scale mean by the number of questions in the scale.

MAP TO THE FATHERING LIFE COURSE

DAD'S STAGE	TRANSITIONS AND CHANGES		
(Child's Age)	Issues facing child:	Issues facing Dad in relation to child:	Adult development issues facing Dad:
ATTACHMENT **Infancy** **(and)** **IDEALISM** **Preschool**	• Leaving behind security of the womb • Going from nursing and being completely dependent to being weaned	Giving up: • Before-birth illusions • Existing control of one's emotions • Degrees of irresponsibility	• Leaving behind free time, time with the "guys" • Leaving old routines, sleep patterns

DAD'S STAGE (Child's Age)	TRANSITIONS AND CHANGES		
	Issues facing child:	Issues facing Dad in relation to child:	Adult development issues facing Dad:
UNDERSTANDING **Grade School**	• Moving away from the view that a child is completely centered on himself to seeing his friends as the definition of his world	• Having less control over part of child's environment • Leaving behind simple structures for relating to child • Having one's fathering on public display	• Reconsidering old definitions of success
ENLIGHTENMENT **Adolescence**	• Leaving behind the security and identity of childhood • Needing to start taking more responsibility	• Surrendering ability to plan and make choices for child • Declining sense of family unity as fewer activities and routines involve whole family, due to child's growing independence • Learning to let down facades in order to be vulnerable with teenager	• Losing one's illusions "de-illusionment"* • Losing one's own youth • Declining physical abilities • Finding more limits to career options
REFLECTION **Young Adult**	• Losing security of structures like school and peer group • Losing parents' full financial support	• Losing one's child! (the empty nest) • Ending some dreams for family activities or goals	• Having large part of identity change as children leave home • Diminishing security and assurance about the future

* Phrase coined by Daniel Levinson in *Seasons of a Man's Life.*

DAD'S STAGE (Child's Age)	TRANSITIONS AND CHANGES		
	Issues facing child:	Issues facing Dad in relation to child:	Adult development issues facing Dad:
GENERATIVITY Parent	• Losing parents' full financial support	• Losing some dignity • Losing identity as responsible leader or disciplinarian	• Giving up the sense of worth coming from one's work (particularly if retiring)

DAD'S STAGE (Child's Age)	GOALS—IDEALS		
	For the child:	For Dad in relation to child:	For Dad:
ATTACHMENT Infancy (and) IDEALISM Preschool	• Trying to figure out the "world" • Trying to control impulses • Learning to relate to others and communicate	• Bonding • Providing for family • Accepting responsibility and developing a job description	• Exploring possibilities of adult world • Creating stable structure for family
UNDERSTANDING Grade School	• Starting structured learning (schooling) • Learning to make friends • Learning to concentrate and communicate ideas	• Introducing child to society, culture, and spiritual matters • Guarding child from bad influences • Finding those who will support us (emotionally and socially in fathering)	• Nurturing marriage • Starting up career achievement ladder • "Finding a niche in society" (Levinson's words)

DAD'S STAGE (Child's Age)	GOALS—IDEALS		
	For the child:	For Dad in relation to child:	For Dad:
ENLIGHTENMENT **Adolescence**	• Searching for new identity • Taking on responsibilities of independence	• Supporting child unconditionally • Training child to take responsibility, (e.g., moral and social behavior) • Developing a new, maturing relationship (e.g., by new joint activities, active listening)	• Questioning where one's at, and then starting to construct a new dream
REFLECTION **Young Adult**	• Selecting a mate • Managing a home • Starting an occupation • Finding a new social group	• Bridging the distance (understanding and receiving signals) • Understanding and respecting differences	• Exploring new areas of life • Finding a new definition of success
GENERATIVITY **Parent**	• Exploring possibilities of adult world • Bonding with our children • Creating stable family structure	• Providing your perspective • Passing on family history	• Preparing a legacy that will last beyond one's life span

POLL HIGHLIGHTS "THE ROLE OF FATHERS IN AMERICA"

Demographics and Methodology

A random national sampling of 793 adults was conducted from January 11–18, 1996, by the Gallup Organization of Princeton, New Jersey, for the National Center for Fathering (NCF). The survey results came from telephone interviews and have a sampling error of plus or minus 4 percentage points. (In addition to sampling error, question wording and practical difficulties in conducting a survey can introduce error or bias into the findings of opinion polls.)

Demographic weighting was applied to the data in order to bring the demographic characteristics of the sample into line with the most recently available Census Bureau estimates to which these results are projected, that is, the total population of adults (age eighteen and older) living in telephone households in the continental United States.

Of the respondents, 39 percent had children under age eighteen, and 45 percent had children eighteen and over. (The two groups obviously overlap.)

Of the parents surveyed, 58 percent had children living with them, and 10 percent had children under eighteen but not living with them. Among the fathers, 17 percent had step- or adopted children.

Twenty items were included in the survey. Highlights of the results follow; summaries of these and other survey items are also included in Father Facts #1, #5, and #8.

Selected Findings

In the following six items, percentages may not total 100 percent because of those who refused to answer or responded "don't know."

"The most significant family or social problem facing America is the physical absence of the father from the home."

Strongly agree	28.4%
Agree	50.7% (Combined agreement: 79.1%)
Disagree	16.1%
Strongly disagree	1.9% (Combined disagreement: 18.0%")

"Most people have unresolved problems with their fathers."

Strongly agree	6.8%
Agree	47.3% (Combined agreement: 54.1%)
Disagree	36.5%
Strongly disagree	2.8% (Combined disagreement: 39.3%)

"It's important for children to live in a home with both their mother and father."

Strongly agree	53.7%
Agree	37.2% (Combined agreement: 90.9%)
Disagree	6.4%
Strongly disagree	1.1% (Combined disagreement: 7.5%)

This high level of agreement that children should live with both their mother and father was even stronger among respondents who had children of their own, 92.4%. Disagreement with the statement was only .4% higher among women than men.

"Fathers make unique contributions to their children's lives."

Strongly agree	43.2%
Agree	47.1% (Combined agreement: 90.3%)
Disagree	5.7%
Strongly disagree	1.9% (Combined disagreement: 7.6%)

"A child's needs are met differently by a father compared to a mother."

Mostly true	68.3%
Somewhat true	23.8%
Somewhat false	2.5%
Mostly false	2.0%

"Most fathers know what is going on in their children's lives."

Strongly agree	4.0%
Agree	38.7%
Disagree	47.8%
Strongly disagree	6.2%

One other notable response was to the following statement:

"You express affection to your children."

(Fathers only)

Strongly agree	83.1%
Agree	12.8%
Disagree	1.5%
Strongly disagree	0.6%

The lowest level of *strongly agree* responses came from the age group of those over fifty; the percentage was still relatively high, 75.4%.

RESOURCES FROM
THE NATIONAL CENTER FOR FATHERING

Author Ken Canfield is the founder of the National Center for Fathering—your *one-stop resource for your most important job.* We're here 24/7 at fathers.com to help you become the best dad you can be.

fathers.com weekly Sign up for our e-mail message, designed to provide insights on relevant topics and give practical action points to use with your children.

FATHERING TIPS Try our list of hot topics or our searchable database. Either way, you'll find hundreds of articles on the topics dads need most: discipline, communication, relating to teens, urban fathering, non-custodial fathering, work-family tension, and more.

Humor—Visit one of the most popular areas of our site, where you'll find Top Ten lists, a joke of the day, and a national humor columnist writing on family issues.

Why We Exist

We believe every child needs a dad he or she can count on. Children thrive when they have an involved father—someone who loves them, knows them, guides them, and helps them achieve their destiny. At the National Center for Fathering, we inspire and equip men to be the involved fathers, grandfathers, and father figures their children need.

What We Do

The National Center for Fathering focuses on equipping men to be the fathers, grandfathers, and father figures their children need. We have training and programming designed for state and local social service agencies, schools, faith communities, and most of all, everyday dads.

We reach a million fathers each year through:

Training—As the premier source for father training, the Center has trained and certified more than 700 trainers and 2,500 small-group leaders through seminars and small-group training. From "Quenching the Father Thirst" to "Connecting with Your Kids" to "Why Bring Dad Into the Picture" to the "Father-Daughter Summit" and "7 Secrets of Effective Fathers Seminar," our programs and training curricula have received enthusiastic reviews from people in the U.S. and around the world.

Programming—Geared toward reaching men where they are, the Center provides leading-edge fathering programs including the Urban Father-Child Partnership, the Father of the Year Essay Contest, WatchD.O.G.S. (Dads Of Great Students), Coach DADS, R.E.A.D. to Kids, and Fathering Court. Currently, 25 states implement one or more of these programs.

Resources—As your resource for practical tips on fathering, the Center offers helpful articles, tips, and information, some of the best books, CDs, and other fathering resources, as well as gifts *for* dad and *from* dad.

MAKING A DIFFERENCE

In a recent survey of dads familiar with the National Center for Fathering and fathers.com, 90.5% of the 2,400 respondents said that their interaction with the National Center has resulted in a significant, very significant, or extremely significant change in their family's life. Here are a few of their comments:

"You are the 'go-to guys' for fathering issues."

Thomas—Ohio

"I have HIGH praise for the Center! It helps me realize the factors that are most important to my small children, and how I can most effectively communicate with them and spend my time in ways that have meaning to them."

Dan—California

"I look forward to the weekly e-mails for fathering tips and advice to help better myself and provide the level of parenting my daughter deserves and requires. This removes the guesswork and allows more efficient use of my time with my daughter."

Michael—Ohio

"As a pastor, it has given me a burden to strengthen the fathers of our church. Many of my men were greatly helped by this seminar."

John—Pennsylvania

"I am not anywhere close to perfect, but thanks to the Center I am hooked to a pipeline of resources that encourage me and also keep me accountable (through the weekly e-mail)."

Clay—Missouri